Zen & the Art of
Pond Building

D. J. Herda

STERLING

New York / London
www.sterlingpublishing.com

STERLING and the distinctive Sterling logo are registered
trademarks of Sterling Publishing Co., Inc.

Library of Congress Cataloging-in-Publication Data

Herda, D. J., 1948–
  Zen & the art of pond building / D.J. Herda.
    p. cm.
  Includes index.
  ISBN-13: 978-1-4027-4274-3
  ISBN-10: 1-4027-4274-6
  1. Fish ponds--Design and construction. 2. Pond animals. 3. Pond
plants. I. Title: Zen and the art of pond building. II. Title.
  SH157.85.F52H47 2007
  639.3'1—dc22

                                        2007033418

10 9 8 7 6 5 4 3 2 1

Published by Sterling Publishing Co., Inc.
387 Park Avenue South, New York, NY 10016
© 2008 by D. J. Herda
Distributed in Canada by Sterling Publishing
c/o Canadian Manda Group, 165 Dufferin Street
Toronto, Ontario, Canada M6K 3H6
Distributed in the United Kingdom by GMC
Distribution Services
Castle Place, 166 High Street, Lewes, East Sussex,
England BN7 1XU
Distributed in Australia by Capricorn Link
(Australia) Pty. Ltd.
P.O. Box 704, Windsor, NSW 2756, Australia

Book design and layout: *tabula rasa* graphic design
Ripple image on pages i, 1, 11, 13, 16-17, 25-27, 31-33,
44-47, 63-64, 67, 74, 77, 86-87, 91, 93, 98-99, 118, 121,
131-133, 154, 156-157, 161-163, 168-169, 178, 181,
184-185, 191-192 ©iStockphoto.com/Felix Möckel

Front jacket: Top left to right: Waterfall courtesy
of Carefree Pools, Highland Park, IL.
Iris © Lilyblooms.com. Waterlily from imageafter.com.
Bottom left to right: Lotus © Lilyblooms.com. Darning needle
© D. J. Herda. Waterlilies © Erika Walsh for Fotolia.com.
Back jacket: koi photo © Weng Chai Lim for Fotolia.
Pond photo © Cindy Haggerty for Fotolia.

Sterling ISBN-13: 978-1-4027-4274-3
        ISBN-10: 1-4027-4274-6

For information about custom editions, special sales,
premium and corporate purchases, please contact
Sterling Special Sales Department at 800-805-5489 or
specialsales@sterlingpublishing.com.

OPPOSITE: Yellow flowering bog plants
reflect off the still surface of the pond.
Photo © Feng Yu for Fotolia.

CONTENTS

one

Water, Water Everywhere

> Before enlightenment: chopping wood, carrying water.
> After enlightenment: chopping wood, carrying water.
>
> —Zen proverb

Forget Jack London. Forget the call of the wild. It's the call of the *water* that counts. Oh, but that's wild, too, isn't it? Isn't water the *most* wild of all natural elements, and isn't it that very wildness—the danger, the mystique, the drama—that is its very allure?

My first real run-in with water, the wild, free-flowing kind, came when I was a kid of five or six. We had recently moved from the inner city of Chicago to the wide-open spaces of suburbia, and when my cousin showed up for a visit one Saturday morning, we found ourselves out the back door and exploring the Great Outside, the hanging willows, the fields of thistles and wildflowers, the endless vistas of nature.

"What's that?"

I turned to him. "What?"

He craned his neck. "What's that sound?"

I listened, craning my neck likewise, but heard nothing. Dale was a full year older than I, and with age, apparently, came better hearing. I shrugged.

"Come on."

Before I could say I didn't think it was a good idea to wander any farther from home, we had wandered farther from home, off through jungles of wild sunflowers, their prickly stalks chafing my bare arms as we beat a slow, steady path through their growth, until finally we emerged on the bank of a stream. Well, actually, it was more of a creek. Oh, hell, it was a *ditch*. But in it was the most remarkable thing I had ever seen: *life*.

Dale was the first to clamber down its canyon-like walls, which must have topped two feet or more; he perched above the slowly moving water. "Hey, look at this!"

"What is it?" I quickly followed his path to the water's edge and scrunched down on my haunches beside him. "What is it?" I asked again. He held up a rock he had lifted from the streambed. There, dangling like a trapeze performer from his precarious roost, was a black, slippery-looking thing.

"I don't know," he said, poking it with his finger. It wriggled. "Looks like some kind of worm ... with a suction cup on one end. See?"

He held it up to the light.

"Yeah," I said. "But it's flat. And slimy."

"Yeah," he said. "What do you want to do with it?"

I shrugged. "Better put it back. It might die out of water."

OPPOSITE: This man-made pond was created by a backhoe and features a small central "island" complete with pine trees. A large pond presents more design opportunities than a small one. *Photo by Tom McNemar for Fotolia.*

"We could kill it with a rock." He glinted at me, a sudden wash of malevolence sweeping his face. I pondered the options: put it back in the water or kill it with a rock. I furrowed my brow.

"Nah, let's put it back and see what else we can find."

Six hours later, we returned home—wet pant legs, wet socks, wet shoes, and covered with mud. There to greet us upon our triumphant return were two complete sets of parents, four scowling faces, eight glowering eyes, not to mention the first of a long series of animated lectures we would receive and predictably ignore over the next few years, lectures that would center on the dangers of water, the stupidity of wandering far from home (actually, it turned out to be less than a couple of blocks from our front door as the crow flies), and the foolhardiness of walking barefoot through water that could house a number of potentially life-threatening hazards.

But neither lectures nor threats nor an endless parade of groundings ("You're not to leave this property for *two whole weeks,* do you hear?") would have their desired effect on us, because we had discovered the simple truth: in water there is *mystery.*

That point would be driven home to us repeatedly until one day, several years later, we would learn firsthand just how much mystery water could contain. On a fishing junket with our fathers, my cousin and I found ourselves on the banks of Saginaski Slough, a semi-stagnant body of water in the middle of nowhere, teaming with bass, catfish, bluegills, and sunfish, where we were about to be taught a lesson in just what dangers those watery mysteries could harbor.

"Come on," my uncle told us. "Follow me."

"Where are we going?" Dale asked.

"Just follow me. You, too," he said to me. "I'm going to show you kids once and for all just how

dangerous playing around water can be." And with that, he led us up the bank to the gravel road, which we followed to where it unfolded onto a concrete-and-steel-beamed two-lane bridge. Several people had gathered around a squad car with swirling lights. A small handful of cops were pulling on a rope threaded between the girders of the bridge down to the surface of the river below and beyond.

"What's going on?" Dale asked.

My uncle stopped a few yards from where the action was unfolding. "I want you kids to see what happens when you're not careful. Somebody drowned out there, and the police are pulling up the body. I want you to see what happens when you're careless."

Wow! A drowning. Just like on TV. And a body, to boot! This was better than *Highway Patrol!*

With the eyes and excitement of youth focused on the end of a long line of hemp snaking its way slowly toward the bridge, we waited patiently for our reward, wondering already how we would manage to come up with an argument strong enough to ward off all of the "I told you so's" that were sure to follow. A gray package broke the surface. Slowly, the cops tugged on the line until the package dangled just below the bridge. With a mighty effort, they popped it up over the edge. It flopped down onto the concrete. We gathered closer as one of the cops cut a rope wrapped around the tarp.

Suddenly, a stench like none I have ever known before or since washed over us, and the small crowd of onlookers parted like the Red Sea, people clasping their hands over their mouths and gagging. As the tarp opened, we spotted the red of what had once been a shirt and the faded blue of a pair of jeans covering the decomposing body of the victim. One of the cops turned the body over with his boot heel. A thick rope bound both of its wrists.

"Looks like a gangland hit," a cop who had

been hunched over the body said. He stood up suddenly and staggered back several steps from the grisly package. "I'll call homicide."

I'm not sure to this day which of those two watery events left the greatest impression on me—the discovery of that very first leech in the ditch near our home or the unveiling of the unmistakably telltale signs of a South Side Chicago Mafia whacking. But to this day, for me, water remains an intriguing element, the very heart of all the mystery and allure that the universe holds deep within its womb.

In between those two events, and well afterwards, of course, my encounters with water in the wild have been a source of fascination and fondness to me. Whether as a boy hunting for frogs and turtles on the edge of a lake in northern Illinois or as a man fishing for brown trout in a stream in southern Wisconsin; whether wading out to a sandbar in the Gulf of Mexico or walking the beaches of Cabo San Lucas—even checking out the mysterious hatchlings of insects inside an abandoned rubber tire in a prairie somewhere—it is the very beginning, and sometimes, too, the end, of life as we have never before known it.

That's what water means to me.

That, and the sound of it ... the softly playing concerti of melodies long ago forgotten. That's part of water's allure, too, its voice. There is something soothing, relaxing, rewarding, rejuvenating about it, all at the same time. Perhaps the sound triggers some distant memories and rekindles the allure in that way. Perhaps it simply sounds pleasant. Whatever the reason, shortly after I grew up, got married, and moved out of my parents' home, I found myself instinctively gravitating toward water. I rented an apartment near the shores of Lake Michigan, took a job editing just a stone's throw from the Great Lakes' breakers, and spent Sunday mornings walking the coarse sands and wondering at what lay beyond.

From there, I moved to Madison, Wisconsin, to a rental unit on the edge of a wildlife preserve, complete with sprawling pond, and then to some farmland with a trout stream running through it, and finally to a home with a pier and a boat on Wisconsin's Lake Mendota. Anywhere, just so long as it was near water.

And then it happened. I was advised for health reasons to head west, and I ended up living in southwestern Utah, in what is affectionately termed the "high desert" (a.k.a. Hell's Kitchen Two), where the deer and the antelope play because, well, hell, there's nothing else for them to do, such as drink from a stream. In fact, streams, lakes, and rivers are few and far between, hell and gone from this piece of desert "paradise." In an environment that receives scant inches of rainfall a year, I soon found myself lusting after water, in any form, in any amount.

That was several years ago. Shortly thereafter, I decided I needed to reconnect with water, pure and simple; if the desert would not come to the water, then the water would have to come to the desert. Which is exactly what happened.

The resulting part-boulder, part-brick, above-ground pond ended up holding 500 gallons of water. Where once only cactus and sandstone stood, today twin waterfalls splay off two slabs of stacked flagstone before disappearing into the pond, where the water is filtered and recirculated back to the falls by means of an underwater pump. A few goldfish, a couple of koi (Samson and Delilah), and a lot of enjoyment later, and the pond is finally fully planted and the focal point of our upper back yard.

It was the first and most enjoyable of the ponds we had built, and I soon found myself working through the day in order to go out in the evening to sit beside it, listening to the cascading water and watching the fish circle around in search of food or

3

This man-made pond features a central planting of cattails and a school of medium-sized koi, which are notorious for eating most other types of water plants. The plants serve as a supplemental source of food as well as a place to hide from sun and various predators. *Photo by Neezam for Fotolia.*

crayfish and a few bullheads and some tadpoles and frogs and toads and a red-eared turtle or two....

It was every pleasant experience with water that I had ever had, every remarkable run-in, every chance encounter. Building a pond might very well have saved my life. Certainly it improved its quality. And then I realized what to some people would have been obvious sooner: if one pond is good, two must be better. It was then, too, that I realized I wasn't alone in my growing fascination with and fanaticism for water.

THE CHINESE HAVE A WORD

They call it *feng shui* (foong SHWAY). It is the art of arranging one's habitat for success—in business, personal life, health, wealth, and more. The thought is that, when all elements in a person's environment are harmoniously balanced, the mind and body are able to function together, leading to greater happiness and success.

Water is one of the most powerful elements in *feng shui*. It can speed up or slow down the positive *ch'i,* which is the invisible universal energy, both positive and negative, found in all things, even inanimate objects. Positive ch'i helps us to acquire health, wealth, and lasting relationships. Water features—whether indoors or out—have a way of creating the energy of ch'i. Placing a tabletop fountain in your home or office is the easiest way to add ch'i into your life and significantly enhance its overall quality. Positive ch'i, in turn, can have an amazing effect on your wealth, romance, and general well-being. To enhance your wealth and prosperity, *feng shui* advises positioning the indoor water feature in the southeast part of your home or office. For success in your career, place it in the north. Another form of feng shui uses a map called the bagua, by which various elements are placed in relationship to the entryway of the whole house or of a particular room. Placing water in the far left of the house (or the room) as you stand in the

a warm and familiar voice. Three months later, on a routine visit to my doctor, I learned that my blood pressure had dropped nearly by half and my cholesterol level had sunk to a point where I no longer expected to live out my life by the number of Seinfeld episodes I'd yet to see. In fact, my doctor said, it was a miracle.

But it wasn't a miracle at all. It was my cousin and I and our first run-in with a leech and some doorway leads to wealth. Placing it at the doorway leads to success in business.

Whichever form of feng shui you follow, one thing is clear: fountains and other water features inside the home are healthful additions to any residential environment.

Fountains also add the relaxing sound of a babbling brook to your environment while adding humidity to dry indoor air. That, in turn, decreases the amount of dust, pollutants, and static electricity in the air. Flowing or moving water also increases the number of negative ions in the air. Too many positive ions (which are created by pollution and other factors) can result in sickness and depression. Water features help reduce that number by balancing them with negative ions. So, for reasons of health, wealth, and overall success, it's water to the rescue.

Now, if all this Oriental philosophical stuff sounds a bit bizarre, don't worry. It does to everyone, at least at first. But the more you see the results of water in action, the more you realize that there is something downright mystical about its healthful and even curative powers. It all centers around *power*— the power to control one's environment, the power to establish lines of wellness with nature, the power to affect one's own success and well-being.

WATER, GARDENS, AND HEALTH

Doylestown Hospital's Health & Wellness Center in Warrington, Pennsylvania, is a unique combination of business success and human wellness. It was designed to combine both traditional health care elements—physicians' offices, an ambulatory surgical center, a medical imaging lab, and rehab therapy—with non-traditional elements, such as a healing garden, pond, waterfall, and stream.

Before any designs were drawn up, ideas were generated from a whirlwind fact-finding expedition conducted by Doylestown Hospital's CFO, Bob Bauer, and his colleague, Dr. Michael Gross. Together, they visited more than 75 clinics nationwide.

"The trip galvanized our sense of what we wanted and, just as powerfully, what we *didn't* want," said Bauer. According to Gross, they didn't find anything that incorporated all of the medical, physical, and spiritual elements they considered essential. So they realized they would have to develop a plan by ear.

To meet their critical demands, their physical building needed first to have the right atmosphere. Rather than a typical medical clinic, they wanted a more sensitive, environmentally appealing environment.

"Hospital management kept mentioning Barnes & Noble," said architect Edward Jenkins, senior vice president, eastern regional manager, Marshall Erdman & Associates, Hartford, Connecticut. "They wanted that kind of upscale appearance and level of comfort."

As a result, the design team worked from the landscaping on up to create a facility that would be more enjoyable and less threatening to its patients. The building, which stands alongside a major thoroughfare leading into downtown Philadelphia, sits at the center of the site. A combination of brick and precast bands and sills makes up the building's exterior.

Rather than a standard flat roof, the designers opted for a sloped roof covered with high-grade architectural shingles. Combined with large expanses of windows, the roof makes the building appear more inviting and less institutional.

The parking areas also received more than the usual attention to detail. As a result, they, too, are more user-friendly. Special streetlights were chosen to illuminate the parking lot without disturbing residents in nearby homes. According to Jenkins, the light source within each pyramid-shaped fixture is invisible; only the light shining on the ground provides a clue to the source above.

Most important of all, the healing gardens that insulate the building from the parking area enhance the facility's inviting appearance. They include meandering pathways of concrete and stone, a pond, a small stream, and a waterfall next to a walking labyrinth complete with several meditation areas. "We decided to place the gardens right next to the building so that patients could look out from almost any window and see flowers and greenery instead of ... cars," Jenkins said.

The tranquility of the healing gardens stretches into the interior of the building's two-story atrium. The bluestone path marking the structure's two main entries literally grows into the atrium's walkways, stream, and yet another waterfall indoors.

Starting near the top of one of two bluestone columns at the atrium's west entry, the waterfall flows down the face of the column until it drops onto a mantel. From there, the water cascades in a 10-foot sheet, falling into a stream that flows through three levels of small ponds, all ringed in bluestone. Adding to the drama and balance of all of this *feng shui* is a school of koi in a pool surrounded by bamboo-style plantings. The overall effect is mesmerizing.

"I remember going to the Center several months ago for my nerves, which were shot," said Fred De Marco, a one-time CEO and self-made businessman. "Basically, I was a walking basket case. I'd had some con man work his way into our corporation, and inside of eight months, he embezzled us into bankruptcy. I lost literally millions. My wife was wonderful, very supportive, and when she heard about the Center, she got in touch with them and we went down for an interview and examination. I don't remember any of that, or not much,

anyway; I was so jittery. But I do recall sitting inside and listening to the waterfall and watching the fish circling in the pond. I started to cry, and my wife asked me what the matter was. I just shook my head. I couldn't speak.

"Several months later, well on the road to being cured, I told her what had happened that day. I told her that the sound of the water had taken me back to a time when I would drive to upstate New York, into the Adirondacks, and park beside one of those towering falls that comes cascading down out of nowhere. I would sit there in the sunlight, listening, feeling the earth trembling beneath me, and count my blessings.

"Somehow, in the Center that day, I'd been transported back to a time before all the garbage, before all the bad stuff happened to us, before we'd been set up for the fall. And I knew deep down inside that I was going to be okay. The waterfall and the fishpond helped me to realize that life isn't over simply because something goes wrong, no matter how bad things might seem at the time. Water put me back in touch with my soul, something I'd lost for months and months and wasn't sure I'd *ever* find again. It was a real blessing."

JUST THE FACTS, PLEASE

Fred De Marco undoubtedly didn't realize it, but there were more than simply pleasant memories involved in his reaction to the water features of the Center. Researchers have known as far back as 1915 that, when water is atomized (e.g., on the impact of a water droplet, for example), negative and positive charges are separated.

Molecules that are torn from the surface of the water bear a negative charge (small negative ions) whereas the entire mass of water is positive. It's these negative ions that explain the refreshing, invigorating effect one experiences when close to a waterfall or a stream or even after a rain. Reactions to negative ions increase overall well-being, as well as physical and mental capacity. Here's how negative ions contribute to good health:

- Negative ions accelerate the oxidative breakdown of serotonin (5-hydroxytryptamine), a naturally occurring chemical within the body.
- Positive ions have the opposite action: they neutralize the enzymes that break down serotonin. Positive ions produce an increase in the serotonin level, which in turn produces tachycardia and increased blood pressure, often resulting in bronchial spasms approaching the severity of those experienced during an asthma attack. Greater serotonin levels also produce the undesirable effects of increased intestinal peristalsis (the contractions and dilations of the intestines that move the contents onwards), increased sensitivity to pain, and increased aggression.
- The *decrease* in serotonin brought about by negative ions results in an overall calming effect and also increases internal bodily defenses against infection.
- Negative ions also produce an increase in hemoglobin/oxygen affinity so that the partial oxygen pressure in the blood rises while the partial carbon dioxide pressure decreases. This, in turn, results in reduced respiratory rate and enhances the metabolism of water-soluble vitamins.
- Negative ions produce an increase in pH and, in particular, an increase in the performance of the mucosa, which contributes to a stronger immune system, with an additional increase in ciliary movement in the airways.
- According to the studies of Fleischer and Pantlitschko, negative ions probably also improve blood flow by increasing the release of proteolytic enzymes with fibrinolytic activity. Improved blood flow contributes to more oxygen reaching the body's vital organs.

- Studies of the adrenal glands of golden hamsters kept under the same experimental conditions showed that the glands of animals treated with positive ions weighed 33% less than those of animals treated with normal respiratory air. In contrast, the weight of the adrenal glands from golden hamsters treated with *negative* ions was 29% higher. Other studies found a 30% enlargement of rat adrenals after 20 days of treatment with negative ions. This finding suggests that the ability of the adrenals to produce glucocorticoids—which have health-giving effects in the body—is reduced by positive ions and increased by negative ions.
- As early as 1959, a considerable increase in vital capacity was observed by M. A. Vytchikova and A. Minkh. In a group of nine sports students, Minkh found that ergometer endurance was increased by 260% in 32 days compared with a normal control group following the inhalation of air enriched with 1.5 million negative small ions per cubic centimeter for 15 minutes a day.
- As early as the 1976 Olympics, air ionization in the sleeping quarters of team members was being used to improve performance in Russian and German sports centers (M. Jokl, Prague).
- Studies by Altmann as early as 1975 showed that the performance of schoolchildren could be increased considerably by simply changing the electrical conditions of the schoolrooms. Comparable effects have also been achieved by the use of ionized air.

According to the latest information in the fields of medicine, biology, and meteorology, atmospheric ions have a significant biological effect on all living things. Atmospheric electrical factors are a component of our environment, and humans are clearly affected by electro-ionic microclimates to a far greater extent than previously imagined.

These findings are especially intriguing in light of the great rise in popularity of artificial air conditioning. The use of air-conditioning units, as well as heating systems, electrical installations, and plastics, means that civilized humans spend between 50 and 100 percent of their time in an unnaturally charged electro-climate. Because of the pollution found in cities, in closed rooms, and in cars, the proportion of negative ions in the atmosphere is markedly reduced compared with those available in undisturbed nature.

An atmosphere with an excess of negative ions, such as frequently arises under open sky, usually induces a complete vegetative turnaround within two to three weeks. In the curative phase of this total turnaround, the vegetative nervous system, which regulates involuntary bodily activity, is restored and the course of infectious diseases is lessened as the body heals itself.

Interior designer Cynthia Leibrock agrees that a healthy indoor environment requires more than four walls and a ceiling. Leibrock is qualified to make her assessment. She has been a notable interior designer specializing in environmental health for 30 years, author of three award-winning books, the proprietor of the Easy Access to Health, LLC, and of the AgingBeautifully.org Web site, and an instructor at Harvard University, where she has taught for more than a decade. In a 2004 interview with *Nursing Homes/Long Term Care Management* editor-in-chief Richard L. Peck, she recently summarized her views regarding health facilities and effective healing:

"The psychological impact of the environment is often overlooked," Leibrock said. "We have design research available documenting that the built environment can reduce stress and depression. In my latest book, *Design Details for Health,* I cite research correlating the soothing sounds of moving water with relaxation, linking sunlight exposure to enhanced well-being and reduced length of stay,

and documenting the therapeutic benefit of healing gardens. Pleasant aromas have been shown by research to reduce the levels of blood pressure, respiration, and pain perception."

The Center for Health Design, based in Lafayette, California, couldn't agree more. In 2005, it began assembling a consortium of hospitals to build new health facilities utilizing principles of healing design centered around nature—one of whose major elements, of course, is water. This consortium is committed to research and evaluation to see how well their new facilities work in practice. To date, their findings have been impressive: unexpected reductions in the overall cost of operation (resulting from shortened patient rehabilitation times and hospital labor) as well as increased patient and family satisfaction, increased staff morale, more efficient use of resources (including drugs), and an overall increase in patient health.

Studies continue to test ways in which natural surroundings interrelate with medical care and illness. This new field of environmental psychology, called *psychoneuroimmunology,* focuses on the correlation between stress and health.

A fresh new wave of health facilities promises to reinvent the concept of the modern-day hospital and revive the spirit of "hospitality" in patient care settings. Health care architects and designers are updating and upgrading hospitals with new facilities across the country, including:

- Bronson Medical Center in Kalamazoo, Michigan
- Doernbecher Children's Hospital in Portland, Oregon
- Northwestern Memorial in Chicago, Illinois
- Woodwinds in St. Paul, Minnesota
- Griffin Hospital in Stamford, Connecticut
- Children's Hospital and Health Center in San Diego, California.

The emphasis on healing design in these new facilities represents a long overdue recognition that patients' surroundings affect their well-being. In a 1998 study to determine how a medical facility's environment can affect medical outcomes, researchers discovered the following:

1. **Medical care.** The environment can support or hinder caregiver actions and medical interventions, making it easier or more difficult for clinicians to do their jobs and aiding helpful or harmful impacts. One example: the sound of a bubbling fountain reduces the stressful commotion and noise of health care workers moving about in and outside of the patient's room.

2. **Health status.** A more natural environment may strengthen or impair patients' health status and personal characteristics by alleviating or exacerbating existing conditions and patients' personal strengths. One example is that loss of sleep due to noise in the post-operative setting may prolong recovery time.

3. **Causes of illness.** The environment can protect patients from or expose them to causes of illness. Circulation of ultra-clean air may protect hospitalized patients from debilitating or even fatal nosocomial infections. One example: air exposed to negative ions created from moving water.

Conversely, research on the impact of the environment on patients actually links poor hospital design to negative outcomes such as increased anxiety, delirium, elevated blood pressure, and use of drugs to control pain.

A July 30, 2001, article entitled "New Woodbury Hospital Uses Natural Ambience to Assist the Healing Process" (*Minneapolis Star-Tribune*) reached many of the same conclusions, saying that the hospital's use of natural ambience assisted in the overall healing process by making the facilities more reflective of nature.

But the overall health benefits produced by water features and other elements found in nature are a result of more than mere stress-level reductions. The white noise produced by the running water of an indoor fountain has been shown to alleviate some types of insomnia while dissolving tension and clearing the mind. Large indoor waterfalls also help to maintain healthy levels of humidity in the air, preventing dry skin and chapped lips.

Outdoors, nearly everyone has experienced the energetic feeling that comes from walking along a mountain stream or along the seashore. That feeling of vitality is due mainly to the high concentrations of negatively charged particles (ions) in the air. With an indoor waterfall, those same negative ions are released in the home.

In the same way that the pounding surf or a fast moving river creates negative ions, so too does an indoor water feature, such as a fountain or a waterfall. These particles have the power to increase your energy level and lift your mood. Negative ions also bond with air-borne impurities, such as pollen and dust, causing them to settle harmlessly to the floor, where they are no longer able to pollute the air. The negative ions produced by an indoor water fountain have also been shown to have a dramatic effect on energy levels and mood. Numerous studies indicate that negative ions may be an effective treatment for depression.

Pure ozone is another potential benefit of indoor water features. It is a molecule containing three atoms of oxygen rather than the two atoms we normally breathe.

Ozone is a naturally occurring colorless gas produced by the ultraviolet rays of the sun. It makes the air smell fresh and the sky look blue. It is the second most powerful sterile element in the world, with the ability to destroy virtually every bacterium, fungus, and virus known. A by-product of highly charged UV rays, often produced in conjunction with water, ozone works 3,125 times faster than chlorine. Occurring quite readily in nature (as with lightning strikes during thunderstorms), ozone produces that fresh, clean, spring-rain smell that we notice after a storm. Although toxic in unnaturally high concentrations, it is found in more normal, healthy levels in locations such as the seashore, in mountain forests, and at the base of waterfalls.

Reacting to the recent discoveries of the positive effects of ozone, some companies specializing in creating custom-made water features are now incorporating ozone-generating units upon request. The ozone cleans the water by oxidizing all organisms that it comes in contact with, creating a healthier indoor environment. A small amount of ozone is also released into the air, sanitizing the air within close proximity to the unit.

While ozone at normal levels is somewhat difficult to generate and maintain within the home environment, negative ions are not. They are a natural result of rupturing water created by fountains, waterfalls, and even some recirculating filters used in aquariums. All generate negative ions, which in turn help to promote both physical and mental health. Even small decorative water fountains that cascade or spray a few inches provide the atomizing effect that produces negative ions, as well as the calming sound of moving water and a strong visual appeal.

If nothing else, imagine introducing a small water feature into the bedroom, where the average person spends at least 6 to 8 hours a day. Imagine one in the living room or den, where a person spends another four or more hours a day. And how about one right outside your back door? Are you beginning to get the picture?

If not, listen to what Marcia Delorean, an assistant escrow officer working for First American Title Company, says about her backyard pond and waterfall.

"I'm under a tremendous amount of pressure when I'm at work. Sometimes, I go a full day without a single break, a glass of water, even lunch. That's how hectic it can be. By the time I come home at five or six in the evening, I'm physically and mentally exhausted. I pour myself a glass of iced tea and sit out on the patio overlooking my small pond and waterfall. Within minutes, I'm swept away by something I call the oasis effect. It's a godsend of sweet, calming sounds and a kind of euphoria I've never felt before.

"Some people might not understand, but I'm sure it's the beneficial effects of the water. I wouldn't live anywhere without a water feature ever again. I simply don't think I could survive."

The author planted this small pond with cattails to help clarify the water while providing oxygen for the goldfish inhabiting it.

THE DOG AND THE BOY

Muddy water,
let stand,
becomes clear.

—Zen proverb

Oaklawn, Illinois. A summer evening, 1955.

I am alone in the house, except for my father, who is in the den, watching television. I am in the bathtub, playing with my toy soldiers and boats.

My Uncle Jim and his wife, Ethel, taking their first vacation in 15 years, asked if they could leave their German shepherd, Chief, with us while they are gone. My aunt and uncle, whom I love dearly, own a tavern on the south side of Chicago.

Three times a day, my uncle walks Chief in the gravel parking lot out back. Well, it's gravel only in the nominal sense, having long ago acquired a generous top-coating of glass shards, bricks, automobile parts, and rusted-out washing machines.

So when they ask if we will watch their dog, I am ecstatic. We live on a half-acre lot in the suburbs, with plenty of open land around us, and Chief loves it.

For 2 weeks, every time I go outdoors, Chief goes with me. He runs and leaps through the air and barks as he never could before. He chases balls and brings them to me and retrieves sticks and does all kinds of things dogs are supposed to do. We even take him fishing with us one Saturday morning, and—like all dogs everywhere—he wastes little time in learning how to swim.

Each day, we play hard, Chief and I, and at night, we enjoy our bath-time ritual. I take my toys into the tub, and Chief comes down the tiled hallway to check in on me. It is his watchdog nature. He pushes open the door, comes up to the tub, and drinks from my cupped hands the water of life. He lets me pat him on the head before he turns around and leaves to go check out the rest of the house.

This evening, as I splash around in the tub, I hear the unmistakable clip-clop of Chief's unclipped toenails on the floor leading to the bathroom. I look up to make sure that the door is cracked open, and I wait for his appearance. I continue playing for several more minutes, and when Chief fails to appear, I wonder what could be wrong. I call for him, but nothing happens. And then I remember.

My aunt and uncle had returned from their trip and picked Chief up earlier that day. Yet I am sure I heard his footsteps on the hard tile floor.

I get out of the tub, dry myself off, and slip into my pajamas before running out, calling for my father. But my father is on the phone. I overhear bits and pieces of his conversation, and I watch as he hangs up.

"Dad," I say. "You'll never guess what happened."

He looks concerned. I am puzzled. My father rarely looks concerned.

"What?" I ask him. "What's the matter?"

My father clears his throat. "Son, that was your Uncle Jim," he tells me. "He called to say that Chief died shortly after they got him home today."

two

The Birth of a Pond

From the pine tree, learn of the pine tree;
And from the bamboo, learn of the bamboo.

—Basho

There's no easier way I can think of to add a sense of tranquility and purpose to life than by building a pond or establishing some other kind of water feature in the home environment. Indoors, ponds are a conversation piece as well as a source of cleansing and environmental control. They add humidity to the air when it's dry and remove particulates and other airborne pollutants, which are almost always present, in this day and age.

They provide an ideal backdrop for house-plants and even allow you to grow some exotic, moisture-loving varieties, such as orchids, as well as bog plants, including cattails, several varieties of bamboo, rush, and even papyrus. And, of course, ponds offer an opportunity to raise fish, turtles, and other water-loving creatures in a setting far more natural than an aquarium (although we have one of those in our home, too, just for fun).

Indoor ponds, streams, and waterfalls create a microclimate that's not only healthy for humans but also beneficial for *all* living things. We know a couple who keep exotic birds. Their macaw is let out of his

OPPOSITE: A series of strategically placed fountainheads form a unique pattern of water in this poured concrete pond. *Photo © Pavel Losevsky for Fotolia.*

cage every morning around 7:00. After begging a piece of toast from the breakfast table, he waddles across the living room floor to the sprawling foyer, where he grooms himself in the indoor pond there, preening his feathers at the edge of a small waterfall. His owners are enamored and in love: it's like living in the middle of a tropical rain forest with all the conveniences of home—and without the *Giardia*.

We created our first indoor pond here in Utah from injection-molded plastic, a scant 3 feet long and 8 inches deep. We bought a couple of turtles and enjoyed feeding them, until we discovered both of them missing one day. They turned up a few hours later hiding behind the schefflera in the corner. Who knew turtles could climb?

Our next pond was larger—some 5 feet across—and deeper, in part to keep the turtles from escaping, a goal that proved only moderately successful. Turtles are nothing if not single-minded in their determination. Thinking they were bored in so large a pond, we introduced several goldfish and a couple of koi, some water plants, and a fountain. The fountain put out a delightfully calming sound; the fish began eating and growing before our very eyes, and the plants made everything look more natural.

It didn't take long for the turtles to take notice of the fish, along with their newly redecorated digs, and their activity picked up. They spent more time swimming around and less time trying to escape. They spent more time eating, too, much to our chagrin and our steadily dwindling supply of fish. So off to the local wildlife preserve the turtles went. (They were indigenous to the area and not exotic introductions—something to remember before releasing *any* animal into the wild.)

As the remaining fish continued to grow in size (the koi were now nearly a foot long and getting rambunctious), we got the distinct impression that they needed more room. Since a bigger indoor pond was impractical, we decided to move our pond outdoors and replace the indoor pond with a small bubbling fountain.

Of course, that didn't work. Like most pond owners everywhere, we came to realize that molded ponds would eventually be too small for our koi no matter how large a pond we bought. Besides, moving to an outdoor pond meant we could leave all of our previously inherited size restrictions behind.

And so was born the first of our numerous outdoor ponds. Originally planned, as with many *real* children, to be an only child, we soon found that the most carefully laid plans.... Well, you know. So, while no longer our only baby, our first outdoor pond was for a long time our largest—the one that still holds our koi and more than half a dozen goldfish, the smallest of which is now about 8 inches in length. The koi—Samson and Delilah—have passed the 2-foot mark and are still growing happily.

Upon completing our first outdoor pond, we felt that, within the scope of a few days' time, we had done something quite unique (for our neck of the woods, at any rate), as well as rewarding. We had created a sanctuary not only for fish but also for birds (hey, desert birds need water as much as other birds). In the process, we had installed a focal piece—a strong central design element—that suddenly drew all of the other elements in our backyard together.

We had also significantly raised the property value of our home, as well as its desirability. With ponds, of course, come additional plantings and fountains and small waterfalls, etc. (No pond is an island!) We had widened the scope of the ecosystem in which we found ourselves living and, in the process, drew in squirrels, chipmunks, raccoons, roadrunners, desert fox, quail, lizards, hummingbirds, and the occasional harmless snake to investigate and partake of the soothing elements, nourishment, and protection that the pond presented.

They, in turn, provided us with a remarkable opportunity to observe wildlife in its most pristine form—the wild. We often sit on our glider just feet from the water and watch intently as beasts that would not normally consider approaching human habitat do just that and more. From them we've learned patience and garnered a new respect for the beauty and diversity that nature has to offer.

Perhaps most important of all, however, we've come to gain a new respect for those full-time inhabitants that led us to build the pond in the first place: our fish.

Now, don't get me wrong. I'm not a fish-lover. Oh, I enjoy a nicely grilled salmon steak every now and again, and fried oysters in a Po' Boy sandwich are awfully tough to beat. But fish—the kind that swim around in water and have the personality of a mushroom—have never held much allure for me. They hadn't, at any rate, until we built our pond.

Suddenly, we discovered that our fish—led by the koi, who perch unmistakably atop the pecking order of the school—have definite personalities. They are also far more intelligent than one might ever imagine merely from dangling a baited hook in a country pond and pulling out an occasional bass or crappie to join you for dinner.

We learned that fish could be trained to look for food simply by feeding them at the same time each day. No great intellectual achievement, that; even our cats begin rubbing up against us when feeding time grows near. We also learned that fish could be trained to come at the sound of a familiar voice. They could be trained to swim to the surface and be petted before being fed. They could be trained to eat from our hands. They could even be persuaded to propel themselves halfway out of the water and into a cupped palm while doing so.

Now, I don't know about you, but that's something I never knew about fish. More remarkable, still, we learned that fish have unique personalities.

Delilah, for instance, is a mere inch or two smaller than Samson, yet she handles herself with grace and aplomb. She swims elegantly and sleekly around the pond and seems to have a brain that is always at work. Her eyes betray far more intelligence than any sucker I've ever pulled out of a meandering stream, and her willingness to socialize is remarkable. Sometimes she gravitates to one spot and watches us as we talk to her. (Hey, I never said we weren't *weird!*)

Samson, on the other hand, is more typically male. He's brutish and arrogant, bulling his way around the pond as if he were its only inhabitant. He likes to have his back rubbed lightly, to either side of his dorsal fin, and he spends minutes on end circling until he gets his way. He also grunts when he eats, a bit like a pig (something Delilah would never do).

The other fish, the goldfish, while smaller and somewhat less social, have similarly begun displaying individual personalities. Or perhaps we've only recently begun noticing them. (It's difficult to admire the lines on a fox terrier when it's surrounded by bullmastiffs!) Several of these smaller fish are beginning to show signs that they enjoy petting, although

they are still more skittish than the koi and have to be approached more slowly.

What all this boils down to, of course, is that we now receive as much pleasure from our fish as we do from the water elements that we originally built to hold them. It's just one of many unexpected advantages to building ponds, streams, and waterfalls. Some of the others we'll unfurl as we move through this book, offering you concrete advice on the best way to incorporate water features into your own home and environment.

Along the way, just keep reminding yourself that you heard it here second: If you build it, they will come. And your life will be changed forever.

The author's lower pond features a shallow area in the foreground, gradually sloping to 4 feet in depth. The fish are attracted to the shallows for feeding and spawning.

A REFUGE WITHIN

Middleton, Wisconsin. Winter, 1976.

My wife and I have recently moved from Chicago to the comparative beauty of Middleton, a bedroom suburb of the Wisconsin state capital of Madison, where we rent a duplex on the edge of a small wildlife preserve complete with obligatory semi-stagnant marsh. I do not realize that our backyard opens onto such arboreal beauty for several months, until the warming weather melts the snows and thaws the ice covering the marsh. From then on, I am in heaven.

We walk nearly every evening along the railroad tracks that skirt the 400 feet or so between our yard and the preserve, and I revel in the fact that there are frogs and toads and snakes (the non-poisonous variety, of course—I'm not a complete idiot) and even bluegills rising in the pond to feed on insect larvae, things I have not experienced since moving to the suburbs from Chicago when I was 6.

At some point in time, I realize that the Great Outdoors is not enough to satisfy me. I want it around me always, so I go down into the basement of our rental house, carrying with me an armload of lumber, and several hours later stand back to admire a wooden-framed, triangular-shaped corner structure of indeterminate use. It is built of 2" x 2" pine boards and lined with clear plastic sheeting, the entire project setting me back some $14.71.

But it is not until I fill this 3-cubic-foot holding tank with water, disguise the lumber with potted plants, and, finally, introduce to the water some bluegills and bullheads caught from the marsh out back and a few goldfish picked up at the local pet shop that I begin to realize nirvana. For the first time in my life, I have built a water refuge in my own home. For the first time in my life, even without stopping to realize it, I have built a pond.

three

Thinking Out Loud

Building a new water feature is like building a new house: all houses are different, yet all houses are similar. They share certain characteristics, but they vary in final layout, design, and decor.

Water features, too, are different yet similar. They have certain shared elements, and they have layout, design, and decor features that differentiate them from other water features.

Of course, not all water features are ponds. Some are recirculating streams. Some are spewing fountains. Some are cascading waterfalls. But most water features share a common element: the basic pond.

Natural ponds are made up of a holding area (the basic pond), a drainage area (either via seepage through the pond's bottom or via outlets in the form of small creeks, streams, or rivers, depending upon the pond's size), and an input area (usually

ABOVE: A simple pond consists of a watertight container and water. Adding plants helps to purify the water and generate enough oxygen for at least a limited number of fish. A simple pond doesn't have to be plain, as can be seen with this well-planned formal circular pond. *Photo by Roy Madero for Fotolia.*

The author created this pond using two pumps: one to power the small fountain within the pond and another to move the water uphill to a spillway, where it drifts down a lined stream to empty back into the pond.

other creeks, streams, or rivers flowing into the pond). Constructed ponds are different. That's where humankind's ingenuity comes in. Create a problem, and you can just bet some human being somewhere will figure out a way to solve it. Such is the case with the most commonly constructed of all water features—the *outdoor pond*.

DETERMINE WHAT YOU WANT

Before you decide to roll up your sleeves and begin building a pond of your own, stop to think about the kind of pond you'd like to own. A wide range of options exists. Would you like your pond to be dug into the ground or raised? Here in Utah, we live on solid bedrock, so that pretty much determines how deeply in-ground we can, or rather *can't*, go.

Would you like your pond to look modern or natural? Take into consideration the style, finish, and landscaping plan of your existing home. Our home lent itself to a combination of natural styles, and we incorporated several of them.

Would you be satisfied with a small container pond, such as a wine barrel, whether or not you decide to add fish or plants? One obvious advantage of container ponds is that they can be filled and drained quickly and can be moved nearly anywhere whenever you want, depending upon your own whims or seasonal requirements.

If you'd like a recessed pond, do you want it to include a waterfall or a stream? If so, construction will be a bit more complicated than otherwise, although well within the reach of just about anyone. If you want a raised (above-ground) pond, do you want the walls and bottom to be made from manufactured materials, such as concrete, ceramic tile, or dimensional framing lumber; or would you rather use natural stone and earth to hold your pond's waterproof liner?

Do you plan on adding a fountain, either in or near your pond? If so, you'll need to take any plumbing requirements into consideration. Do you want your pond to hold fish? Often, even if you don't want them in the beginning, you will decide to add fish after completing the project and stepping back to see what's missing. To be safe, plan on keeping the option of adding fish open.

There are literally hundreds, perhaps even thousands of different types and shapes of ponds and nearly as many different ways of sealing them to hold water. Remember: there is no right or wrong pond. There is only what pleases *you*. While we can't give you advice on which type of pond to build or the one and only way in which to build it, we *can* share with you those tried-and-true methods that we have encountered that will work for any water feature you might have in mind, beginning with the ubiquitous *holding pond*.

THE HOLDING POND

The basic centerpiece of any artificially created water feature is the holding pond. This is the main body of water, or pond, from which all other activity flows. Whether your holding pond is shallow or deep, you're going to have to have a place for water to congregate. If your pond is a basic bowl-shaped design, you're talking about building a *simple pond*. If, beyond building a simple pond, you plan on adding a stream or waterfall, you're venturing into the realm of a *recirculating pond*. Recirculating ponds are part of a larger close-looped water-circulating system, featuring a holding pond from which water is pumped up to a waterfall or the head of a streambed so that it may return to the pond via gravity. Here's a closer look at what's involved in deciding which kind of pond to build.

THE SIMPLE POND

A *simple pond* is pretty much what the name suggests—a basic bowl-shaped pond designed to hold water. It consists of one-piece construction most often made waterproof via the use of a thick rubber or vinyl material called pond liner, and it's ideal for anyone who has no plans for adding a stream or a waterfall in the near future. A simple pond can hold plants and fish, and you can landscape it in whatever way you want to achieve the finished effects you desire.

For example, we built our first pond primarily out of concrete landscaping bricks interspersed with boulders we moved into place for drama. We like the natural look because we miss the wild beauty of ponds, streams, and waterfalls that we enjoyed when we lived in Colorado and wanted to bring them here to us in the Utah desert.

Building a Simple Pond

Before building a simple pond, you should decide where in your landscape you want your pond to be. Mark off the size and shape of your pond with spray paint or landscaper flags, and then take a couple of days to decide if you've chosen a good location. There's no sense in rushing into this project. Once completed, your pond is going to remain where you put it for a long, long time.

Walk around your property and try to envision what the pond will look like from various points of view. Take into consideration one important fact: once it's there, it's *there*. Oh, sure, you can tear it down, dig it up, expand it, alter its shape, or start a

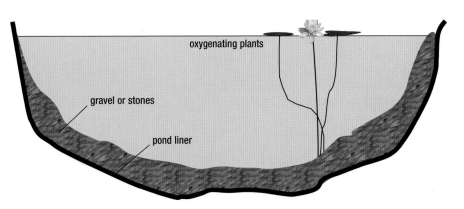

A basic pond consists of a waterproof membrane or pond liner and plenty of water. Some gravel or stones to cover the bottom of the pond and a few plants are basic add-ons.

oxygenating plants

gravel or stones

pond liner

new pond from scratch later, but why not simply do it right in the first place?

Also, pay attention to the placement of your pond in relationship to other permanent landscape elements, such as barbecue grills, property lines, fences, trees, and large shrubs. Later we'll talk more about the consequences of building a pond near existing landscaping and hardscaping.

Once built, a simple pond will provide a place for birds to drink and fish to swim. It's great for installing a fountain. (Even a small one makes a beautifully relaxing sound.) It's ideal for growing water plants. And, of course, it provides moisture to the surrounding environment and negative ions for your health. See the simple pond diagram for a cross-section of the main features of pond.

Yes, all things considered, a simple pond is very possibly the best pond a person could choose to build. Unless you decide to build something more elaborate.

THE RECIRCULATING POND

For some people, simple is not necessarily better. If you're one of them, then you already know you're never going to be content with just a simple pond. That's where the recirculating pond comes in.

A recirculating pond is a simple pond on steroids. In addition to the pond, you'll use a pump and hose to move the water from the pond to some point higher up in elevation, where the water will empty either into a streambed that flows back down to the pond or to a waterfall that drops the water back into the pond. Recirculating ponds are limited in size, scope, and design only by your own imagination and the size of the pump you use to move the water. Some are no larger than a simple pond with an additional circulating pump. Others are quite large and complex. Our largest pond, for example, includes a 500-gallon holding pond from which

water is pumped 24 feet up and away, where it dumps via a waterfall into a 50-gallon holding pond. From there, the water cascades over a spillway into a streambed that meanders some 20 feet to another spillway, which dumps water into a 150-gallon pond. From there, the water flows over a third spillway into a small stream that feeds back into the holding pond. See what I mean?

Building a Recirculating Pond

When you set out to build a recirculating pond, you'll start with a basic holding pond, just as you do when building a simple pond. That's because you're going to need a place for the water to congregate, which will be the lowest point on-grade. It's easier and more efficient to pump water from a low-lying location, where gravity deposits it, to a high-lying location, where some mechanical means will function as the delivery boy. From there, Mother Nature will take over the task of returning the water to the holding pond. See the diagram of the typical recirculating pond for an overview.

This makes selecting a site for a recirculating pond pretty important. You're going to want to have a site that's lower than the stream or waterfall that will feed into it. And, of course, you're going to need to make sure that you have enough physical space to accommodate the stream or waterfall in addition to the holding pond without inconveniencing anyone.

Choosing a Headwater Location for the Recirculating Pond

Once you've decided to build a recirculating pond, you'll want to determine where you want to set the headwater—that point where the water pumped out of your pond will be released to begin its journey back down to the pond. If the headwater is to be at the top of a waterfall that spills directly into the pond, your options are fairly limited. Locate the best place for the waterfall visually and plan on situating the head-water there. Don't worry about the fact that your waterfall site isn't any taller than your pond site. We'll show you how to raise the height later.

stone spillway
oxygenating water
skimmer box/pump
gravel or stones
pond liner
hose

If you can't decide on just where you'd like your waterfall, no problem. You can build two falls nearly as easily as one, and they can both be serviced by the same pump. See? I told you this was a piece of cake!

If, instead of a waterfall, the headwater for your pond is to be a stream, you'll need to plan on providing a slope from highest point to lowest (the pond) so that the pump can move the water up to the headwater point and gravity can take over from there. Of course, if you have the space, you may want to incorporate a stream *and* a waterfall, or even several falls and smaller ponds. And that's workable, too.

If you're lucky enough to have a natural slope leading toward your pond, congratulations. You hit the jackpot. More likely than not, you're going to be working with a flat piece of ground. That means you'll need to bring in soil, rocks, logs, dimensional lumber, or other elements to raise the grade of your stream above that of the pond. Don't worry about the appearance of your pond, stream, or waterfall yet. Remember: effective landscaping forgives all sins.

Once you have decided where and how your water is going to flow, you'll need to determine the approximate placement of the pond pump, filter, and hoses. You'll also need to provide access to electrical power; and having a water source nearby isn't a bad idea, either.

A typical recirculating pond includes the elements of a basic pond plus a means for recirculating the water. In this case, the circulation is achieved via a skimmer box/pump combination that takes water in, runs it through a filter, and pumps it via a hose to an outlet point—in this example, a small stone spillway at the far end of the pond. When installing a skimmer box, try to place it as far away from the water discharge source as possible in order to create a natural turnover of water and to avoid unoxygenated or stagnant areas. As the pump draws water and debris into the box from the pond surface, the water is filtered and returned to the pond by means of a hose that is usually buried or otherwise hidden from view.

THE POND PUMP

A pump, I once foolishly believed, is an optional addition to a pond. That is to say, it's optional if you don't mind stagnant, slimy water that's rife with mosquito larvae. If that's not your idea of the perfect landscaping feature, plan on buying a pump. You'll use it, even in a simple pond, to keep the water circulating in order to keep it oxygenated and clean (which might also require the addition of a filter, below).

For a simple pond, you can use a small pump or a pump-and-filter combination in which the pump sits in a filter box, draws unfiltered water through a filtering medium such as charcoal or foam padding, and discharges clean water out the other end. Such pumps often come equipped with a fountain so that the clean water is spurted from the holding pond into the air in any of a number of pleasing patterns.

For a recirculating pond, you'll need a pump to move the water from the holding pond to a discharge point higher up in grade. The pump will draw the water from the pond and force it uphill through a hose that stretches from Point A to Point B.

Larger pumps come equipped with two discharge openings—either one suitable for moving the water through different hoses or for powering a fountain or two, should that be your goal.

There are many types and sizes of pumps on the market, some more suited to lifting and

A ground-level view of the pond created by the author with two pumps.

moving water over greater distances than others. Some are able to do little more than aerate the water or shoot a small spray into the air. Others can lift water a dozen feet or more in elevation and carry it a distance of 20 or 30 feet. We'll talk more about which pump is right for your needs later.

THE POND FILTER

In addition to a pump, you should seriously consider using a pond filter. Especially if you plan on introducing fish to your pond, a filter is a near necessity. That's because fish give off by-products (hey, all that fish food has to go *somewhere!*); as these by-products decompose, they release into the water various waste products such as ammonia and nitrites that can be deadly to fish.

A good filtration system can help prevent the buildup of chemical toxins by removing waste products, along with uneaten food, plant debris, and anything else subject to decomposition, *before* it has a chance to do any serious damage.

There are exceptions to the necessity of using a commercially manufactured pond filter. If you're not planning on introducing fish into your pond, you *can* get by without one. A pump alone should be sufficient to keep the water moving and prevent it from stagnating and becoming a breeding ground for mosquitoes and other undesirables. Likewise, if your pond will contain only a few fish and *lot*s of live plants, you can probably get by without a filter, since the plants act as living filters, taking in nutrients during the decomposition process and giving off life-sustaining oxygen in return.

But, in order for this natural type of filtration system to be effective, you'll need a lot more plants than fish, and maintaining the proper balance can become a daunting task.

Here's an example of a pond using an external sealed filter, meaning it is leakproof under pressure. It functions in the same manner as does a typical underwater filter, by drawing unfiltered water in one end, passing it through some type of filter medium, and expelling filtered water out the other end. The major advantage of using an external filter is that it is easy to access when it needs to be cleaned. Make sure when sealing the filter box that all fittings are tight and that there are no leaks.

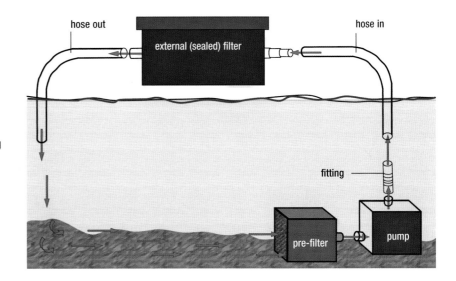

hose out

hose in

external (sealed) filter

fitting

pre-filter

pump

CAREFUL PLANNING

If you plan on building your pond near existing trees and shrubs, expect at least some minor inconveniences, and possibly more. For example, ponds love shade—at least partial shade. That's because algae and algal blooms thrive in full sunlight. Besides looking bad (you know, lending water that greenish, stagnant, sewer-water look), algae robs water of oxygen, thus creating even *more* problems, especially for fishponds. By shading your pond for at least part of the day, you'll have fewer problems with algae and enjoy generally healthier water.

But shading your pond can be a problem. If you use trees—the obvious choice for shade— you're going to have to face additional maintenance. Deciduous trees, those that go bare during winter, drop their leaves once a year. When they do, you can virtually bet that every last one of them is going to end up in your pond. You'll need to remove the fallen debris regularly before it decomposes in order to prevent the buildup of nitrites and nitrates.

Flowering deciduous trees are even worse, since the flower blossoms fall off in spring and the leaves, in fall.

The obvious solution might appear to be to build your pond beneath a pine tree, which remains evergreen all year long. That might *appear* to be the solution, but it's not, since pine trees shed a good number of their needles throughout the year, as witnessed by the "pine straw" matting piling up below evergreen trees. One good wind or rain storm, and you'll quickly see how much of a nuisance those "evergreen needles" can be.

Fortunately, there are *some* evergreen and semi-evergreen trees that are fairly clean alternatives to pines. These include oleanders (actually tall-growing shrubs), cypress, and eucalyptus trees, which may or may not be suitable to your climate. These plants rarely drop leaves, don't have needles, and—with the exception of oleanders—don't flower. For other possibilities, check with your local state horticulturist or nursery owner.

We view the maintenance of cleaning up tree debris to be a small price to pay for a partially shaded pond, especially here in the high desert of southern Utah where summer days often tip 120° F and cloudy days are next to nil. Of course, you can add skimmer boxes (which skim the water and pick up floating debris from the pond's surface), vacuums, and other devices to help keep your pond clean of fallen debris and, thus, nitrite-free, if you like. Regardless, you should be aware that the benefits of shading your pond are not without a few drawbacks.

Similarly, you need to be concerned if there are other elements too close to the pond for your own good. An adjacent barbecue pit might sound appealing, but all the smoke, grease spatters, and other residual pollution from outdoor cooking could cause harm to your pond's fish and plants.

Likewise, building a pond too close to a fence without careful consideration can be awkward. You'll want to leave plenty of access room so that you can regularly check on and service pumps, filters, and other pond elements, which are traditionally stored out of sight around the back side of the pond.

Above all else, think twice before locating a pond beneath a high-power electrical line. If the line should ever break in a storm and end up in the water, you'll get quite a fireworks display. Better to keep *any* pond construction clear of overhead lines.

And, while we're talking about safety first, check with your local utility company to make certain that no electrical, telephone, coaxial cables, or water lines are buried where you plan on digging. An ounce of prevention—and a 3-minute telephone call—could be worth your very life or at least help you avoid having to pay hundreds or even thousands of dollars in repair costs.

Now, if you wonder just what kind of idiot would tackle a job like this—putting together all of these necessary ingredients just to be near water or, more succinctly, to have water be near you—let me assure you, we are not your run-of-the-mill idiots. We are not your everyday loons. We are possessed.

QUICK CHECKLIST

- Choose the type of water feature you want— simple pond, recirculating pond, container pond, fountain, or a combination.
- Decide on whether to construct your pond in-ground or above ground.
- Select the approximate size and placement of your pond, taking into consideration all of the pre-existing landscape elements on your property.
- Decide upon the look that you'd like to achieve—either natural or manufactured, modern or traditional.

THE FISHERMAN AND THE BRIDE

Student says,
I am very
discouraged,
What should I do?
Master says,
encourage others.

—Zen proverb

Chicago, Illinois. Lake Michigan. Summer, 1969.

I have accepted my father-in-law's invitation to go smelting. I do not have a clue as to what smelting is, but I learn soon enough. Smelting, he tells me, is netting a small, inconspicuous Lake Michigan fish called, appropriately enough, a smelt. The purpose of smelting is to bring home as many of the little buggers as possible in order to make a tasty meal. Since I have never eaten a smelt in my life—and, for that matter, have never known anyone else who has—I take him at his word.

On Saturday morning, he calls for me at our apartment. I share the place with his daughter, whom I married a mere year earlier. It is a small two-bedroom four-plex in the suburbs just south of the city. It is 3:30 a.m. I have been awake since 2.

In a heartbeat, I am out the door, dressed as warmly as I know how for the middle of the city in the middle of summer, having been forewarned about the biting cold winds off the lake, even in July. Within 45 minutes, we are parked at the shore, unloading a world of exotic looking paraphernalia, the most important of which, even I have already figured out, is the net.

As we run the guyline out into the choppy water and string the netting so that it runs the line after it, we sit back and wait. My father-in-law and I make small talk. Rather, he talks and I listen. This much, too, I have already figured out.

Forty minutes later, my father-in-law feels the net, smiles appreciatively, and begins pulling it in. I rejoice. Not because we have caught a mess of fish, but rather because I mistakenly believe that his action is a sign that we are finished smelting and will soon be on our way home. The wind bellows off the lake. My feet are frozen to the sand. My hands are numb. My light jacket is absolutely useless against the cold damp air. I am frozen to the bone. Worse, still, I have to pee.

We remove the two or three fish that had the great misfortune of impaling themselves in the netting and slip them into a bucket, where I'm sure they'll be flash-frozen in no time. Thirty minutes later, we repeat the scene, with only slightly more success.

After about the fifth time, with the first damp gloomy glow of daylight hovering low over the horizon and the rain beginning to fall, we decide to call it a day. We give our dozen or so minnows to another hapless idiot fishing near us, and we head for home.

I am cold, I am aching, I am tired, I am wet. I cannot wait to get back to our apartment, to settle into a bath and then into some warm clothes before doing something enjoyable, such as slitting my wrists.

"How did it go?" my young bride asks me.

"Great," I say as I straddle the toilet and breathe a sigh of relief. "Although, we didn't catch many fish."

"I didn't think you would," she says. "Dad never does."

I look at her blankly, at this woman with whom I would years later have my one and only son, and I wonder for a moment if I had not made a mistake when I asked for her hand in matrimonial bliss. That evening, I find out.

We share dinner at my in-laws' home, and high up on the menu is something called breaded fried smelt. The smell is manna from heaven. And when it arrives golden-brown on a plate playing near me, I cannot resist. With seafood sauce, without, with fries on the side, without...there is no wrong way, I soon learn, to eat breaded fried smelt.

Deep into my second helping, I turn to my father-in-law and ask where he got the fish. He tells me that a friend of his had been out that day, as well, and had caught more than he could handle.

"Seems we were using too small a net," he tells me. "We were using a number four and needed a number three or a number three and needed a number four or something like that. Anyway, all the smelt were hitting our net and bounding off instead of getting caught."

"Well, I'll be..." I say, stuffing an entire fish into my mouth. Nothing, I think to myself, should taste this good.

"I'm thinking of giving it another try next weekend," my father-in-law adds absently. If you want to come..."

My brows instinctively rise as I glance first at my wife and then at my mother-in-law and pause for the briefest of moments. I bite into the fish, chew for several seconds, and swallow.

"Count me in," I say, turning to my mother-in-law. "Mom, are there any more smelt?"

four

Construction Zone

There is no work that can be done without honor: Thus, in the beginning was the word. And the word was with honor. And the honor came from God. And God made man. And man painstakingly began to build ponds. By carving. And whittling. And digging. And crafting. And stacking. And honing. And gluing. And tearing apart. And starting all over again.

In those first days, when we realized that we needed to move our molded pond out of the house and replace it with something larger that we could fill with yet more water, expose to natural light, and equip with a fountain—an honest-to-God fountain spraying high into the air!—we were the children of God. We were the blessed innocent. We were the saints of the realm, the wide-eyed newly born babes ready to take a leap of faith.

In time, we would become the warriors.

ABOVE: Water lilies, water lettuce, and water hyacinth all thrive in clear, clean water with at least 8 hours of sunlight a day. *Photo © Cindy Haggerty for Fotolia.*

We began our inside-out transformation by surveying our land. We had owned the property for nearly 2 years but had never gotten around to spending much time outdoors. This was no mere oversight, and it was no reflection upon our philosophical bent. My wife and I love the outdoors. But, in a climate where summer temperatures are grueling; where all living things are confined to greenery resembling, albeit remotely, blades of grass beneath the life-sustaining succor of built-in sprinkling systems; where trees are root-fed-and-watered; where rocks the size of small Volkswagens bulge out of the scorched earth everywhere, we spent little time outside the walls of our air-conditioned hacienda.

So when the time came to pull the plug on our inside pond, we were forced to stop and survey our options. They were limited.

SELECTING A LOCATION

On one side of our house: a house. On the other side of our house: another house. In front of our house, a covenant-restricted greenbelt. In back of our house: 25 acres of rock, gravel, sand, cactus, and heat.

We had a sudden stroke of genius. We would build our pond in back of our house.

And so we began. Not in the cool wonders of winter, where temperatures here hover at a civilized 40° F. Oh, no. Instead, we began in the fetid disillusionment of summer, which day after day glared down upon us, not a cloud in the sky, not a breeze breaking the day, and certainly not a raindrop within a hundred miles, until I began to believe the sun would never set for all eternity and the heat would never move off the horizon.

We were lucky, I guess, in that someone of some insight had 20 years earlier planted—oh, God, dare I say *lucky?*—a redbud tree. An Eastern redbud tree, no less, the kind that blooms out each spring in a profusion of pink-on-white flowers and that drops each spring a profusion of pink-on-white flowers, followed by a few months of relative shade and then the ceremonial dropping each winter of a profusion of brown-on-brown leaves.

Nonetheless, we were lucky.

We knew from our reading that ponds do not do well in scorching sun. For one thing, algae flourish in sunlight and heat, and algae are an aquaculturist's scourge. For another, fish fry beneath relentless heat, and those kinds of fish fries are *not* what we were seeking. For yet another, people in the high desert are reluctant to sit out at night, admiring the sweat of their brows, when their lungs can barely function.

But this tree, this single prolific Eastern redbud, with all of its mess and all of its clutter, would be our first pond's salvation. And we knew it.

We grabbed our shovels and picks and our hardened steel bars, and we began the dubious task of chipping away at solid bedrock. Two days later, a couple of incredulous and remarkably dimwitted people grasped the true meaning of life. If the mountain will not come to the people, the people will have to schlep to the mountain.

And schlep we did.

We went to our local home improvement center and bought three pallets of concrete bricks. It was a cheap fix—a buck-plus per brick—and the brick stacked easily to conform to relatively conventional shapes, which was important to us because of the lay of the land.

By now, it had become pretty obvious to us that our brick pond would rise from the existing grade to as great a height as we felt practical, and stretch from the redbud tree on one side to the bedrock boulder on the other, bumping up against the 6-foot cactus in the rear. That would leave us enough space in between the front wall of the pond and the back wall of our house to allow for a small redwood glider and some passageway.

PLANNING 101

We began our project by first drawing out the shape of our soon-to-be pond on paper, and then we transferred that drawing to the ground, using spray paint manufactured for just such a purpose. It was not until some time later that we realized just how foolish this endeavor was, since our space dictated the size and shape of the beast, and no amount of paint on the ground would change that.

We next got the brilliant notion to utilize some of the plethora of natural stone boulders—we're talking 4 feet long by 3 feet wide and plenty heavy—to form part of our pond's walls. In doing so, we reasoned, we would both save on the cost of concrete bricks that we would otherwise have to purchase and add dramatic natural appeal to the finished product. (The interior we would cover with a waterproof pond liner … but, judging by the length of time we had already been toiling away with little to show for it, that event would unfold no time soon.)

Our rationale had been nothing short of brilliant. Not only did we manage to incorporate the natural beauty of Utah's high desert country into the man-made efficacy of a manufactured concrete brick wall, but we also came to learn several important principles of modern physics that soon enough grew clear to us both: rectangular bricks and irregularly shaped boulders make strange bedfellows, indeed.

As we plodded along, we found ourselves setting two or three courses of concrete brick, struggling to make them butt up against the asymmetrical exterior of a boulder, tearing out a course or two of brick, chipping some bricks in half and in thirds to fit better the natural contours of the boulders, and then repeating the process all over again with the next course of bricks.

Time and again.

All this we managed to accomplish, of course, while perspiring like stuffed pigs in an underground spit. I could imagine a group of ravenous Boy Scouts awaiting the outcome of the porker's unveiling while anxiously licking their lips.

More than once I had to tear my wife from her self-effacing tasks in order to take in water and electrolytes, just to keep her from perishing. After all, I love her dearly, and I needed the labor. By nighttime, we would turn in to bed like beaten pups, tired and subdued, aching from head to toenails; and we slept like babies.

The next morning, we would marvel at just how little pain showed up at breakfast and how great the willingness to tackle head-on yet another day of sun, heat, and unpredictable obstacles could be.

On our weekends and holidays, we would indulge in early morning sustenance and head back outdoors to begin work anew. In time, as the walls neared completion, we decided to go out to purchase the ubiquitous pond liner, from which virtually all ponds flow (obviously, stacked bricks butted loosely against sandstone boulders would never hold water), and when we returned, we couldn't resist setting the liner in place. Once it was there, it looked beautiful, serene, as if it had been born to the landscape, yet one more harshly, stunningly dramatic piece of Utah's painfully stark surroundings, like the black lava stone and the red quarry rock that cover the state in general and our building site in toto.

SMOOTH!

But we weren't ready for water yet. Not by a long shot. We took the liner back out, confident that it was large enough to do the job once we set it in place again and began filling it with water, and we removed or blunted as many of the sharp pebbles and sandstone edges as we could find. We also brought in several courses of sand, which, combined with natural stones, we arranged throughout the bottom of the pond area in a step-like fashion in order to create different depths beneath the liner. Next, we put down a soft underlayment to prevent any unforeseen objects puncturing the liner, which we finally set in last.

Once we had draped the edges of the liner over the top of the pond wall—an oval wall now standing roughly 3 feet above grade—we anchored it lightly with stones and pulled the garden hose out of hiding. Saying a small prayer to the Vishnu God of Non-Collapsing Pond Structures, we began dumping the water in.

We started first by turning the hose on full and filling a 5-gallon bucket with water. We clocked the length of time it took to fill the bucket at 45 seconds. After that, we turned the hose into the pond and began the job of filling what seemed to be a gigantic raised hole, noting the total amount of time that it took to do so, so that we could, at the rate of 9 seconds per gallon, determine the overall capacity of the pond.

Now, I would have done that clocking thing even if I'd had no other reason do so besides my intrinsic curiosity about just such things. It is a bad trait I picked up long ago that has gotten me into a lot of trouble over the years. But, beyond that, I read somewhere that it's a good thing to know the exact capacity of a pond. In that way, when it comes time to treat the pond for algae or medicate the fish for fungal disease or parasites or anything else that comes along down the line, you'll have a pretty good idea of how much water you're actually dealing with. It beats guessing.

We determined by the time we had filled our pond to capacity that it held 450 gallons, give or take a milliliter.

Once we had filled the pond and stepped back for a better look, we were blown away. It was beautiful. It was spectacular. It was absolutely breathtaking! All right, not beautiful. Not spectacular. And far from breathtaking. More like massive, awesome, and foreboding. It looked as if we had just invested a ton of blood, sweat, and tears in building an oversized bathtub. Which is exactly what we had done. But it was our oversized bathtub. And, by God, it was outdoors.

As I looked at my wife, she looked back at me. *Okay,* we seemed to say to each other. *It lacks style and grace. And it's a bit short on overall allure.* But, we knew that some carefully placed plants and a few other decorator goodies would take care of *that* problem. What we didn't know was just exactly *how.*

QUICK CHECKLIST

- Take into consideration all existing outdoor landscaping elements before selecting a pond site.
- When deciding where to place your pond, consider factors such as shade, access, and convenience.
- Work up a sketch of your pond and include notations on construction materials and techniques before you begin to build.
- Make sure you rid your pond site of all sharp obstacles, from rocks and stones to branches and twigs.

STUDENTS IN THE STORM

We do not learn
by experience
But by the capacity
for experience.

—Buddha

Lake Mendota, Wisconsin, 1980.

A midsummer's day. It is pushing 4 p.m., and the lake is growing choppy. We are half a mile from shore, from the University Union where the sailing club is situated. The wind howls in from the west, and a dozen skiffs scurry for shore. I have the tiller, and my instructor is barking out orders. I have aced the test, and the license is mine. Three others aboard have probably done likewise. One, possibly not.

I feel good. I feel nervous, though, those old familiar knots forming once again in my stomach, and I expect the instructor to take the helm to guide the boat to its moorings. I have done it many times myself, but the waves are kicking up now to 4 and in some places 5 feet. A huge wall slams hard against the starboard hull and washes over us. I shake the water from my eyes. I have never moored a boat in 4- or 5-foot swells. The instructor motions toward me, and I move sideways, holding the tiller out to him.

Suddenly from off starboard we hear a scream. The boat behind us, 70 feet or so, catches a sudden gust and turtles. Its hull bobs up and down against the waves, three of its crew clutching their life vests and flailing like mad, while the fourth, the helmswoman, grabs at the boat's keel. Her hands slip and she goes under for a split second before bobbing back to the surface. She cries out once more and loses contact with the boat as it rolls farther out toward the middle of the lake with each inbound wave. Lightning cracks in the distance and thunder rocks the afternoon sky. The clouds are now dark and ominous, emptying in faster than I could have imagined, *pouring* in, low and ugly, mean and glowering. They open up all at once and a sheet of water and hail washes over us.

In a second, the instructor hands the tiller back to me and shouts for me to take the boat in. I look him in the eyes as he tightens his vest and I tell him okay. I glance at our three other passengers, all terrified. The instructor takes one mighty leap up into the squall and lands with a crash against an in-coming wave. Within moments, he has broken clear from our boat and is on his way to help.

I look off toward the pier and see the dock screaming toward us. I sheet the sail to half mast and shout "Prepare to come about," and in a second, the boat's prow edges into the wind at the eye of the storm. "Coming about!"

The boom snaps wildly from port to starboard. The wind switches around to our port. The maneuver works. The boat slows in the water, and in a heartbeat, the sail slackens slightly, the telltales, revealing anything *but* the wind's true direction, swirling around in angry little circles.

As we edge our way to within 30 feet of the dock, I lower the sail to quarter mast, watching the approach of the pier. My heart races as I see the harbormaster's assistant working feverishly dockside, scurrying to reach the other students caught by the storm. Beyond her, off the far side of the dock, I spy two more boats upturned, and I pray to God we won't soon join them.

Another sudden flash of light precedes more deafening booms, a sudden gust of wind, and more shouting. We edge to within 20 feet when a gust swirls suddenly around and bears down on us from the south, catching our sail and launching us up out of the water and racing once again toward the dock. I lower the sail slightly and pull hard on the rudder as the prow noses once again into the wind. I adjust the tiller as the boat's momentum carries us to within 10 feet of the dock.

"Prepare to come about," I yell again, and the students duck their heads as the mast swings about. Five feet from the dock. Four. Three. I drop the sail and call out for everyone to hold on. Two. One. As the boat reaches the pier, I pull hard on the tiller, edging the prow into the wind, where it suddenly stalls, the hull brushing the dock with a soft thud as we sit there, bobbing up and down with the surging waves.

The student up fore throws a line out across the pier and quickly scampers up after it. He holds the boat off as I help the others out. Safely unloaded, I climb out behind them and shout for them to walk the boat to shore, to get it away from the dock as three other boats hit nearly in unison, hit hard, sending another student overboard. I reach down to help pull her up out of the water. She begins to cry, sputtering while brushing at her suit, and runs down the dock toward shore.

As the pier weaves and bobs, I look out toward the capsized boat and our instructor. He has managed to right the skiff and is helping to pull the students back onboard. Someone grabs my arm. It is the harbormaster's assistant.

"Help me with these two, will you? Christ, what a time to be low on instructors. Get these students out and tie off the lines until we can pull the boats ashore!"

"Okay," I yell back sheepishly, "but *I'm* a student."

OPPOSITE: Koi love to congregate in schools, as these 3-year-old fish are doing as they await feeding time. *Photo © Weng Chai Lim for Fotolia.*

five

Gone Fishin'

The 356 Porsche speedster, the "bathtub" Porsche, is one of the most extraordinary automobiles ever built. It was German inventor Ferdinand Porsche's first driving machine to be named after him. Before that, Porsche had contributed to the development of the Ferry Morse, the Lohner-Porsche, and the Mercedes SS and, more important, had developed the Volkswagen Type 60, the original "People's Car," back in 1938.

But the Second World War delayed the VW's production and Porsche's dreams. Under orders from Hitler's Third Reich, the designer was forced to use his energies to create a military jeep based on the Type 60. It wasn't until 1946 that the Volkswagen "Beetle" went into series production.

Finally, on June 8, 1948, Ferry Porsche came face to face with his singular opportunity to break out on his own. And break out he did.

The Porsche 356 speedster, made of Volkswagen parts and featuring a lightweight metal body, quickly became one of the most emulated cars in the world. Boasting a 1.1-liter engine that delivered a blistering

40 horsepower, it soon caught the attention of auto aficionados everywhere.

Although Porsche had anticipated maximum sales of the car to be fewer than 500 units, by the time the assembly line shut down in 1956, the company had produced more than 81,000 of them. Today, the 356 remains one of Porsche's most sought-after and coveted collectibles.

I knew all of this, of course, before we'd ever even dreamed of building our similarly remarkable "bathtub" pond. Thus, for me, hope sprang eternal. What at the time looked to be a good example of a perfect waste of time and space would, I was sure, turn into something eminently more elaborate, more spectacular, and more prized. Why, someday, I might even place my own name on its design and put it into mass production. Uh-huh.

My wife, on the other hand, knew nothing about Ferry Porsche and his collectible 356 speedster. She knew nothing about taking a Volkswagen and turning it into a sports car. She also knew very little about my tenacity for accomplishing just such feats.

So, as we stood there surveying our work, I calmly suggested to her that what the pond needed most to transform it from an architectural work of wonder into an aesthetic work of art was a waterfall or two. She paused, glared at the bathtub, and turned slowly toward me.

"What the pond needs most," she said resolutely, "are plants."

Never one to knock good fortune—how often is a man blessed with a woman who recognizes the need for labor and then actually volunteers to supply it?—I readily agreed with her. Inside of an hour, we were at the local nursery, rooting around for appropriately pond-friendly plants, for growing, living things that would reflect our desire for what we hoped would become an even larger growing, living thing. While we scoured the nursery's offerings,

I was already drawing up in my head plans for a waterfall, which is what the pond really needed after all.

Recognizing a willing heart, the value of two strong pairs of hands, and a desire to work from sunup to sundown, I soon enough came to the conclusion that having two people build a pond is not only desirable, it is absolutely necessary.

Oh, sure, one person can do the job, but at twice the cost in blood, sweat, and tears. He or she is also likely to age a decade overnight, regardless of the time spanned.

With two people working shoulder to shoulder, the work is easier, and the job takes on a life all its own. A snap decision becomes an exercise in democratic principles. A quick turn of a shovel becomes a lesson in communal thinking. A stone's placement becomes a boardroom meeting. Even the situating of a plant goes more smoothly when one person is there doing the actual situating while the other steps back to evaluate the results—*A little to the left, please.*

So, we labored on, completing the first of our Utah desert ponds in Spring 2001. We'd had a few setbacks along the way.

We hadn't leveled our building site when we began laying bricks, so that, by the time we completed the first course, the concrete blocks looked a bit like the Great Wall of China, winding and wending, rising and falling in every direction. We also very nearly rolled a 2-ton boulder onto my wife as she lay sprawled onto her back and the dolly we were using to haul it down the hillside broke free.

We needed to move a foot-tall redbud volunteer next to the main tree and pulled and tugged at it for nearly 2 hours before finally giving up and building the pond around it. Today, the baby tree is actually taller than the parent and will someday soon take over the main responsibility of shading the pond.

All these things we viewed as minor setbacks, mere annoyances that cost us more in time and frustration than anything else. And, in time, we worked through them. We finished the pond and the planting by fall. That's how long it took for us to get the damned thing situated the way we wanted it.

Of course, we thought we were finished that fall, but the following spring, we pulled out half of what we'd planted the previous year and replaced most of those plants with others that we felt worked better. The best-laid plans.

I had also that fall constructed a small spillway consisting of water rolling off the top of several large rocks stacked one upon the other on the back wall of the pond so that a small stream trickled slowly, steadily downward. Okay, so it wasn't Niagara Falls, but it made a nice sound, and the water's movement was fun to watch.

That next spring, as my wife replanted the pond, I developed plans for a new and improved spillway, something that would sit on the back pond wall ... a new backdrop, new aesthetics, with more new plants and a more dramatic and efficient cascading water feature. This time, instead of dribbling a small stream of running water off a stack of rocks on the pond wall, I decided to do something far more interesting. I designed a rustic wooden planter to hold some spreading yews. Beneath the planter, I crafted an opening through which a wide stream of water would emerge, as if by magic, to go tumbling over the lip of the pond's back wall and into the water.

Once I saw how well the planter/spillway worked, I decided that a second unit next to the first would create an even more dramatic "wall-of-water" effect, and I built a companion. Here are my suggestions for building a planter-box spillway. Construct the planter box first. When that's complete, build the water trough in the same length and width and approximately 2 to 4 inches deep. Before attaching the trough to the bottom of the planter box, waterproof the trough to prevent leaks. When the waterproofing is dry, attach the trough to the planter box using galvanized screws from the inside of the planter box into the $1" \times 2"$ water trough frame, and set the completed project where you want it. Attach the hose fitting and hose from your filter box or pump and turn the system on to check for leaks. See page 36 for details.

Today, after several more plantings have been removed, we are finally satisfied with the results. As you walk by the pond now, with its ivy-covered walls and asparagus ferns and rosemary and baby

Close-up view of a spillway planter.

TO MAKE THE ACTUAL PLANTER SPILLWAY:

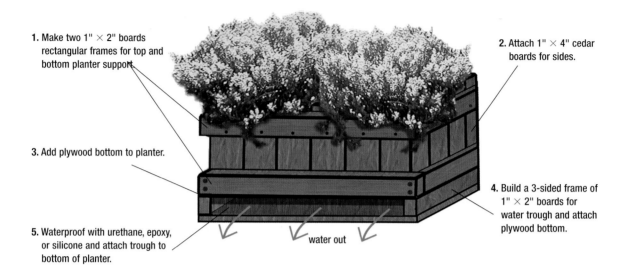

1. Make two 1" × 2" boards rectangular frames for top and bottom planter support.

2. Attach 1" × 4" cedar boards for sides.

3. Add plywood bottom to planter.

4. Build a 3-sided frame of 1" × 2" boards for water trough and attach plywood bottom.

5. Waterproof with urethane, epoxy, or silicone and attach trough to bottom of planter.

water out

DETAIL

6. Drill hole through trough back and attach fitting; seal against leaks with silicone caulk.

7. Run hose from pump or filter and secure with clamp.

You can build your own spillway planter out of scrap lumber. (Cedar or redwood stand up to the elements the best.) The planter sits atop a three-sided waterproof wooden trough. As the water from the pump enters the back side of the trough via a hose connected to a watertight fitting (silicone sealant works well here), it flows forward and out the front side of the trough, creating a soothing waterfall effect and lots of oxygenation.

tears peppered with violets, sweet alyssum, and vinca, you can't help but feel the drama and excitement of it all. You can't help but feel, as well, that this pond has been there as long as the house itself, what with the lichens and moss and other spreading ground-cover fighting to fill in every square inch of concrete brick still visible.

Neither one of us said so, but we both knew intrinsically that we wanted our pond to look natural, or—if not natural—as natural as possible. That was one of our "hidden" agendas when we began

building the pond. Certainly we wanted it to look old, settled in, permanent. The last effect we were shooting for was the "plastic-pot-on-the-patio" look.

For us, landscaping our pond became a practice in evolution. As in life itself, we found that inanimate objects such as ponds, when integrated with living things such as plants, take on a life all their own. As with any life, ponds live through infancy, into childhood, through adolescence, past middle age, settling finally into their senior years. Our pond, I would estimate today, is probably in young

DISGUISING THE BARE SPOTS

Whenever you build a pond—whether it's raised or sunken—you're going to have a lot of disguising to do. You know, those places where the liner shows and you wish it didn't ... or where you've placed a rock or two and they stand out like the proverbial throbbing thumb.

One of the best ways to cover up both the bare spots and the "mistakes" is by using moss balls. Take a wad of Spanish moss (available at garden centers and hobby and craft shops) and wrap it around a handful of soil. Place the ball wherever you want to hide something, and cover it with baby tears, which is an amazingly fast-growing and resilient ground cover.

With the moss ball in place, the baby tears will begin spreading within a few weeks, moving out from the moss to spread across other areas of the wall or bank, as well. It's a quick, easy, and natural-looking fix for nearly any spot that needs help around the pond!

For a quick and easy way to make vertical walls look more appealing, try concocting a moss cocktail.

In a blender, combine 1 cup buttermilk with 1 can stale beer (let the beer sit open overnight). Then add one small container of live moss (honest to God), such as Scotch or Irish moss, available at most nursery centers.

Turn the blender on and blend until the moss is finely chopped. Empty the mix into a container and, using a paintbrush, paint it onto those surfaces where you'd like to see moss grow. Make sure the surfaces are damp and that they're kept damp during the moss's lifetime.

The moss roots will burrow into the stone, brick, wood, or other porous surface and make their home there, sending up a thick mat of moss, usually within a few weeks, depending upon growing conditions. In time, your newly crafted wall will look as if it's been there for centuries!

Baby tears.

Scotch moss.

adulthood—settled enough to appear dignified but not enough to resist the embrace of change.

Our pond, too, has a personality all its own. It has evolved from a big, brusque, bristling bully of an object into a backdrop of peace and tranquility. It is still relatively tall at over 3 feet in height, so it hardly disappears into the landscape. But the plants and details surrounding it help settle it into the background quite comfortably. If anything, it is eloquent instead of brash. It is pleasing instead of piercing. It provides a nice place to hang out after work, sipping on a glass of red wine and smoking a pipe.

After all, water is engagingly calming. The reflections are mesmerizing. Sharing an environment whose atmosphere is enhanced by the fracturing of falling water is healthy. That's one of the reasons ponds have been popular for thousands of years and one of the reasons they are the wave of the future for our health and well-being.

Of course, one could make the same argument in favor of eating a pile of raw seaweed: the more you eat, the healthier you become. But, while I

A closeup view of the author's planter-box spillways on the rear wall of his upper pond.

don't mind the elegance of sushi, I would just as soon forego the subterranean grass.

It is just that way with ponds. Anyone can drop half a wine barrel onto a lawn and attach a fish figurine spewing water from its mouth. There is nothing wrong with that. But, with very little additional effort—the extra mile that it takes to go the distance—you can create something more soothing, more reposeful, and quite a bit more attractive. As for us, we created a joy to behold, not to mention the first stage for an entirely new chapter in our lives.

What's more, it worked!

FOOD FOR FISH

Once we had completed our pond and finished our first round of planting, we were feeling pretty smug. After all, neither of us had ever built so large an outdoor hardscaping element before—and above ground! I say "pretty smug" because something was missing. That something was what we had intended for our pond from the very beginning—a place to house our fish.

Now, ponds and fishponds are about as similar as Yorkies and bullmastiffs. They both look like dogs; they both act like dogs. After that, the similarities come to a screeching halt.

So, too, it is with ponds. Oh, you have in both types of ponds all of the general elements necessary for the successful construction and operation of a pond—and, in the case of fishponds, then some. The "then some" are those peculiarities that help to keep your fish alive, healthy, happy, and growing. Whereas plants only require a little light, a little water, and an occasional feeding, fish are more demanding. *By far!*

OXYGEN, OXYGEN EVERYWHERE

For starters, fish breathe through their gills. They take in water, from which the fish's gills extract oxygen, and they expel the water mixed with a dilute ammonia by-product back into the pond. Therefore, a fishpond must be well oxygenated. The more so the better. Since dissolved oxygen is created by aerated water, you'll need to add a waterfall, fountain, stream, pump-powered bubbler, or whatever other means available to you in order to increase the movement of the water and, thus, its oxygen content.

It's true that goldfish and koi, being related to the native American carp, require less oxygen than, say, rainbow trout and northern pike. Nevertheless, too little oxygen for any species will produce sluggish fish with weakened immune systems, placing the fish at risk of contracting a host of diseases. If severe enough, oxygen deprivation can kill—quickly and silently—often before you ever have a chance to learn that something is wrong.

To provide oxygen for our pond, we installed those two waterfall planters by which the pump in the bottom of the holding pond takes in the water, moves it through two hoses, and ejects it beneath the twin planters, where the water's own momentum forces it out the front for a 16-inch free fall back into the pond. As the cascading water hits the surface, it fractures the water molecules, causing both aeration and ionization, i.e., oxygenated water for the fish and cleaner, healthier air for us.

We initially also used a second pump to power an in-pond fountain. The pump—smaller than the main one—took in water and forced it up a vertical tube. When the water reached the top of the tube, a specially constructed interchangeable head produced a variety of special effects, ranging from a simple bubbler and a flowing bell to an elaborate spray. It was something similar to Chicago's Buckingham Fountain, only less so. The idea of the fountain was to stir up the water surface and create still more oxygen.

Although the fountain worked well, we decided in time that we didn't like it in that pond, so we pulled it out, comfortable in the knowledge that the twin planter spillways generated more than enough oxygen for whatever number of fish we decided to introduce.

pH: THE ACID TEST

Never satisfied with merely oxygenated water, fish also require their homes to fall within a certain pH range (pH is the measure of a body of water's alkalinity vs. acidity content). A low pH indicates a higher level of acidity in the water, while a high pH indicates a higher level of alkalinity. (Simple, inexpensive pH tests are available at most pet shops and over the Internet, and most of them are relatively accurate.) Although pH levels vary wildly, most water levels range from 6.0 (very acidic) to 8.0 (very alkaline), with 7.0 being neutral.

While goldfish and koi are tolerant of a fairly wide pH range (they're perfectly comfortable in water with a pH ranging from 6.0 to 8.0), they prefer neutral to slightly alkaline readings, somewhere within the 7.0 to 7.2 range. Most aquatic plants, too, do best within that neutral range. Various chemical additives to alter the pH balance of your pond's water are as near as your local pet shop or pond supply store.

Of course, as with nearly everything else having to do with ponds, you can count on them being expensive, depending upon the volume of water you need to treat and the degree to which the pH level must be altered. Here's how they work.

If your water is acidic, adding a pH-raising water conditioner such as pH-Plus™ will raise the pH level. If your water is alkaline, adding water conditioner such as pH-Minus™ will lower the pH level. The conundrum comes in when you are trying to determine just how *much* pH-Plus or pH-Minus to add in order to raise or lower the water's pH to the desired level. It's mostly a trial-and-error, hit-or-miss proposition. If you think that sounds awkward and cumbersome (if not outright confusing), you're right. Over time, we've found pH adjusters to be relatively inefficient and far too costly to use in most ponds.

Enter a newer approach to treating water: the all-purpose neutral regulator. It stabilizes either acidic or alkaline water to around 7.0 pH, regardless of how much of it you use. It works by precipitating calcium and magnesium in the water while removing chlorine, chloramines, and ammonia, all harmful to fish. The regulator is simple to use and safe for fish and plants, and it maintains a constant pH level for a month or longer under average conditions.

Today, thanks to the introduction of these regulators, maintaining proper pH, whether in a thousand-gallon pond or a 5-gallon aquarium, is a piece of cake.

CHEMICAL POLLUTANTS

It goes without saying that fish are sensitive to chemical pollution. We've all heard horror stories about fish die-offs following a chemical spill in a local lake or an oil spill in the ocean. Well, it can happen even more quickly in a self-contained pond; so, to protect your investment, you need to avoid using *any* chemicals not specifically labeled harmless to fish anywhere *near* your pond. That includes herbicides for your lawn, nitrate fertilizers for your flowerbeds, and insecticides around your house or patio.

Two other chemicals that can prove deadly to fish are nitrites and nitrates, which are created by the natural decomposition of decaying plants, uneaten fish food, and fish waste. These chemicals act against fish by entering their bloodstream and preventing the fish's gills from utilizing the oxygen in the water. An overdose of nitrites, which eventually turn into

nitrates, can quickly and silently suffocate your fish to death. Worse, still, these two silent killers have no readily available neutralizer: filters don't remove them, and there is nothing you can add to the water to reduce their toxic levels except more water (through the process of dilution).

If your water tests high for either chemical (test kits are available at your pet shop or pond supply outlet, and no fish keeper should ever be caught without one), you should do an *immediate* major water change—draining at least one-third to one-half of the water and replacing it with fresh water. The fresh water, of course, doesn't actually combat the nitrites or nitrates, but it does dilute their concentration to a more fish-friendly level.

When adding water from the tap, remember that most communities use chlorine or chloramines to kill off bacteria and other human-unfriendly critters. Too much of either of these chemicals can also adversely affect your fish, resulting in weakened immune systems and occasionally even death.

Fortunately, unlike nitrites and nitrates, chlorine and chloramines *can* be neutralized safely by adding inexpensive chemicals, including those pH regulators we spoke about earlier. Several other commercial products for removing chlorine and chloramines, such as AmQuel,® are also widely available.

TO HEALTHY FISH!

Fish enjoy early morning and late afternoon sunlight. They are cold-blooded animals, meaning that their internal temperatures adjust to match that of their surrounding environment rather than staying at a relatively constant temperature, as do human beings and other mammals. That said, fish—much like people—prefer to rest in the shade during the hottest part of the day. Therefore, you should provide your pond fish with some direct sun, but also give them access to shade for whenever they require it. As we found out in Utah, shading a naturally sunny pond is far easier than adding sunlight to a pond built in total shade.

To provide shade for our pond, we rely on existing trees, nearby fences, and a small man-made planted "bridge" that runs from the front wall of the pond to the back. It's built out of rough-cut cedar to resist rotting and covered with Spanish moss. We planted the bridge with baby tears and several types of grasses to make it appear natural. As a bonus, the plants' roots hang down into the water, giving the fish something to nibble on and helping to keep the water clean.

Other excellent sources of shade are floating plants, such as water hyacinths, water lettuce, parrot's feather, and duckweed. These plants, which sit on top of the water, block out the sun, providing a natural canopy for the fish below. Water lilies can also be useful as shade generators, in addition to providing a profusion of colorful flowers all summer long.

Besides shade from direct sun, fish also require enough physical space to grow properly and to avoid stress, which lowers their immune system and makes them more susceptible to disease and parasite attacks.

Fish also enjoy rooting around various floating and underwater plants—the kinds that are commonly available from pet shops, nurseries, and pond-supply outlets. Some of our favorites are cattails, hardy water lilies, water hyacinth, marsh marigold, and water lettuce. The fish love to nose around them in search of food and sometimes enjoy nibbling on the leaves, which probably taste to them a bit like a fresh Caesar salad. Plants are also useful in that they take in pollutants and excessive nutrients for their own growth and give off life-sustaining oxygen in the process. It's a win-win situation.

One word of caution, though. If you have koi, be prepared to replace plants often, as the fish are notorious grazers. One medium-sized koi can

Cattails. Photo © *Lilyblooms.com*.

denude a dozen or more water lilies over the course of a single growing season. While goldfish can be mildly destructive on occasion, they are far less so than their Japanese cousins.

WHAT NEXT?

If all this information about fish and water quality sounds a bit overwhelming, believe me, it's not that bad. Oh, it will take some getting used to. After a while, though, testing your pond's water and deciding what to add or when to make a water change becomes second nature.

One word of advice to small-pond owners: be especially vigilant. Since small ponds contain relatively little water, their chemical makeup can change dramatically within a very short time. Large ponds with more water, greater surface area, and a larger turnover rate, on the other hand, can handle more chemicals without endangering fish in the short run.

So, if you're thinking of building your own fishpond, take a moment to reflect upon the two pond scenarios described below.

BEST-CASE FISHPOND SCENARIO

Are you looking for the best pond you can possibly own? Here it is. You have a 1,000-gallon or larger pond stocked with 20 medium-sized goldfish and small koi. The pond is equipped with a large-capacity pump and filter. The pump moves the water through a hose 20 feet uphill to a spillway, where the water is dumped into a small holding pond filled with cattails before cascading over a

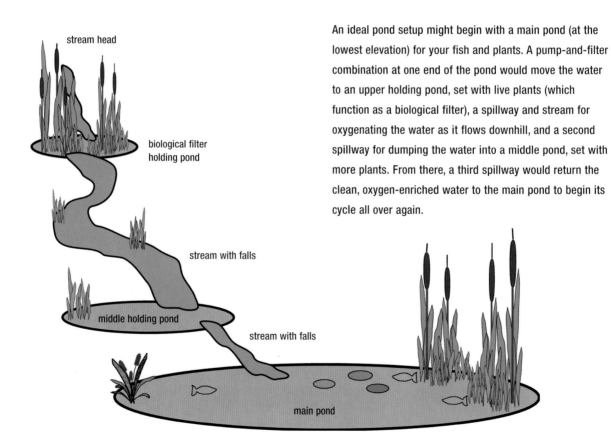

stream head

biological filter holding pond

stream with falls

middle holding pond

stream with falls

main pond

An ideal pond setup might begin with a main pond (at the lowest elevation) for your fish and plants. A pump-and-filter combination at one end of the pond would move the water to an upper holding pond, set with live plants (which function as a biological filter), a spillway and stream for oxygenating the water as it flows downhill, and a second spillway for dumping the water into a middle pond, set with more plants. From there, a third spillway would return the clean, oxygen-enriched water to the main pond to begin its cycle all over again.

second spillway and into a meandering stream lined with watercress, bullrush, and other living plants. From there, the stream washes over a third spillway into a larger holding pond also filled with living plants, including water lilies and hyacinths. Finally, the water spills over a fourth spillway and down another short planted streambed before emptying back into the main pond.

Advantage: You will nearly never have to worry about a sudden buildup of nitrites, nitrates, ammonia, chlorine, chloramines, or virtually any other naturally occurring chemical pollutant.

WORST-CASE FISHPOND SCENARIO

You have a 50-gallon wine barrel with a small pump-and-fountain and six small goldfish.

Disadvantage: You will nearly *always* have to worry about a sudden buildup of naturally occurring chemical pollutants, and you'll *constantly* have to monitor the condition of your water to keep your fish healthy.

Of these two scenarios, one pond isn't necessarily *better* for you than the other; it's just part of the game, something to be aware of. In the end, isn't that what being a responsible pond owner, a responsible human being, is all about? Watching, observing, learning, acting, *reacting*—being in tune with Nature so that you can be in tune with yourself?

Remember what one experienced old-time pond keeper once told me. If you're looking for a maintenance-free hobby, set up a pond. If you're looking for a maintenance-free hobby with a hook, set up a fishpond. And it's true. If you're going to own a fishpond, you're going to have to spend anywhere from several minutes to several hours a week observing, testing, treating, and worrying about what's going to happen next or how to react when it does.

In the end, of course, the decision about which pond to build is yours. Then again, so are the rewards.

QUICK CHECKLIST

- If you plan on adding fish to your pond, make sure the location is "fish friendly."
- Learn the role that oxygen, pH, and chemical pollutants play in the health cycle of pond fish.
- Unlike architecture, when it comes to fishponds, less is not more; plan on building the largest pond you possibly can for healthier fish.

THE LAST GLIMPSE OF FALL

Be soft in your
practice. Think
of the method
as a fine silvery
stream, not a
raging waterfall.
Follow the stream,
have faith in
its course.
It will go its
own way,
Meandering here,
trickling there.
It will find
the grooves,
the cracks,
the crevices.
Just follow it.
Never let it
out of your sight.
It will take you.

—Sheng-yen

Algonquin Provincial Park, Ontario, Canada. September, 1983.

We pull our canoes from the water at the end of the first day just as the last golden spires of light dip down behind the trees. I am delighted, overjoyed—depressed, despondent. It is turning out to be one of those trips where everything goes right except for the reason you came in the first place.

"Don't worry. They're here. We'll find them."

Dean Jenkins, our guide, looks younger than his 29 years, with rugged features and a lanky build that betray his backwoods savvy. He has been plying the waters of these lakes all his life. His family grew up on the shores of one of them. His father was a park ranger here for most of his career.

I give him a weak smile and a thumbs up before turning toward the smell of slow-roasting quail over an open pit. Half an hour later, I am out like a light.

Algonquin is home to 20 different kinds of reptiles and amphibians, 40 types of mammals, and over 130 species of birds, making this a birder's paradise. The haunting call of the loon cries out morning and eve, and the lakes bulge with large families of mallards and merganser ducks, with beaver and muskrat, and with otter.

But we are not out on this trip for loons or ducks or otters. On this trip, we are after the park's mightiest quarry, its largest and most elusive species. On this trip, we are hunting moose.

I came to Algonquin to capture on film for all posterity a moose or two—possibly a bull, if lucky enough, or at least a cow with her calf. I left a book deadline dangling in my office in exchange for the opportunity—the first and possibly the last of my life.

The next morning, we wake to the call of the loon. After a light breakfast, we slip the canoes into the spring-fed lake and start once more in the general direction of the sun, already drawing the mist off the lake's sparkling surface.

By lunchtime, we have seen several loons and more ducks than I knew existed. We round a corner and scare up a pair of golden eagles scavenging a dead fish in a shallow inlet. We slip silently past majestic blue herons and white-plumed egrets. But no moose. We have 5, maybe 6 more hours of paddling before returning to camp. The following morning, we realize, will be hopeless, for we will need to head back to the launch and civilization shortly after sunup.

Back once again in our canoes, we spread out wherever the lake widens, our guide signaling with his hands to split into two smaller groups, each taking a different tack around an island before regrouping on the far side. We seem an eternity away from a sighting—if that close.

By the end of the day, as the sun's rays pour down on us, we break upon a small cove off the main channel, and I motion for Dean to follow us in. The sun is drawing close to the horizon, and the other canoes have already turned back toward camp. It is now or never.

Dean draws his canoe alongside ours. "Well, what do you think? Should we call it a day?"

I look left. I look right. The stronger current heads in that direction. "Let's just drift along awhile," I say. He shrugs.

After 15 minutes, he holds one hand up to his eyes. As if on cue, the prickly ash begin to shake and the leaves tremble. I turn to Dean, his eyes glued to the shoreline.

I motion Mark to paddle in for a closer look and pull my camera from its bag. I prop my elbows against my knees and wait for the hollow thump as the canoe touches shore. Suddenly, the thicket splits in two and a gray-brown head peers out. I snap away furiously as the head is soon followed by a body too large for its own good. The beast stands peering downwind at us, straining to see. Suddenly, another head pokes out, and then another body, smaller than the first—a yearling calf. It is too much to hope for, a cow and last year's offspring.

"Psst!" Mark says, motioning me to the front. "Let's switch places. You'll get a better shot."

We manage to slide past one another without overturning. As the cow and her calf disappear back into the brush, I stand up, one foot in the canoe, the other anchored firmly atop the rocks holding our craft on shore.

Within seconds, a loud roar belches up out of the woods. Several trees shake, their canopies trembling overhead. A huge rack breaks free from the thicket, followed by a massive head and an even larger body. I zoom back to fit the entire creature into the frame and goad the camera into action. My eye glued to the finder, I hear Dean whisper that the bull is mating with the cow, who still has last year's bundle of heaven at her udder.

I zoom back again as the bull grows larger. Again I snap away, zooming back several more times to keep the beast in full view, when finally I realize that I am zooming back because the bull is moving ... *forward!*

I lower the camera from my face and stare—not 30 feet away—into two dark, malevolent eyes made darker still by the setting sun. My heart leaps. My pulse pounds. My breath comes in short staccato pants. I hear Mark behind me struggling to dislodge the canoe with his paddle, pushing against the rocky bottom.

The bull lowers his head, raises it to sniff the air, and then lowers it again. He takes one short, ominous step forward.

"My God," I say softly, not wanting to make a sudden move. Moose have poor eyesight, but they can hear a heartbeat a hundred yards away.

"Can you push off?" Mark whispers. I watch the bull crane his head to pick up the words, the wind suddenly rustling the shrubs behind it. In an instant, it will all be over. Head lowered, rack straining, the beast will charge us, and before I can get my damned foot back into the canoe, we'll be upended and ripped to shreds as we frantically try to out-swim a solid ton of muscle with attitude.

Suddenly I see the shrubs behind the beast open up again, and the cow emerges once more. Eyeing the bull lasciviously, she bellows once, twice, before taking a bite from the grass at her hooves.

The bull turns his massive head toward her, back once again toward us, and finally toward her again before turning slowly around and walking back toward the thicket. Within moments, both of the animals have disappeared into the wilderness, the thrashing and trembling of the growth around them sending shivers up my spine.

Thank God for lust.

"Let's get the hell outa here," Mark says, and I need no coaxing. We shove off and paddle furiously to catch up with our guide.

The following morning, the thick mist has opened up into a cold, light drizzle as we paddle our way out of camp. It is enough to darken anyone's spirits. I think it is the most beautiful thing on earth.

As we approach the dock and the launch waiting to take us back to civilization, the clouds open up and a thin ribbon of blue shines through, illuminating a path across the water, just before closing, again, for good.

"Did you see anything?" the skipper of the launch calls out as we dock our craft. "I heard the moose have moved deeper into the woods, what with snow moving in tonight. Too bad, eh?"

I pull myself clear of the canoe, turn toward Mark, and wink. "Oh, there might be one or two still around," I say. "You never know."

six

If You Build It, They Will Come

Are you ready, now? Are you all set to dig in and begin building your own outdoor pond? Are you sure?

Before you take your first giant step, step back. Look at all of those little sketches of what you want your pond to look like. If you don't have any little sketches of what you want your pond to look like, make some.

Building a pond takes planning. It takes dreaming. It takes thinking ahead. In that sense, it's little different from planning a dream house or that perfect surprise birthday party. Building a pond, even a small one, is a major step. If you do it wrong, you'll regret it. If you do it right, it will transform your garden, as well as your life, into something you never thought possible. I guarantee it.

ABOVE: Ponds come in all shapes and sizes. This one, made from poured concrete, is rectangular in shape to fit into a more formal setting than would a free-form pond. The owners lined it with pond fabric in order to prevent leakage.
Photo © by Monja Wessel for Fotolia.

A bird's-eye view of a pond-lover's dream might include: 1, a front entryway water feature such as a fountain; 2, a side-yard multi-level pond with one or more spillways and holding ponds; 3, a main pond for raising fish and plants; 4, a deck with a small decorative water feature and possibly a fountain; 5, a geometrically shaped pond with deck seating on two sides for ease of access to feeding fish; and 6, a hidden pond with bench accessible via a narrow meandering path.

Here are a few questions to ask before you take that first big step. Do you know what kind of pump and filter you're going to use, if any? If not, check out some options in Chapter 7. Will the pond be lighted for dramatic effect? If so, you'll need to provide for an electrical outlet (better yet, a whole battery of them; pumps need outlets, too).

Are you planning on introducing fish into your pond? If you are, the pond will need to be at least 3 feet deep—deeper in harsh winter climates. How about plants? Of course, you're going to set new plants around the perimeter of your pond, but why not also plant some exotic-looking water plants, such as marsh pickerel and water lilies, within the pond?

Will your pond have a spillway, a waterfall, or a stream feeding into it? If so, make certain that your sketches show where they will go so that you can keep them in mind as you begin construction. Will there be a fountain nearby or in the pond? Depending upon the size and type, you may need to prepare a special foundation for the fountain first. See the pond plan illustration, to give you some idea of the possibilities.

LINER POND OR MOLDED POND

There is one more thing you need to determine before you begin building your pond. Are you going to build a liner pond—a pond in which water is retained by use of a flexible rubber or vinyl liner—or a molded pond? A liner pond is more flexible because you can build the pond to any size or configuration you desire. A molded pond is simpler to install because it is constructed of stiff plastic resin and is virtually freestanding. The drawback to molded ponds is that they're limited in the number of sizes, colors, and configurations available.

Despite their limitations, molded ponds have a place in the world. Although they are not the most natural-looking of ponds (even though you can do a lot to disguise the walls with rocks, stones, moss, and plants), they're ideal when used to create a modernistic water feature or one of regular shape. You can build a molded pond into the ground (recessed) or above-ground (raised). If it's above-ground, you'll need to shore up the walls of the pond with rocks or soil to prevent them from bending, sagging, or even cracking under pressure from the water.

For a more formal look, you can situate a regularly shaped molded pond on-site, build a wooden frame around it, and finish off the frame with stucco, brick, stone, or any other material available to you. If, on the other hand, you want the most natural-looking pond possible, choose to build a liner pond. A liner pond is easiest to disguise because the liner can be trimmed back right to water level, leaving little evidence of human endeavor.

Regardless of the type of pond you choose to build, once you've answered all the necessary questions, you're ready to go. You've selected a suitable site for your pond. You've done some preliminary clearing of the area. You've settled on the right size and shape for you. You know what building and pond materials you're going to use. Now, it's time to roll up your sleeves and get to work.

THE RECESSED POND: PREPARING THE SITE

There are a couple of good reasons for building a recessed pond. For starters, it will look more natural than a raised pond. It will also be easier to approach for cleaning and planting than a raised pond. In addition, it will allow you to create varying pond depths easily, thus enabling you to grow a wide variety of water plants with different depth requirements.

If your pond is going to be recessed, you're virtually assured of having to do some digging. If it's going to be a large pond and you can maneuver the machinery into your yard, hire an experienced backhoe operator. Make sure to get a written contract that provides for the removal of excess dirt and debris from the site. Also, get a copy of the contractor's insurance declarations sheet, just in case something goes wrong. And always, always, ALWAYS have the utility company come out to mark off any underground lines and pipes before you begin digging. Where utilities are concerned, you always want to err on the side of caution.

If your pond is going to be relatively small, you can do the digging by hand. That's going to require a few simple tools, such as a round-point shovel, a blunt-nose shovel, a rake, and a hoe. It's also going to take a whole lot of muscle.

Start the project by marking out the pond with spray marker paint or chalk. Tamp the perimeter of the pond area down firmly so that once all of your

DETERMINING POND DEPTH

When planning your pond, keep in mind that it should be wider and longer than it is deep for several reasons. First, a pond deeper than 3 to 4 feet is considerably more difficult to maintain. Even with a filter, you'll have to clean the bottom of the pond periodically to remove organic debris, such as leaves, grass clippings, and flower heads, to prevent them from decaying. Also, underwater plants, which are valuable in helping to turn toxic nitrates into oxygen, require sunlight to grow. If the pond is too deep, they won't do well except in the shallow areas.

If you plan on introducing fish to your pond, you'll want the pond to have the greatest surface area possible. The more surface area your pond has, the more you'll be able to enjoy your fish and the more oxygen the water will be exposed to. A profusion of underwater plants will offer fish a place to hide when they feel threatened and a place to spawn when the time is right. Water that's approximately a foot deep makes an excellent spawning ground.

49

A WORD OF CAUTION

If you're like most people, you'd be amazed at the number of different utility lines being buried below ground these days. You'd be even *more* amazed at just how costly it would be if you were responsible for breaking a line or two.

I came across a rural job site once where a contractor had brought out a backhoe to clear a drainage ditch of some dirt and debris. There were overhead electrical power lines, so the hoe operator assumed there were no utilities buried underground. He was wrong. Inside of 10 minutes, he had sliced through a buried cable TV line and a fiber optics line in three different places. (It had taken him a while to realize what he had done.)

As a result, the contractor received a bill from the cable company for more than $400 for cable repair and replacement. He also received a bill from the fiber optics company in excess of $80,000! The last I heard from the contractor, he was headed to court.

pond's weight is on it, the dirt won't compact, causing the pond liner to sag. For large jobs, you can rent a soil compactor at most equipment rental shops, or you can make a hand compactor from an 8-foot 2 × 4 to which you've attached a 12"-square plywood foot. Put on a pair of gloves and begin tamping—straight up and down, the harder the better. (Pond building is also good exercise!)

Once the soil is tamped, begin digging the pond's perimeter. Work all the way around, piling the excavated dirt in a wheelbarrow or plastic trash container. When the dirt receptacle is full, dump it where you think you'll need it most—

along the pond's bank, for example. Try to create a gently sloping "lip" around the pond. In that way, you'll get double the depth of pond for every shovelful of dirt you remove—the depth of the shovel and the depth of the material piled up outside the hole. The lip will also help prevent chemical-laden runoff from your neighbor's lawn from poisoning your waterway.

When you have completed digging out the perimeter of your pond, step back and take a good critical look. Once the perimeter has been dug out, it's easier to envision the size of the pond. Is yours going to be large enough to satisfy your requirements? Is it too large?

Continue digging toward the center of the pond, piling the excavated dirt up around the perimeter or stacking it where you might want to create a waterfall, a streambed, or a raised planter. Create a grade that slopes gently up from the excavation for a nice, natural look.

When you've removed a shovel's depth of dirt from the entire pond, step back and look it over once again. This is a good time to determine where your shallows will be. You'll want some areas of your pond to be shallower than others in order to plant shallow water plants, to provide fish an area to sun themselves during the cold days of winter and to offer pregnant females a safe haven for their eggs and fry.

Try to envision an area where cattails might look good. You'll want that part of your pond to slope gradually from water level down to around 8 inches in depth. Also determine where you want the deepest part of your pond—most likely toward the center. Fish will use that area for safety from predatory animals such as raccoons and waterfowl. It's also the part of the pond that will remain open in winter when the shallower areas freeze over, if you live in a cold climate.

Make sure you dig the deepest part of your pond 3 feet deep or more. To determine the depth, run a string across the middle of the pond from a stake on each side. Then take a carpenter's rule and measure the distance from the bottom of the hole to the string.

If the pond isn't deep enough, dig a little more. If it's deeper than you want (although there's really no practical limit to the depth of a pond), replace some of the dirt you just removed.

Also, now is a good time to shovel away space for a skimmer box/filter/pump combination, if you plan on using one (and I highly recommend that you do for all but the smallest of ponds). If you plan instead on using an underwater pump with an external filter box, you can add that after your pond is lined and filled with water.

INSTALLING A BOTTOM DRAIN

For the sake of convenience, you might want to install a bottom drain, which will make cleaning your pond much easier. You can purchase a drain at most home supply centers or plumbing supply shops. It will come with a drain casing, a dome to keep fish from being sucked into it, and a flange to seal the drain to the pond liner. Silicone sealant applied liberally to the gaskets above and below the pond fabric helps immensely in preventing leakage. A pre-manufactured bottom drain consists of a domed lid to prevent fish and large debris from passing through the drain system. The lid is attached via a series of gaskets to a bottom flange, which extends through the pond lining. A bead of silicone seals the flange against the lining, preventing leaks. As the pump draws the water past the domed lid and into the drain system, debris from the pond bottom is drawn into the filter box, where the filter removes most of the larger particles before returning the water to the pond. A bottom

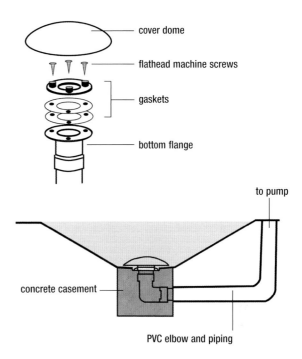

Components and cross-section of a typical bottom-drain assembly. It includes several component parts that, once assembled, create a watertight seal between the inside pond liner and the outside world.

drain is also an effective way of emptying a pond prior to cleaning. Instead of returning the water to the pond, it can be pumped into a sewer system or onto a lawn or flower beds, where the nutrient-rich water will help feed your plants. (See the bottom drain diagram.)

To install the drain, dig out a small "box" where the unit will sit. Run a small trench from there to a point outside the pond area. Attach the drain to whatever length of PVC pipe you'll need to extend clear of the excavation site. Then mix enough fast-setting concrete to fill the box. While the concrete is still wet, wiggle the drain with the attached pipe down into the cement, leaving the top of the drain flush with the top of the concrete. Allow the cement to set up overnight before inspecting it, and give the concrete 2 to 3 days to cure before laying the liner into the pond. Once you're satisfied with the preparation that you've completed for your recessed pond, you're ready for the next step.

THE RAISED POND: PREPARING THE SITE

Oops, but wait a minute. What if you don't *want* to build a recessed pond? What then? The answer, of course, lies in building a *raised* pond.

There are several good reasons to build a raised pond. The first and most obvious is that, for one reason or another, you're unable to dig your pond into the ground. Perhaps there's a concrete slab where you'd like to place your pond. Or maybe you're "blessed" with solid bedrock mere inches beneath the soil surface—something we refer to here as "The Utah Syndrome."

Perhaps you have young children in your family or neighborhood and don't want them playing around a recessed pond, where they might slip and fall in. Maybe you don't want the runoff from the surrounding lawns working its way into your pond—runoff containing all sorts of chemical additives. You may want a raised pond to butt up against the house or some other architectural feature.

Whatever the reason, if building a raised pond makes sense to you, start out the same way you would if you were building a recessed pond. Locate the pond area and, if you can dig a few shovels worth of dirt from the center of the pond, all the better. That's just a small head start on the game. If not, don't worry. It will all work out in the end.

The simplest way to build a raised pond wall is to use manufactured landscape bricks. They come in all sizes, colors, shapes, and finishes. Some bricks have a lip on the back, which is a

Ponds such as this one provide the perfect showcase for colorful flowering water lilies. *Photo © Erika Walsh for Fotolia.*

great aid in helping to interlock the bricks so that they don't move under pressure.

Once you have settled on the type and style of brick that's right for you, make sure you order enough of them to complete the job. There's nothing more frustrating in the middle of a project than to run out of bricks and have to bribe your neighbor to go to the store for three more. If math isn't your strong suit (I think it might even be beyond math to something like algebra or—ugh!—*geometry!*), your home-supply store should be able to determine the number of bricks if you tell them the height of the wall and the shape and length of the pond's perimeter.

The bricks will be delivered on pallets that will be removed from the truck with a small forklift, so, you'll need to have an accessible space where they can be stacked. Make sure it's not so close to the building site that you end up stumbling over them for the next 3 weeks and not so far away that you'll be cursing your own stupidity.

One word of advice before you begin stacking any bricks. If your property is not level (i.e., sloping), take some time to add sand, dirt, pea gravel, or even kitty litter to get the pond footprint as level as possible—whatever it takes. If you try running a first course of bricks from level ground to sloping, the finished job is going to look sloppy. In addition to that, you'll have one helluva time trying to tie the bricks together later.

After you've laid out the first course of bricks on your pond's perimeter, step back and take a look at your future pond. Is it large enough? Too large? Shaped just right? Situated in the right spot? If not, now is the time to make adjustments—*not* after you've laid six full courses of bricks around the pond.

In addition, if you're going to use a skimmer box/filter/pump combination (best for all but the smallest of ponds), you'll need to leave a "cutout" or opening in the wall where the skimmer box will sit. The pond liner will run up and over the top of it, just as if it were part of the wall. (It's difficult to envision, I know, but trust me on this!) If, on the other hand, you're using an underwater pump and separate filter box, you won't need to make any special concessions. You'll work that into your completed pond layout later.

Once you're satisfied with the placement and size of your pond, begin laying the second course of bricks, overlapping the centers of the second course with the ends of the first. In that way, the bricks will "lock together" more tightly than if you stacked them one directly over the other.

After you have finally reached what you assume will be your top course of bricks (which means, in effect, that you've probably run out of material), stretch a string from one end of the pond to the other. Crawl into the pond and use a carpenter's rule to measure the deepest part. If it's 3 feet deep or deeper, your pond will be just fine. If not, add more bricks to the wall or dig the center of the pond down deeper, if possible.

Next, decide where you're going to want to place your water plants. Keep in mind this generally good planting advice: place taller plants toward the back and sides of your pond and shorter plants in front. Build up some shallow areas inside your pond, using stacked bricks, rocks, or even plastic buckets turned upside down. Remember that everything is going to be covered with pond liner before the water goes in, and the liner will be covered with pebbles and rocks—so don't worry about the look of your shallow areas right now.

Don't know how deep different plants need to be placed? Check out the planting depth references in Chapter 11. Then adjust the height of your shallow areas to meet the various plants' requirements.

Whatever you do, definitely create shallow areas. Not only will you be grateful you did when it comes time to set your water plants, but also you'll be thankful when you watch your fish swim into the shallows, looking for food. I don't care how much they come to the surface in deep water, there's absolutely no joy the equal of watching fish cavort in the shallows.

Just remember that, wherever you set the depths of your shallow areas, that's where they're going to stay. Once you lay the pond liner over everything and start pumping the water in, it's going to be too late to make any adjustments, so do all of your homework and fine-tuning now.

Next, if you're installing a bottom drain in your raised pond, this is the time to put it in. Follow the instructions above. If not, stop right here. Take a deep breath. And get ready. The big moment has arrived. The thing that turns a bunch of stacked bricks into something much, much more. It's time to install the pond liner.

LAYING THE POND LINER

Regardless of what type of pond you're building—recessed or raised—once you've prepared the site for the liner (sometimes called pond fabric), you're ready for the scary part. I say "scary" because most new pond builders are apprehensive about working with a waterproof liner. They don't realize how resilient liner is and how much abuse it can take without puncturing. And, even though a punctured pond liner isn't something to strive for, if your liner *does* get a hole in it, patch kits are available and easy to use. (Remember how you once patched your kid's bicycle tire?)

Before you go out to purchase your pond liner, take one last look around. Are there any sharp rocks or exposed edges? If so, remove them, blunt them, or cover them with padding so they don't present a problem later. If you're still uncomfortable with the roughness of various protruding objects in your site, consider using a pond underlayment—the equivalent to a carpet pad—in order to protect the liner from punctures. The underlayment is in effect a second waterproof layer that provides added protection against punctures and leaks.

You'll need to know just what size liner to buy. Measure the pond along its longest dimension. This figure will be the length of the liner and/or underlayment you'll need. Use a flexible rule so that you can run the tape from the top of the bank on one side, down into the deepest part of the pond, into any other depressions along the way, and up to the top of the bank on the other side. You're measuring the verticals as well as the widths, because those surfaces will take up liner also. Keep the tape as tight to the ground as possible for the most accurate measurement. Then add 4 feet to your results. This figure will be the *length* of the liner you'll need to buy. For example, if your measurement turns out to be 12 feet, adding 4 more feet will give you a total of 16 feet in length.

Next, measure the pond at its widest point, perpendicular to its length in the same way, including the vertical distances. Again, add 4 feet to the results. That will be the *width* of the liner you'll need.

Liner and underlayment most often are sold from large rolls, available at home centers, nurseries, and pond-supply shops. The width of the rolls varies. If you determine that you need a liner measuring 16 feet in length by 11 feet in width, and the liner comes in 8-foot, 12-foot, and 18-foot widths, you'll need to buy 16 running feet of the 12-foot-wide liner or underlayment in order to provide for the 11-foot width you need.

Three basic types of liners are commonly available: PVC (plasticized polyvinyl chloride), polyethylene, and EPDM (ethylene propylene diene monomer). Of the three, by all means, buy the EPDM. It's flexible, easy to work with, and stretches or "gives" to conform to irregularities in your pond. It also has the best puncture and abrasion resistance of the three. In fact, EPDM liners are so durable that most come with a 20-year warranty.

Although some people insist that PVC works just as well and is less costly, it's simply not so. PVC doesn't hold up well to ultraviolet rays (the sun), doesn't resist puncturing nearly so well, and actually costs more than EPDM in some outlets. If your local stores don't carry what you want in the size you need, check out the numerous online vendors who can usually supply exactly the size you need, often for a better price than you'd find locally.

Once you've purchased your liner, you're ready for the installation. This is where you're going to need some help.

Unfold the liner so that it's flat on the ground (either side up—it doesn't matter). Bribe two or three neighbors to help you out. With four people, have each one take a corner and walk the liner over to the pond, where you can center it over the hole before gently laying it in. If you have only two people, fold the liner in half and walk it over to the pond. Align the fold over the center of the pond, lay the liner in, and unfold it.

Next, take off your shoes (an old liner-laying tradition!) and climb into the pond. Use your hands, working from the center out, to remove as many of the creases as possible. You won't get them all out, because you're fitting a two-dimensional object into a three-dimensional space. Push the liner into all of the holes and crevices, trying to "use up" as much of the material as possible. Depending upon how carefully you measured, you should have between 1 and 2 feet of excess fabric hanging over the bank. (This is infinitely more desirable than being 1 or 2 feet short!)

Once that's accomplished, climb out of the pond, get the garden hose, and fill the hole to a depth of about 1 foot. The weight of the water will help draw the liner into every nook and cranny. You can help with your hands, wherever possible.

At this point, if you've made plans to install a bottom drain, you should remove the water using the hose as a siphon. I know it sounds ridiculous— wax on, wax off—but trust me on this. It's the right way to do it. You can distribute the water around the lawn or your flowerbeds.

Once the water is out, use some old rags to wipe dry the area above the drain. Take a sharp knife and make an incision near the center of the drain. From there, cut the shape of a cross into the fabric, slightly smaller than the diameter of the drain.

Next, squeeze a generous amount of silicone between the drain and the liner, and thread the drain up through the hole, tucking the four corners of the liner underneath. Squeeze another generous bead of silicone on top of the liner just beyond the cutout area so that when you place the flange on the drain and screw it down, the silicone will be sandwiched between the flange and the liner.

Now you have a drain with two layers of silicone to act as a water barrier—one below the liner and above the drain, and the other above the liner and below the drain flange. Tighten the flange down as much as practical and smooth out the excess silicone on the liner. Allow the silicone to dry for at least 24 hours.

During this time, you can complete the connections among the discharge pipe, your filter box, and the pump. (Or you can do what we usually do at this point—go out and spend a bunch of money on plants.)

If you've elected to use a skimmer box to hold both the filter medium and the pump, set the box in place behind the liner in the cutaway you left for it and follow the installation directions for cutting an opening in the side of the liner. Have the silicone ready for a sealant, just as you would when installing a bottom drain. Once again, allow 24 hours for the silicone to set up before filling the pond.

FILLING THE POND

Once those 24 hours have passed, it's time to grab the hose and begin filling your pond. To determine how much water your pond holds, you can either buy or rent a flow meter to attach to your hose, or, as an alternative, you can estimate the amount by measuring the length of time it takes to fill a 5-gallon bucket. Divide that time by 5 to determine the time it takes to fill 1 gallon.

Note the length of time it takes for the hose to fill the pond and divide that time by the amount of time required to fill a gallon. That should give you a relatively close indication of how much water your pond will hold.

For example, if your hose takes 1 minute (60 seconds) to fill a 5-gallon bucket, dividing

60 seconds by 5 gallons gives you 12 seconds per gallon. If your pond takes 1 hour (3,600 seconds) to fill and you divide that time by 12 seconds per gallon, you come up with 300 gallons. It's not absolutely foolproof, but it's pretty darned close!

Once your pond is filled, it's D-Day ... Delirium Day. That's the day you get to fire up your pump and get set to be deliriously happy. *If* everything works as it should. Which means if you did everything the way you should have done it, and *if* the equipment works.

Which brings up an interesting point. If you hit the switch and nothing happens, don't panic. Check that all of the electrical connections have been made. Test the outlet to make sure that it's getting power. Wiggle the plug to make sure it's making electrical contact. If the pump still doesn't work, check your home's breaker box to make certain it hasn't tripped. If that doesn't do the trick, you may have a faulty pump—rare, but certainly possible. To be sure, try plugging the pump into a different outlet. If that doesn't work, take the pump back and exchange it for a new one.

Assuming nothing malfunctioned and everything seems to be working just fine, take a tour around the pond, checking the hose and pipe fittings for leaks. If you find something dripping somewhere, simply tighten the fittings until it stops. This is also a good time to check your stream, waterfall, or spillway to make certain that the water is running where it's supposed to and not where it shouldn't. Depending upon how well you did your homework and how diligently you prepared for this moment, you shouldn't have any major adjustments to make, although it's not uncommon for streams and waterfalls especially to need some tinkering to get them working exactly right.

Once you're convinced that everything looks good, your next step is absolutely critical. Place both hands on your hips, shake your head from side to side, and say out loud, "Well, I'll be damned!"

Then go into the house, pop the top on an icy cold one, and settle back into a chair near the pond to watch the thing run. And, realize that you have broken free from the pack. You have done what few others you know have done. You have built your very own living, breathing pond. It's Miller time.

QUICK CHECKLIST

- When building a recessed pond, mark the location and have on hand all of the tools you'll need.
- If you're going to install a bottom drain, buy the kit beforehand and pick up a bag of quick-drying concrete for pouring a slab beneath the liner.
- If you're building a raised pond, have the brick or other construction material on-site before beginning to build the walls.
- If you plan on using a skimmer box, buy it before excavation or construction begins and leave a space for the box in the wall.

POND BUILDING 101

Twenty Basic Steps to a Two-Level Pond

When professional photographer and fellow pond-lover Chris Evans decided to build a pond in his own backyard, he set about doing it right. After reading the most up-to-date information on pond-building he could find, he sketched out the pond, marked out its shape on the ground, completed all of the necessary excavation, and purchased the materials and equipment he knew he would need to complete the job. Naturally, his pond plans changed as construction unfolded (they always do), but the results were predictably rewarding: a fully functional, aesthetically pleasing, biologically stable man-made pond offering nearly all of the advantages of a naturally existing pond with few of the inherent limitations imposed by Mother Nature. *(Pond Building 101 photos by Chris Evans; www.scipie.com/photography)*

6-1. The excavated pond site. The different depth levels provide for varying water depths.

6-2. An aerial shot shows the upper pond all ready for fabric. The ledger rock at the spillway will provide for a dramatic small falls.

6-3. It doesn't matter what your raised pond is built from, so long as the material is sturdy and water-resistant. A liner will hold the water inside, and soil and plants will disguise the outside.

6-4. Closeup of the upper pond under construction, with a low spot toward the rear of the photo.

6-5. A side view of the upper and lower pond shows the different water depths of the lower pond and the ledger rock for the upper pond falls.

6-6. Where soil is rocky or otherwise less than smooth, lay a pond liner down first to prevent the next layer—the waterproof vinyl fabric—from puncturing and springing a leak.

6-7. After the liner has been set, lay out the vinyl pond fabric.

6-8. As the pond fills with water, many of the wrinkles will flatten out from the weight of the water.

6-9. Filling a pond can take from several minutes to several hours or even days, depending upon the pond's size.

6-10. Once the pond is filled to the brim, let it sit for an hour or two before checking for low spots and possible leaks.

6-11. To ensure that the upper pond loses no water en route to the lower pond, run the pond fabric from the lower pond up over the spillway of the upper pond in a single sheet.

6-12. Once the ponds are filled, set up your pumps and filters and do a maiden run to see that water isn't spilling out the side of the falls or otherwise escaping from the pond.

6-13. Now is a good time to begin thinking about how you will disguise the pump hosing and fabric.

6-14. This pond builder placed some plants in the pond to give him an idea of how they'll look before he finished the pond off.

6-15. Experimenting with the placement of various flat stones on a spillway will help you get just the effect you desire.

6-16. This system features a pump in the lower pond and a filter box that will be disguised later with plants in the upper pond.

6-17. Stacking rocks around the pond to hide the raised wall.

6-18. Closeup of the spillway.

6-19. Note how natural the placement of spillway rocks makes this pond look.

6-20. The finished pond, planted and with a slate tile approach.

FREEDOM AND THE FISH

Man stands in
his own shadow
and wonders
why it is dark.

—Zen proverb

Blue Mounds, Wisconsin. Summer, 1979.

I make it a habit. Every afternoon around 5, I pull myself from my labyrinth, leave my typewriter, reference books, and manuscript behind, and force myself to walk three-quarters of a mile down the gravel driveway to the bridge. From there, I skitter down to the stream below and locate a good spot to step in.

In the 3 years or so that I have been fishing Blue Mounds Creek, I have come to the point where trout fishing is no longer a sport. It is a passion. I am so taken with it that I no longer desire to catch fish so much as to master the art of fishing. It is the presentation that I crave. I do not catch to keep, I catch to release ... or, that is, I catch to release all but the last fish of the day, which I hurry back to the ranch, fillet, and fry up in butter and fresh garlic for dinner.

Today, I am especially hungry, and I am fishing a hole I know to be deeper than my waders and deeper than my own 6 plus feet. It is as deep as forever and as wide as ... well, no one knows. I glance up at the sun hovering just above the ridge to the west, and I know that this is the best time of day to be here. I take my hat off my head, select a suitable offering, and work the fly free. It is a brown hackled nymph, a lucky fly if ever there was one, and one of my favorites. I tie the fly off gingerly, dust it with floating agent, and wet it in the spring-fed water running just below my thighs. I take up the slack line onto my reel.

I lift the line from the water and whip the rod back. Flicking my wrist sharply, the rod flies forward with the line in hot pursuit. I continue this back-to-front motion several more times until I have worked enough line free from the reel to let it sail to where I want it, which is just above the deep hole that I am fishing and alongside the undercut bank that I intend to explore.

The fly lands softly in the middle of a small eddy, circles once or twice, and then begins its downstream journey back toward me. I want to float the nymph past the undercut bank as closely as I can manage in the hopes that the current will draw it in.

Suddenly, the line twitches. I freeze. Again it moves. I wait a brief second or two before yanking up hard on the rod.

Wham! The water swirls. The fish is off and running, out from beneath the undercut bank and into the very depths of the pool. I loosen the clutch on the reel as I feel the power tugging at the other end. I have a 2-pound leader on, and it would not take much to snap it.

After a while, the clutch stops singing, and I pull up gently on the rod until I feel the weight stacked against me. "Shit." I am snagged. The fish took my favorite fly, ran it beneath a log or root, and now I'm hopelessly ensnared. "Shit!" I say again, louder this time, as I feel the constant pressure against the line. No movement, no twitching, just the endless singing of the rippling water. I pull some line back in before it suddenly jerks out of my hand and the fish is off and running again.

"What the ..."

I play the line cautiously, even though I am tiring of the game and my stomach is rumbling; I promise myself that I will eat well tonight, no matter how long it takes to bring dinner home.

Back and forth we go, the fish coming in for the landing and the line peeling off for the chase. I look up at the sun, whose last golden rays have disappeared beneath the aspen-covered ridge, holding the line as taut as I dare without putting too much pressure on it. When the fish wants to run, it runs, and I stand there watching in awe. When it tires of running, I pull it gently toward me, closer, inch by inch, to home.

I put a little more pressure on the fish and feel it pull back, and I decide to give it more line, to give it some leeway. I will lose him that way—he is no longer merely an "it"—and my battle will be over. Either that, or I will tire him to the point where I can finally reel him in.

Sure enough, he turns and runs again, this time back toward the undercut bank from which he came. If he gets under there, I'll lose him for sure. The sun is by now far below the ridge, and several bats fly by. I see the sky darkening, very little of the luminescent blue of dusk left to it, and I know it is now or never.

I tighten the line again and bull the fish back out into the stream, into the pool and the strongest part of the current, where he is forced to fight the moving water as well as the power of the line, the rod, and my aching arms. I work him slowly left to right, back and forth, struggling against all of the forces of man and nature, until I feel it is safe to try to bring him in. I tug on the line, slowly, cautiously, and except for one small effort at the end, the fish—his energy spent—finally succumbs.

"Holy Christ," I say out loud as I reach down, grip him through the gills, and pull him up out of the water. "Jesus." I scamper out of the stream and scurry awkwardly up the bank where I lay the fish on the grass. He is the largest brown trout I have ever caught. Hell, he's the largest brown trout I have ever *seen!* I stretch out my hand and measure him off. Nearly three hands long, more than 22 inches. I look at him, at his magnificent coloring, at the strength and power rippling beneath his skin. I look at him and estimate his weight at more than 6 pounds. How on earth can a 2-pound line pull in a 6-pound fish against a moving current?

As I open his mouth to remove the nymph that was his downfall, I notice his eyes. Or, rather, I notice one of them, the one looking up. Not merely looking up.

Looking up at me. I look into that eye and I see it move, as if surveying the land, a foreign land, a land that it has never known before, a land that it has never seen and probably never even dreamed existed. A land stripped bare of life-sustaining water, a land of frighteningly vivid colors and beasts crawling the ground and soaring through the air, like so many fishes out of water.

I watch as his eye moves to me again, to my own eyes. I watch and I look at him looking at me, and my stomach growls and I know in a heartbeat it is over. I know what must be done.

As I lean down, straddling the banks at a narrow stretch just upstream from the bridge, the fish cupped in my hands, I lower him slowly, allowing him a few seconds to reorient to his surroundings. His gills begin pumping oxygen again. His tail twitches rhythmically. I open my hands, and the fish hangs suspended in eternity. As I lean closer to the water, I swear to God he looks back at me, up over his shoulder, with his left eye—the same eye that had looked at me when he was prone on the bank. Suddenly, with one mighty swish of his powerful tail, he shoots through the ripples and back to the safety of the pool.

It will be a long, cold walk back to the house, I know. And when I get there, I will step out of my waders, hang them beside the fireplace, and slip into some dry slippers.

My creel will be empty. But that will be all right. I will not go hungry. Not this night. This night, I have been fed.

seven

Pumps and Filters for Life

A flower falls even though we love it, and a weed grows
Even though we do not love it.

—Dogen Zenji

Water, water everywhere, and not a drop to ...

Well, you get the point. Today, there are nearly as many different types of pumps and filters to move and clean water as there are fish to benefit from them.

When my father first began keeping tropical fish in an aquarium back in the early fifties, he knew little more about what he was doing than I did. He knew what the man at the pet shop told him, which was nowhere near enough. Predictably, inside of a week, the fish were dead, and we were back at the pet shop, asking the questions we should have asked earlier. The very first one should have been this: "Why do we need a filter?"

FILTERS

Filters play an integral role in fish keeping. They are also valuable—although not absolutely essential— for pond keepers without fish. They help to keep pond water clean and clear, and they make life for a pond owner easier and more enjoyable.

OPPOSITE: In addition to sporting water hyacinth and water lilies, this pond boasts a robust spillway to keep the water circulating while providing an excellent means of oxygenation. A flat rock acts as a ledge from which water cascades down into the main pond. *Photo © digitalphotonut for Fotolia.*

But with all the filters on the market today, what type should you use? Let's take a few moments to take a look at just what kinds of filters are available and how they vary.

As you might imagine, different types of filters do the same job in different ways. They filter, or strain, debris from the water. Some filters are good at removing large pieces of debris; others are good at removing smaller particles. Although different filter types employ different filtration principles, all end up processing waste.

Of the different types of filters on the market today—from mechanical, vortex, ultraviolet, and sand filters to biological, vacuum, skimmer, and trickle tower filters—the most popular is the mechanical filter. It strains debris from the water, usually by means of some sort of membrane through which the water passes and in which the debris gets trapped. Most of the waste you're going to be removing from your pond will come from your fish. I know this for a fact, because we have had fishponds and we have had non-fishponds, and believe me, fishponds are messier!

GARBAGE IN, GARBAGE OUT

Think of a pond as a giant trash can. What you put into it stays in it. A filter, contrary to popular belief, doesn't remove waste. It simply collects it. *You* have to remove the waste, or it will remain there inside the filter, contaminating the water in one form or another, forever. That's worth repeating: What goes into your pond stays in your pond until you remove it.

Dry fish food? It's there. Oh, it will have changed from fish food to fish feces, but the waste matter is still there. Chemical additives? They're there. Salt? Medication? Fallen leaves? Still there. The only time that you actually clean your water of all those waste products is when you back-flush or clean out your filter. That's one of the reasons you need to be diligent about maintaining your filter, as well as about making frequent partial water changes. Water changes reduce waste matter, including potentially toxic chemicals, through dilution. A good rule of thumb is to provide a 10% water change each week for fishponds and once a month for non-fishponds.

What about a naturally occurring pond? Who changes the filter there? I thought you'd never ask. A natural pond contains far fewer fish than a man-made pond. In a natural pond, the water is constantly being replaced—usually more than 10% a week! Every time it rains or a stream overflows or somebody leaves the sprinklers on too long, the water makes its way downhill and eventually ends up in some creek, stream, or pond.

The number of fish and other creatures a natural pond can support was established eons ago by nature. That's not the case with man-made ponds. Of course, we could build ponds and stock them in the same ratio as nature intended ... say, one fish for every 500 gallons of water. But that wouldn't be much fun. That's where the filter comes into play.

Filtration, or the act of removing waste from water, is accomplished in the pond primarily via one of four means: mechanical, chemical, biological, or ultraviolet. Here's a look at the strengths and weaknesses of each different type.

MECHANICAL FILTRATION

Mechanical filtration is a means whereby waste is physically removed from water. Just as if you were to take a net to clear the surface of your pond of fallen leaves, a mechanical filter sifts the waste from the water, separating the wheat from the chaff. A good example of a mechanical filter is a *skimmer box*.

A skimmer box is designed to "skim" the surface of your pond. It sits with an intake manifold at approximately the same height and a little below the pond's surface. It's powered by a pump, usually held inside the skimmer box, and has a filtration pad situated between the intake manifold and the pump. As the pump moves water from the skimmer box out through a hose, more water is drawn into the box through the intake, where it passes through the filtration pad. The clean water goes out the other end, and the crud remains trapped in the filter pad. That's why, at least once a week, depending upon the amount of waste in the pond, the skimmer box needs to be checked, debris should be removed from the chamber, and the filtration pad should be cleaned of debris with a garden hose. We use a skimmer box in our largest pond, which features a 500-gallon holding pond tied in to two smaller ponds, four waterfalls, and two streambeds. So far, the box has worked perfectly.

Another type of mechanical filter is a *settlement tank*. It's usually a flat tank situated next to the pond. It works by pumping water from the bottom of a pond into the tank, where the collected debris settles to the bottom. The debris remains there until it's removed.

A more elaborate type of settlement tank is a *vortex filter*. It's usually cone-shaped and ranges from 2 to 6 feet in height or higher. As water passes through the filter, it swirls around the side of the tank in a circular motion (thus, *vortex*). The waste settles on the bottom, where it remains until it's removed. Although vortex filters are efficient, their large sizes make them counter-productive for the small pond owner.

CHEMICAL FILTRATION

The second type of filtration, called *chemical filtration,* is a bit misleading. Instead of adding chemicals to clean the water, you add something to the water to absorb the chemicals.

The most basic form of chemical filtration is carbon. Carbon helps to clean water through absorption. Millions of microscopic pores on the surface of the carbon absorb ammonia, nitrites, and other types of potentially toxic organic waste.

The drawback to a carbon-based system for use in a pond is that carbon becomes saturated quickly, after which it actually begins releasing ammonia back into the water, which is not a good thing. Furthermore, saturated carbon cannot be cleaned; and, it's impossible to tell when the carbon is saturated and no longer doing its job. That negates any really positive values carbon might have for use in pond-keeping.

Another material, zeolite, works similarly to carbon and can actually be cleaned, or "recharged," by soaking overnight in a bucket of salt water. The salt draws the ammonia out of the zeolite, thus enabling it to be used again.

The problem once more is that it's impossible to tell when the zeolite has reached its ammonia saturation level. Also, while it might be suitable for use in a small pond, the more water you have to treat, the more zeolite you have to lug from the pond to the saltwater bath and back again, making it less than ideal for use in all but the smallest ponds.

BIOLOGICAL FILTRATION

A third filtration method is *biological filtration*. It works the same way in a pond as it does in nature.

Placing a filter medium inside a box creates a living Petri dish where beneficial bacteria can grow, just as they do in nature (although in nature, the Petri dish is usually peat moss or plant roots or anything else that bacteria can cling to). As bacteria grow, they consume waste by-products. That makes a biological filter the single best type of filter for fish-ponds, because beneficial bacteria actually consume toxic ammonia and nitrites. And, if you have fish—especially koi—you're going to have ammonia and nitrites.

Fish, like all animals, produce toxins in the form of ammonia (NH_3). They excrete it through their gills and in their waste. If too much ammonia builds up in your pond, your fish's gills will become irritated. Long-term exposure to ammonia will eventually harm a fish's internal organs. In nature, the aerobic bacteria *Nitrosonomas* remove the hydrogen and add oxygen to each ammonia molecule, thus converting it chemically from NH_3, or ammonia, to NO_2, or nitrite.

Nitrite, a highly toxic chemical, is a by-product of the naturally occurring Nitrogen Cycle. Another bacteria, *Nitrobacter,* converts nitrite into nitrate (NO_3), which is much less toxic to fish.

Biological filtration works by attracting and holding both *Nitrosonomas* and *Nitrobacter* bacteria. When exposed to oxygenated water (the kind you would find in a pond!), these two bacteria begin converting ammonia to nitrites and nitrites to nitrates. To be effective, a biofilter must have a large surface area on which the bacteria can form. This surface area is known as *biomedia,* literally a medium on which beneficial bacteria live.

In the past, many materials have been used as biomedia. These include hollow plastic tubes, orange bags, lava rock, foam sheets, and even hair curlers. The problem is that most of these materials take up a great deal of space, meaning that your filter box is going to have to be immense to provide enough growing surface for the bacteria you need to do the job.

In our pond's biofilters, we use a combination of foam sheeting and soda straws. Yes, the kind the kids like to drink from. We bundle them up and weight them down (so they don't float away) and then place them in the filter box. Each straw, because of its length and shape, offers a large surface area for the bacteria to congregate. When you multiply the surface area of a single straw by a hundred straws all tied together, you begin to get an idea of just how much beneficial bacteria your biofilter could be generating! Best of all, drinking straws are available everywhere dirt cheap!

As effective as straws are for use as biomedia, a new product is supposed to be even better. It's called Alfagrog filter medium. It's extremely porous and is filled with tiny "tubes" into which bacteria can find their way. We haven't tested it yet, but we plan on doing so soon.

Once a biofilter converts ammonia into nitrites and nitrites into nitrates, the nitrates (which, you remember, are only mildly toxic to fish) can be removed through regular water changes. They can also be removed by *massive* numbers of water plants, which absorb the chemical through their roots, while giving off oxygen in return. Since the numbers of plants required to accomplish this task are far beyond the scope of most pond owners, frequent water changes are still considered the best way to remove excessive nitrates.

While biological filtration is of obvious value to the pond owner, there is one drawback to using it. Although it's a minor one, it could be deadly for newly established ponds. It takes from several weeks to several months for the bacteria in a biofilter to build up to a level where it can complete the nitrogen cycle and begin protecting your fish. In the meantime, although your new pond will look clean and healthy, there will come a time when the ammonia, nitrite, and nitrate levels will spike sharply up.

In order to prevent a sudden die-off of your prized fish before the nitrogen cycle takes hold in your pond, you're going to have to make partial water changes frequently, especially for the first few months of your setup.

CHOOSING THE BEST FILTRATION SYSTEM

Now, are you sufficiently overwhelmed? Confused? Wondering which type of filtration system would be best for you? That depends upon what type of pond you're filtering. If you have a simple whiskey barrel, a small pump-and-fountain combination will work fine. If you add fish to the barrel, you should probably add some sort of biological filtration medium. Virtually anything will do. We use foam pads in our small ponds, as they allow water to pass through the pads easily while trapping larger waste products and encouraging bacteriological growth. When the pads get dirty, we rinse the larger waste products out of the pads, being careful not to wash out all of the beneficial bacteria. We clean the pads weekly from spring through fall.

If you have a larger pond with a number of goldfish or koi in it, you should definitely use a combination of filter types that includes both a mechanical and a biological filter. A skimmer box that removes waste from the pond's surface can be fitted with a foam pad and bundled straws for a combination of mechanical and biological filtration. You can purchase mesh bags of carbon and drop a couple of those into the skimmer box, too, once a month. In that way, you'll have three types of filtration working for you—mechanical, chemical (the charcoal), and biological.

You can also use more than one filter to provide different types of filtration. In our large pond, for example, we have a skimmer box equipped with a heavy duty pump at one end (the deep end) that does the majority of filtration. We also have a smaller PondMaster filter in the shallow end. It contains a small pump, filter media, and a grate to keep the fish out. The entire unit sits submerged on the pond bottom, so it is virtually invisible. The only part of the PondMaster that is visible to the eye is the electrical cord, which we disguise with Spanish moss, rocks, and plants.

VEGETATIVE FILTER

We also use another natural means of filtration known as a *vegetative filter* to help hold down the nitrate level of the water. It consists of a separate holding pond loaded with plants. As the water flows through the pond, it filters through the plants' roots, and the plants take in the nitrates while giving off oxygen.

Why go to all the trouble? The answer is simple: we have koi. Koi generate an enormous amount of waste, which means they are living, breathing ammonia machines. Our biofilters convert the ammonia to nitrites, which are still highly toxic, and then to nitrates, which are considerably less toxic. Our vegetative filters remove the nitrates.

Most koi pond owners don't use vegetative filters because the koi will dig up and swallow most of your plants nearly as quickly as you can introduce them. In that way, koi are a bit like infants. If they can reach it, they're going to put it in their mouths. (That includes floating thermometers, by the way—so don't use them!) That's why koi ponds often have high nitrate levels.

Enter the vegetative filter. When you run your pond water through a vegetative filter consisting of a heavily planted pond or even a streambed, you're encouraging the nitrates in the water to be absorbed into the plants' system and transformed into oxygen, and that's a very good thing. That, alone, is reason

The spillway in this pond (on the left) empties into a small holding pool planted with cattails, which act as a natural vegetative filter, before the water empties out the right side of the pool and down a man-made stream leading to a larger lower pond.

enough to do your best to incorporate live plants into your pond environment.

ULTRAVIOLET (UV) CLARIFYING FILTERS

There's one last type of filter that we strongly suggest you consider using. It's called an *ultraviolet clarifying filter*. It consists of an in-line sealed box through which water passes. Inside the box is a waterproof compartment housing an ultraviolet light fixture. As water passes through one end of the box, past the ultraviolet light, and out the other end, the light kills off algae.

Of several types of UV filters on the market, the most effective ones use a quartz filter. The intense light that a UV filter generates penetrates the walls of the algae, causing them to die off and clump together. The clumps can then be removed as they pass through a mechanical filter.

A WORD ABOUT KOI

One last word about koi. While they're one of the most popular fish for outdoor ponds, they take special consideration. Koi eat a lot, and they can get quite large. They also grow extremely quickly. Remember: this is a fish that can get as large as a salmon! The more a koi eats, the more ammonia it generates. The larger a koi grows, the more waste it produces.

Sound like a losing proposition? Not really. After all, koi are such fun! They respond well to people. They're extremely colorful. And they never hesitate to beg for a handout! So, what do you do? Why, you feed them, of course.

We've read a lot over the years about how overfeeding is the primary killer of koi. That's simply not true. Koi do not overeat. They eat just exactly as much as they need in order to grow just as fast as they possibly can. You can feed them all day long, if you want, and they'll thank you for it. In fact, some breeders feed their koi seven or eight times a day! But these breeders have the gigantic filtration systems necessary for keeping the water clean.

So, it's not overfeeding that is deadly to koi, but rather the ammonia they produce as a result of overfeeding. Take special care to remove the ammonia from the water, holding the production of nitrites and nitrates to a minimum, and you'll be way ahead of the pack!

The main drawback to using a UV filter is that it needs to run continually to be effective, so a light bulb normally lasts for no more than a year or so. You should change the bulb and clean the quartz filter annually, ideally in spring before algae have a chance to take hold. Even if the bulb still works after a year, change it anyway, since the power of the UV rays greatly diminishes after that time.

One thing about UV filters and algae: they don't get rid of *all* forms of algae, such as the string types that cling to the rocks and sides of your pond. They only get rid of the suspended algae. But, since that's the algae that makes water appear green and dirty and robs the water of oxygen, killing off suspended algae will help keep your water clearer, cleaner, and safer.

UV filters have a coincidental benefit to fishponds, as well. Just as they manage to kill off suspended algae, the UV rays are effective in eliminating some types of harmful bacteria, fungi, and parasites. That means a UV filter can benefit pond owners not only cosmetically by keeping the pond clean but also physiologically by keeping the fish healthier. Don't believe me? Since adding a UV filter to our largest pond, our water has never been clearer or our fish healthier.

One important consideration in buying a UV filter for your pond: In the case of ultraviolet light, less is definitely *not* more. If a UV filter is rated for a pump that pushes 1,200 gallons of water an hour, buy one rated for at least half again as much, or 1,800 gallons of water an hour. Trust me on this. The more intense the UV rays are, the cleaner and clearer your pond's water will be.

Okay, so that's quite a lot of information to digest. Once it's all boiled down, what *is* the best filtration system for your pond? I suggest a combination of different filter types—all of the ones I've mentioned, if possible. If not, then at least rely upon the two

The author prepares to add an ultraviolet filter to his raised pond. Note the two wooden planter-box spillways sitting atop the rear pond wall.

most commonly used filter types—mechanical and biological. Remember, no single type of filter can possibly accomplish everything you want.

By combining mechanical, chemical, biological, vegetative, and ultraviolet filtration methods, you'll be creating the cleanest, purest, healthiest pond possible. Mixing filtration types ensures a well-balanced, well-functioning pond. And a well-balanced, well-functioning pond produces healthy, happy fish.

PUMPS

Pond pumps come in one of two basic types: submersible and non-submersible. That means you'll need to decide whether you want your pump to be under water (inside the pond) or not (outside the pond). Submersible pumps are probably the most popular, simply because of their placement: out of sight means out of mind. With your pump sitting inside a skimmer box or at the bottom of the pond, there's no need to disguise it or hide it from view.

The purpose of the pump is simple: It moves water from here to there. That's necessary in order to keep the water clean (by running it through a filter) and to create oxygen (by fracturing the water molecules and stirring the water's surface). A pump can move water from a pond to a streambed or it can power a fountain, which in turn provides additional aeration for the pond.

The most important thing to remember when buying a pump is that it should be capable of turning your pond's water over two to three times an hour. That means that, if you have a 1,000-gallon pond, your pump should be rated to deliver at least 2,000 to 3,000 gallons an hour. For a 500-gallon pond, you'll need a 1,000- to 3,000-gallon-an-hour pump. Here, as in few other things in life, bigger actually is better, because the more water you funnel through your pond's filtration system, the better off your pond will be. And your fish—including those koi—will thank you for it!

QUICK CHECKLIST

- Choose the method of filtration you're going to use—mechanical, biological, chemical, UV, or—better still—a combination of the four.
- Decide on what type of pump you're going to use, submersible or non-submersible.
- Try to build into your pond a vegetative filtration system by planting part of the area with water plants.
- Determine how much water you'll need to pump in order to turn your pond's contents over 2 to 3 times an hour.
- Purchase the largest pump (with the greatest flow rate) you can afford.

THE LAST TEARS OF SUMMER

Lake Wisconsin. Summer, 1986.

I am sitting next to my golden retriever in a rented cabin on the lake, which is a misnomer, since it is a lake purely by design. It was formed when the Army Corps of Engineers put a dam across the Wisconsin River, the resulting backwater creating a waterfront real estate boom such as the state has rarely known.

I am sitting in the same place in the cabin that I have been sitting for most of the summer. I have only a few more weeks left before I move back to town, into my own home, which I recently purchased and upon which I am scheduled to close soon, ending a chapter in my life.

It has been a quiet summer, which is exactly what I had been looking for. The solitude has given me a chance to do some research and begin writing a children's book I am working on about famous Supreme Court cases: *Roe* v. *Wade* or *United States* v. *Nixon*.

The sun darts behind a bank of low clouds. I reach around to turn on the light behind my desk and continue pecking away at the keyboard. A crack of thunder sounds from somewhere far across the lake. I look out and wonder if I'm going to need to close the windows soon. The dog looks up. He is not a big fan of thunder.

Suddenly a lightning bolt splits the afternoon sky, and a deafening crack booms ominously down from heaven. The dog lunges for the bed, and before I can get up, rain is pouring down, hammering everything in sight. I close the window closest to my desk and head toward the screen door when I hear someone scream. I freeze. I listen, trying to determine the direction from which the sound came.

Another scream, and I see the waves of the lake lapping at the pier as the wind whips up wildly. I see, too, through the torrent, someone struggling in a canoe offshore. I glance up at the sky, throw the door open, and race to the water's edge. Another lightning bolt, another crack of thunder. I shout to the young girl in the craft, some 20 feet from shore. She is struggling with her paddle and heading out from shore.

"Hey!" I shout. "Hey! Can you swim?"

She peers at me.

"I say, can you ..."

"No," she shouts back. "I'm in trouble. Help!"

I take my shoes off and leap into the water. It is warmer than the rain that has already soaked me to the bone.

"Help!" she cries again.

"Hang on!" I yell back, and in a matter of seconds, I bob up beside the craft.

"I can't swim!" she cries.

"Just hang on," I tell her, and I grab the rope trailing from the bow of the canoe and begin pulling her toward shore. "We're almost there!"

I feel the gravel bottom of the lake beneath my feet, and I stand up. I turn toward the girl and pull the canoe up and out of the water onto shore. I take a closer look at her. She is 14 or 15, soaked, frightened. She is sobbing hysterically.

"It's all right," I tell her. "You're safe."

I help her out of the canoe and onto land. I look into her eyes and they are dilated. Her breaths explode in short, rapid spurts.

"Here," I tell her, taking off my shirt and throwing it around her. "Just kneel down for a minute and catch your breath." She drops to all fours, and I tell her to lower her head and slow her breathing down, to take deeper, longer breaths. She begins to quiet, and as I try to shield her from the pelting rain, I ask her where she lives. She looks up at me but cannot talk.

"Come on. Come on into the cabin. I'll get you some dry clothes, and we'll call your parents."

She looks up at me, begins to stand, and nearly topples over. I grab her by the shoulders to steady her. Upshore, I see some people running toward us. They are waving their arms and shouting something unintelligible.

"Do you know them?"

She looks up and nods. She takes off my shirt and hands it to me as they reach us.

"Janine, what happened? What's the matter?"

She begins to sob again, and one of the women in the group cradles her.

"I think she just got scared," I say. "She was hyperventilating. I pulled her canoe to shore."

"Come on," a man says. "Come on, Janine, we'll take you home."

And as I stand there watching, they turn and slowly begin retracing their steps along the shore until they are out of sight.

As I walk back to the cabin, the rain stops. By the time I reach the door, a thin shaft of brilliant yellow light splits the charcoal sky. I turn and pause briefly. All is as it was before. The lawn, the beach, the pier, the motorboat. And a small aluminum canoe with a rope hanging from its bow.

eight

All Flowing Things

> Let your mind wander in simplicity, blend your spirit with the vastness,
> Follow along with things the way they are, and make no room for personal views—
> Then the world will be governed.
>
> — Chuang-tzu

I admit it. We're spoiled. It's difficult for either my wife or I to look at a pond—at any pond—without thinking to ourselves, "Gee, wouldn't a waterfall or a stream have made it just perfect!"

And, you know, we usually find ourselves saying, "*Yes!*"

So, without proselytizing too much, I think the time is right to consider adding a waterfall or a stream to your pond. In fact, I'm betting on it. What's so hot about waterfalls and streams? Just this: they oxygenate the water; they filter out debris; they help to dissipate chlorine; they provide visual dramatic impact; and they're too, too cool.

Best of all, you can build streams and waterfalls nearly anywhere with the aid of an efficient pump and that miracle of aquaculture, the pond liner. Streams can be a mere foot or two in length or meander around for hundreds of feet. (I told you they're cool!) They can incorporate a small pool or two plus a waterfall, spillway, or just about anything else your own imagination can conjure up.

Waterfalls can be as simple as a thin bead of water trickling a mere inch or two over the lip of a rock or as dramatic as a wall of water free-falling

OPPOSITE: A rock wall provides the perfect opportunity for showcasing a spillway that empties into the pond below. Planting the crevices lends the illusion of a natural setting to the scene. *Photo © Seraphic06 for Fotolia.com.*

RIGHT: The author created this spillway using several cans of black pond foam, which he assembled into the desired effect. The foam spillway sits atop a concrete brick wall, the bottom portion of which is lined with pond liner to prevent leakage.

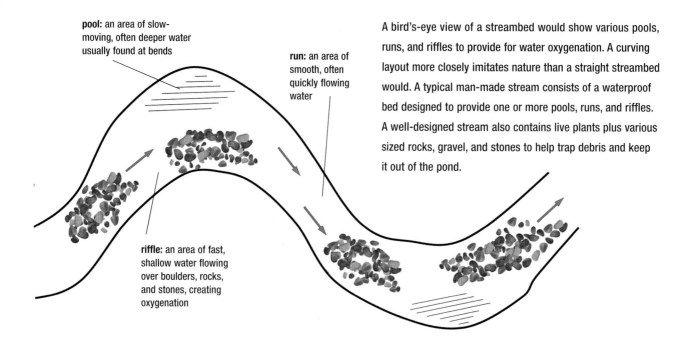

pool: an area of slow-moving, often deeper water usually found at bends

run: an area of smooth, often quickly flowing water

riffle: an area of fast, shallow water flowing over boulders, rocks, and stones, creating oxygenation

A bird's-eye view of a streambed would show various pools, runs, and riffles to provide for water oxygenation. A curving layout more closely imitates nature than a straight streambed would. A typical man-made stream consists of a waterproof bed designed to provide one or more pools, runs, and riffles. A well-designed stream also contains live plants plus various sized rocks, gravel, and stones to help trap debris and keep it out of the pond.

several feet or more. Although streams and waterfalls often appear naturalistic, many ornate formal gardens incorporate them as well. And, just as you began building your pond, your waterfall or stream should begin with a layout.

PLANNING A STREAM

Before designing your stream, take some time to study the way natural creeks, brooks, and streams run. Visit a local park. Spend time looking at pictures. Pay attention to how a stream cuts its course, how the banks are situated, where rocks lie, and how plants grow. Notice that some rocks are in the stream, and some line its banks. Notice, too, how nearly all rocks are only partially exposed, the balance of them being buried.

Take a close look at the plants, too. See where they grow, whether they're alone or in bunches, and how they look. Observe how small falls and pools develop. Nature, remember, is our best teacher.

Naturalizing a stream is the key to making it look as if it were part of your original landscape—as if you bought a house in which a stream ran through the backyard. I can't tell you how many times someone has seen our streams and falls and told us how lucky we were to have found a piece of property with water running through it! Someday, I swear, I'm going to respond with, "Yeah, but you should have seen it last fall when the salmon were spawning!"

BUILDING A STREAM

Before you actually begin creating your stream, sketch it out on paper. Take into account the contours of your landscape. Remember the obvious: water flows downhill. Buck that dictum, and you're inviting a headache.

You can sketch out a stream just about anywhere on your property. If your yard is sloped, half your battle is already won. If not, you'll have to build up the streambed. You'll need at least a 1- to

2-inch fall *minimum* for each 10 feet of stream in order to keep the water flowing. Otherwise, it could pool up and back flow or overflow the sides.

What material should you use to build up a slope for your stream? Well, since it will be covered by pond liner and disguised by landscaping, you can use anything that's handy and will remain relatively stable. That includes rocks, stones, compacted soil, lumber (preferably cedar, redwood, or treated pine so that it doesn't rot over time, causing your streambed to sag), old tires, etc. Stay clear of organic materials such as hay and straw since they will biodegrade, causing the stream to settle.

How long and how wide are you going to make your stream? That's another consideration. While no hard rules apply here, you should use some common sense. Sketching your yard out on a sheet of paper will give you a good bird's-eye view of how your stream will fit in with the rest of your landscaping. You want it to look natural and inviting, not overwhelming or inconspicuous.

As a rule of thumb, if your stream is going to tie into a pond, the total length of the stream should be a minimum of twice the length of the pond in order for them to be in scale with each other. Don't put a 3-foot-long stream together with a 12-foot-long pond and expect it to look natural.

As for the width of the stream, common sense again prevails. The wider the streambed, the more leisurely its current. The narrower the bed, the faster the current. Of course, current is also determined in part by the size of your pump. A unit that pumps 4,000 gallons an hour will move water four times faster than one that pumps 1,000 gallons an hour; so, you can have a rapidly flowing stream in a wide bed, for example, if your plans—and your budget—allow for a large pump.

If you're looking to emulate nature (and that's usually the plan in adding a stream to the landscape),

include a series of short, nearly level sections in the streambed. These sections, which are actually small holding ponds, should be level enough to hold some water even when the pump is off. You can connect the sections by drop-offs of just a few inches, resulting in a natural-looking series of stepping pools.

Don't forget to vary the direction of the stream. Most streams in nature bend and weave around boulders, trees, rocks, and other elements, and so should yours. Avoid running your stream straight downhill. Large rocks in the stream create rivulets as they divert water around them. Small rocks and pebbles produce ripples as the water moves over them. Both produce oxygen and negative ions.

Once your stream and waterfall sketch is complete, take your design outside. Mark out the watercourse with landscaper's spray paint or chalk. If your design includes a waterfall, read the next section. Here's a summary of points to remember about building a stream:

- Keep the dimensions of the stream—both length and width—proportionate to the landscape. Don't build a 4-foot-wide, 20-foot-long stream to service a 100-gallon pond.
- To make your stream look more natural, vary the size and placement of the rocks, stones, and boulders you use both in the stream and along its banks.
- Also vary the width of the stream, from narrow to wider, as well as its general lie. A meandering stream will look more natural than a straight one. Remember that in nature, nearly nothing is straight.
- Before fitting your stream with pond liner, build up the sides of the stream with rocks or dirt so that they are fairly level throughout the stream's length. Don't make the right bank 4 feet tall and the left bank 1 foot tall. For most streams, a 1- to

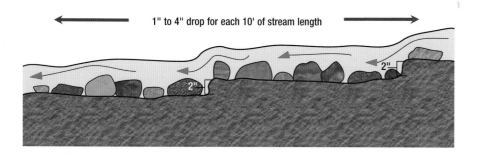

1" to 4" drop for each 10' of stream length

In this cutaway side view of a typical stream, note how the streambed falls in elevation 1 to 4 inches for each 10 feet of stream length. The greater the change in elevation, the faster the water will flow (up to the limitations of the size of your pump).

2-inch drop in elevation for every 10 feet of stream length will keep the water moving, while a 4-inch drop will create a fast-moving stream.

- Finally, don't cut the excess liner along the stream banks to size until you have given the stream a trial run. You may find places where you will need to build up the sides to prevent water from snaking or splashing out. It's always easier to do that when you have plenty of liner available to work with.

PLANNING A WATERFALL

A streambed is boundless. It can be low and rambling or steep and dynamic. Will it have waterfalls? And, if so, how many? That's pretty much determined by the lay of your land and your own desires. A streambed can have no falls or can be nothing but a series of falls placed one after the other. The height and width of the falls are up to you.

Various types of waterfalls exist in nature, and nearly all can be emulated for the backyard pond, depending upon the dimensions of the area with which you have to work. The two most common types of waterfalls are the free-falling and the cascading. The free-falling waterfall carries water over a flat stone extending out past the pond wall so that the water falls in a straight vertical line from the lip of the stone into the pond. A cascading waterfall releases the water at the top of a series of stacked rocks or stones, where it cascades, or winds, down the rocks and into the pond. Each type of waterfall

creates a different water sound. The one you choose to build is solely a matter of personal taste.

You should keep in mind one rule when creating waterfalls: they should be in scale with the pond into which they empty. A small trickle will be lost emptying into a large pond and will contribute little in the way of oxygen and negative ionization. On the other hand, a torrent of water will produce a dynamic effect

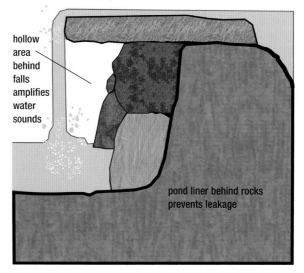

overhanging stone creates a curtain of water

hollow area behind falls amplifies water sounds

pond liner behind rocks prevents leakage

A cutaway view of a typical waterfall shows the overhanging stone used to create the fall, as well as the stones and smaller rocks behind the waterfall for visual effect. The pond fabric and liner run in a single sheet behind the waterfall to prevent leakage.

Waterfalls cascading over a cliff into a large pond.
Photo © Carefree Pools, Highland Park, IL.

and a ton of oxygen, so is less really more when it comes to spillways, or just the opposite?

Enter the header pool. A header pool (a 10-inch or deeper pool at the top of a waterfall) can create a more natural look than water simply spilling from an outlet pipe. Header pools emulate nature. One header pool, or catch basin, drops water over a spillway into the stream, which deposits the water into the next header pool, and so forth.

While you're in the planning stage, think about what type of falls you want: a smooth, broad, unbroken curtain of water that plummets into a header pool or a narrow, frothy cascade. The surface of the spill stone (the stone that forms the lip of the fall) determines the way that water falls. For a curtain of water, use a smooth, flat stone. For a

frothy cascade, find a spill stone with ridges and bumps, one that funnels water somewhat toward its center. For a trickling effect, use a series of rocks stacked up vertically that spread out gradually toward the stream below.

But remember this: the best-laid stream and waterfall plans mimic nature. Make yours meander lazily throughout your landscape while incorporating a variety of stones and plants scattered around in a seemingly random pattern. Remember: "random" means natural. Nothing in nature is ordered.

EXCAVATING

Once you're satisfied with how your waterfall and stream look on paper, you're ready to start moving a little dirt around. If you have an existing slope or hill, its fall line will largely determine the pitch of your water feature. But if you're creating a watercourse on relatively flat land or if you want a greater pitch to your feature than naturally exists, you'll need to build a berm, or high spot.

On either a natural incline or a constructed berm, start by defining the layout of the stream or waterfall on the ground. Use stakes and twine along the sides of the streambed as you define exactly where your stream will twist and turn. Once you've finalized the course (or, at least, once you *think* you've finalized the course), use more stakes and twine to indicate the height of your finished project. In that way, you'll know at a glance where you have to remove dirt and where you have to build up a berm. Use a level, if necessary, to make sure that both sides of the layout are at the same elevation and that the streambed moves steadily downhill. Otherwise, the water will want to overflow the banks.

Also, remember that water tends to want to travel in a straight line. If your streambed features a sharp turn, make the outside bank at that point approximately 25% higher than the opposite bank. When the water hits that spot, it will tend to climb a little higher on the wall before bending around to follow the stream downhill. You don't want to lose any water along the way. This is supposed to be a closed loop, after all.

While we've read widely about the niceties of digging a channel beneath a stream in order to run electrical piping or hose from the pond to the stream head, we strongly advise against that. If anything ever goes wrong with your water-delivery system, you don't want to have to tear out the entire stream to fix or replace it.

Instead, make provisions to run the pipe or hose alongside one bank of the stream or the other. It can always be disguised with soil, rocks, and plants. And in that way, if you need to get at it for any reason at all, it will be much simpler and less costly to do so.

INSTALLING A STREAM LINER

Once you're satisfied with the placement of your stream and waterfalls, lay down some underlayment (if necessary) and fit the liner to the entire excavation site. Try using a single piece of liner for the most problem-free design possible. If you must use more than one section of liner, make sure that you start at the lowest end of the stream and overlap the pieces on your way up. Lap each upper section over the lower piece and seal the seams with adhesive or tape made for use with pond liner. (Make sure the liner sections are dry before attempting to seal them.) Sealing will allow the water to flow over the seam without any leakage.

As a rule of thumb, overlap the liner for the streambed by 6 to 12 inches on each side. That will leave you enough extra material to work with should your trial run show that you need to make some adjustments to the height of the banks.

TAKING A TRIAL RUN

After laying all of the liner, sealing the seams, and making sure that everything is in place, set your pump into the lowest part of your pond. Place it on bricks or on a flat rock so that it won't take in silt from the pond's bottom. Attach the pump to the supply and outlet lines, and fire it up.

The pump will quickly begin moving the water to the top of your streambed, where it will begin running downhill, filling up the stream and any ponds or deep pockets along the way. If the water gets too close to the top edge of the liner at any location, build up the bank there with rocks, stones, or soil. Remember that nature will provide for some settlement over the course of time: you don't want the settling to be on the banks, where water could escape your system.

This is a good time, too, to check out your waterfalls. Make adjustments in the rocks, and be sure that the water going over the falls remains inside the liner. (Waterfalls have a nasty habit of trying to send water off to the sides to run out of the liner and outside the stream.)

At this point, you're going to be tempted to trim off the excess pond liner on each side of the stream. Don't do it. Trust me on this. Instead, begin disguising the liner with soil, rocks, plantings, and any other landscape or hardscape elements you wish. You can always come back and trim away the excess afterwards. Remember: it's easy to cut away; it's damned hard to replace!

GRAVEL, STONES, AND ROCKS

Once you're satisfied that your stream is functioning properly, begin laying rocks along the outer banks. These rocks, called edging, help to hold the liner in place while disguising its presence. They also help to create an optical transition from the streambed to the surrounding landscape.

Edging stones can be flat or round, laid in one course or stacked, depending upon your personal

ROCKS, ROCKS, ROCKS

Nothing makes a water feature look more natural than rocks. If they're used wisely. We've seen rocks that have been laid from one end of a stream to the other that absolutely ruined the entire water feature. That's because rocks aren't "laid" in nature. They're set in, exposed by wind and rain, grown over by moss and lichens, and more. Here are a few tips when working with your own hardscape.

• **Gravel and pebbles.** Use these elements as a bottom layer inside your pond to cover the liner and create a gravel bed, just as you'd find in nature. Pea gravel is widely available at most home centers and local quarries, and it's less expensive than, say, aquarium gravel. Stick to natural colors for obvious reasons, and use gravel and pebbles sparingly, since they encourage the growth of algae more so than larger rocks and stones.

• **Rocks and stones.** Medium-sized rocks and stones are great for holding the liner in place and for raising the banks of a stream from underneath. Choose rocks and stones that look as though they might be native to your area. Flat flagstone is great for edging and lining the inside of stream walls and spillways. Choose worn or weathered stone whenever possible.

• **Boulders.** Boulders can be costly to buy. If you're lucky enough to have a naturally available supply nearby—and have the horsepower to handle them—good for you. Otherwise, you'll probably use only an occasional boulder as an accent element.

Why use boulders at all? Well, they add drama to the landscape by drawing the eye to them. They also make great backdrops for plants and shrubs. For the most natural effect, partially bury boulders in soil. When a boulder is used in the water, keep at least half of it below water level, once again emulating nature. Set huge boulders on a concrete or brick footing to prevent them from settling.

This pond features a series of holding pools, spillways, and riffles, all powered by a single pump. *Photo © Julianna Tilton for Fotolia.*

sound of the flowing water. Make sure that you rinse away any excess mortar and drain the pond completely of all sediment before adding fish. Uncured mortar is toxic. Always wait at least one week before adding fish to a water feature containing mortar.

If you want a spillway for your waterfall—a series of fairly flat, stacked rocks over which the water from the falls can trickle down— begin laying the rocks from the bottom up. Leave a few prominent lips for the water to spill from one level to the next. Tilting the spillway stones slightly forward will keep the water moving forward and increase the volume over the face of the spillway.

Next, begin laying stones, rocks, and gravel in the streambed. Use a variety of stone types and sizes so that the finished product looks natural. Large rocks help to hide the liner and add splash and movement to the stream. Small rocks and stones fill in the gaps. Standing rocks on edge along the walls of the stream will help conceal the liner. If the rocks won't stay in place on their own, use a dab of spray foam or adhesive designed for use in streams and ponds.

tastes. Although we prefer to use freestanding stones so that they can be moved around whenever desired, you can also set stones in mortar, should you so desire. Mortar prevents water from flowing under and around the edging and softens the

As you continue landscaping with rocks and stones, turn the water on periodically to check your progress.

ADJUSTING THE SOUND

Sound is an important element in creating your stream and waterfalls. What, after all, is moving water without sound? You can help control the sound of your watercourse by the way you create waterfalls and position stones and other elements along the streambed.

Sound in a water feature is determined by the water's speed and volume. It occurs when moving water meets an immovable object. Large amounts of quickly moving water produce a gushing sound. A slowly moving rivulet produces sounds more like that of a ripple on a lake. Although pleasant if adjusted properly, a ripple that's too weak can sound like a leaky faucet.

Not surprisingly, the more falls and spillways you design into your water feature, the louder the sound. Different types of falls create different sounds. A flat fall where water sheets over the edge of a single rock and free-falls into a pool below makes a subtle—even peaceful—sound. A fall where water cascades down several stacked rocks makes a greater splashing sound. Positioning stones behind the falls creates hollow spaces that amplify and echo sound.

Placing large stones in the stream not only makes the stream look more natural but also increases the splashing. Add, move, or remove large stones until the stream or waterfall looks—and sounds—exactly the way you want.

Once you've fine-tuned your stream and waterfalls, sit back and enjoy the sights, the sounds, and the scent of your new water feature. Watch the water as it cascades over the falls. Listen to it as it wends its way along the streambed. Marvel at the rings it forms when it settles in a pool. Imagine the course of every single water molecule in your water feature, how each one moves from one end of the pond to the other, traveling through the pump and hose and up to the top of the streambed before starting its journey of life back down toward the holding pond and a brand new cycle.

Feel good about what you've accomplished. Feel great about what you've accomplished. But, this time, forget the brewski. *This* calls for Merlot.

QUICK CHECKLIST

- When planning a naturalized stream, include some bends and turns, the way you'd find them in nature.
- Berm the curved corners of a streambed to keep water from overflowing the banks.
- Sketch out your stream on paper and transfer the layout to the ground before beginning construction.
- If you plan on installing a waterfall, design it in advance and build it to provide maximum aeration.

THE STARFISH AND THE POOL

All rivers
run to the
ocean without
filling it up.
All water
comes from
it without ever
emptying it.

—Zen proverb

St. Petersburg, Florida. Summer, 1959.

Growing up in Chicago and finding myself standing at the edge of the Gulf of Mexico, gazing out at the sea and the waves, I am awed. The young boy in me remains strong. I want nothing more than to explore. I walk along the beach. It is just after high tide, and the lapping waves have begun to recede.

I come across a shallow depression in the sand and, upon closer inspection, find that it is ringed with rocks and coral and driftwood, ringed as if by encircling the water. The ring has created its very own pond, a microcosm of the ocean from which it sprang.

I learn later from a beachcomber that the pond is called a tidal pool. When I look more closely at the water, I see tiny shells moving about. When I pick one up, two oversized claws are all that are exposed to my view—a hermit crab. I place the crab back in the water, and it quickly side-slips away.

I decide to look deeper into the pool, and there I find a starfish. I pick it up, turn it over, and see a thousand tiny threaded feet wriggling around rhythmically. I study it closely before I put it back into the water. I look deeper still into the pool, and there I find a diminutive octopus. I make a motion to pick it up, although I would never do so, and it looks warily at me before darting away toward the safety of some coral. Before I know, it is gone, hidden amongst the jagged edges of the living skeleton.

I look deeper still into the pool, and I see tiny mollusks moving slowly across the sand on the bottom. I pick one up, and it disappears into its shell.

That evening, over dinner, I relay to my companions what it was that I had found earlier that day. They smile and tell me what a wonderful story I have shared with them and how my fifth-grade classmates will enjoy hearing it.

Back in Chicago, I tell no one of my discovery. I covet the experience while silently laying plans to build my own tidal pool one day.

nine

Lighting the Way

There came a time not too long after we had built our first pond and waterfall that we decided the days weren't long enough in order to admire their beauty. Either that, or we were just plain bored. For whatever reason, we decided the time was right to add some light.

Light is another element of your overall landscape. Chances are good that, if you've bought a new home lately, you've already installed some low-watt

ABOVE: One of the author's ponds features a small fountain, several low-wattage outdoor lights, and strategically placed plants and rocks to simulate a more natural effect. Note that the black water-system tubing toward the bottom of the photo is being overgrown by plants and will soon be completely covered.

outdoor lights to act as focal point for various plants and hardscaping. Now the time is right to expand that lighting to include your pond.

You can create remarkable effects for your pond, stream, and waterfalls with lighting. You can make a fountain glimmer, illuminate the underwater world of your pond from within, highlight your waterfalls, and even liven up your stream—all with the addition of a few lights.

All water feature lights require basically the same things: a GFI (grounded) electrical outlet, a low-voltage transformer, a cable to deliver power to your lights, and the fixtures. Lights are available for installation outside of or under the water. If you plan on using underwater lights, make sure they're specifically designed for that purpose. Otherwise, you could end up getting the shock of your life!

Before you invest in lights for your water feature, do a little experimenting with a strong adjustable flashlight after dark. Try lighting up various areas to see how they look. Play light against shadows. Your goal here, as in using outdoor lights anywhere in your landscape, should be naturalness. You want the minimum amount of light placed unobtrusively for maximum natural beauty. Don't fall victim to the "light-itis" trap. If you want your property to look like an amusement park, move to Disneyland.

Basically, outdoor lights come in four different types: spot, dome, floating, and critter. Dome lights have a top on them and cast their glow down in a 360-degree circle. Spotlights concentrate their beams in a narrow direction and can be adjusted to shine on different objects. Floating lights, designed to float on the surface of a pond, are held in place by anchored cords. Critter lights (oh, come on, you've seen them) are generally plastic figurines with soft lights illuminating them from inside.

Use dome lights to illuminate the ground. Use spotlights to emphasize a particular plant, rock, or waterfall. Use floating lights to brighten up the surface of the pool. Use critter lights never. *Period.*

SUBMERGED (UNDERWATER) LIGHTS

There are several types of submerged lights on the market, each one creating its own special effect, depending on how you position it. Most submerged lights come with dark colored casings so that the lights "disappear" into the darkness of the pond. They can be set either to illuminate an area or a feature under water or to shine up out of the water to illuminate a design element outside of the pond.

Waterfall lights add drama to waterfalls and spillways when placed beneath or behind them, bringing a new dimension to your pond after dark.

Fountain lights, either in white or in colors, give a fantasy effect to a spray. Some come equipped with transparent wheels of several colors. Use colored light sparingly, though, since they can quickly become garish.

Some light sets feature transformers that include built-in timers to allow you to set the time period during which the lights remain on. Others are equipped with light-sensing cells so that the lights go on at dusk and off at dawn. Be sure to check that you're getting the type of timer you want before you buy. Timers not only take one more task off your already busy little hands but also provide for maximum safety and security even when you're away from home.

PLACING LIGHTS

When trying to decide where to place your lights, try to remember a couple of things.

• First, underwater lights work best in clear water. Your water should never be murky anyway, so this is a no-brainer.
• Second, never light up your entire fishpond.

Fish need dark places in which to hide and feel safe. They also need darkness to regulate their body cycles. You wouldn't like to live in an environment of constant light, would you? People near the Arctic Circle have been known to go stark raving mad after months without any darkness. It also makes catching nightcrawlers a near impossibility! So, throw a couple of spotlights onto certain areas of the pond, and you'll be amazed at how the fish gravitate to them. Light up the entire body of water, and you'll stress your fish and risk the wrath of your neighbors.

- Third, position dome lights and spotlights where you can conceal their cables and connecting wires. We usually cover everything with bark and plants, which works relatively well until we need to reposition something and have to scratch around, looking for the cable. As an alternative, you can place lights around shrubby plants, next to a large rock, or anywhere else where the wiring can be hidden more easily.

INSTALLING LOW-VOLTAGE LIGHTING

Unlike normal 120-volt lights, installation of low-voltage landscape lights can be done safely by nearly anyone. Because they're low voltage, you don't run the risk of being fried if something goes wrong, the way you would in installing a 120-volt system. As a bonus, low-voltage lights can be exposed to moisture and even sit in water without shorting out, something that's good to know when laying lights around a water feature.

To install a low-voltage system, you'll need a transformer to reduce regular 120-volt household current to 12 volts, the same amount of power used to run your car. Many low-voltage lighting system kits featuring transformer, cable, and lights are available at a reasonable price. Although you can purchase low-wattage lights, cable, and

transformers separately, we prefer to buy them in kits for several reasons. For one, kits contain everything you need to get started fast. For another, all of the items in a kit are compatible, so there's no guesswork about how many watts you'll be running or what size transformer or cable you'll need to do the job. Also, kits are nearly always less costly than buying the same number of components individually.

The major drawback to buying a lighting kit is that not all styles of light fixtures come in kits. But even if you need to buy a few extra fixtures to add to your lightscape, you'll probably still be dollars ahead by buying a kit.

- To set up your lighting system, place the transformer near the GFI receptacle closest to your water feature.
- Next, run exterior electrical cable from the transformer along the route where you want your lights to be. Keep in mind that the lights will need to be within 6 inches or so of the cable in order to make the connection.
- Make sure when choosing a low-watt outdoor lighting set that you select one that features a transformer and cable of the right size to run the number of lights you want. To determine the maximum number of watts you'll need, simply add the number of watts used by each light bulb. Say, for example, that you want to install ten dome lights of 4 watts each and two spotlights of 10 watts each. That's a total of 40 watts plus 20 watts, or 60 watts. Your transformer and cable, therefore, must be rated to handle 60 watts of power. The more wattage the transformer can handle, the more expensive it will be.
- The cable must be rated to carry the total amount of wattage your lights are going to draw from the transformer to the light fixtures. That translates to

Water lilies in bloom make a dramatic, colorful statement against the dark green foliage of the mother plants.

#14 wire for up to 144 watts, #12 wire for up to 192 watts, and #10 wire for up to 288 watts.

- When laying the cable, cover it lightly with bark or plants. Do not bury it.
- Once the cable is laid out, begin attaching the light fixtures. Some attach with clips of various types while others need to be wired into the system. Refer to the instructions in your lighting kit for more help.

The joy of having your pond, stream, waterfalls, and fountains lit up well into the night will help turn an everyday spectacular landscaping feature into a magical, mystical, after-dark wonderland.

QUICK CHECKLIST

- Choose the best outdoor light type for your landscape—outdoor, dome, spot, but not critter.
- Use underwater lighting for drama, but only sparingly.
- When purchasing outdoor lights, consider buying a kit to make sure that everything functions properly together.
- Conceal exposed cable and cords with wood chips, plants, or other design elements.

THE MOUNTAIN AND THE LAKE

Whistler-Blackcomb, British Columbia, Canada. Summer, 1991.

It is early in the morning when we awaken—my companion and I—and take the stairs down to the village where we rent a couple of mountain bikes. Inside of 20 minutes, we are peddling furiously uphill, far from the maddening crowd, which for the mountains usually consists of four people with packs on their backs and granola bars in their pockets.

After nearly an hour, we stumble across a high-mountain lake that has been there for far longer than we can imagine. The sun, peeking above the peaks, throws its orange glow across the water, spreading out before us as still and peaceful as the day portends to be. We are already warm—the sun's rays at this altitude are merciless—and taking off our jackets and sweaters, when my companion says that she has always wanted to take a dip in a mountain lake.

Now, since my mother didn't raise any stupid kids, I know instinctively that bathing in the buff with someone who will remember the experience for the rest of her life is simply too great an opportunity to pass up. Within minutes, we have set our bicycles on the gravel path and stripped to the bone, preparing for the plunge.

"Last one in..." she yells, and although I much prefer entering a pool (or even a bathtub) gradually (one tepid limb at a time), I throw caution to the wind and race off behind her until I feel the water up to my thighs. I dive in head first.

In a sudden lunge of energy, I leap as high out of the water as humanly possible and begin paddling for my very life. When I get to shore, I can hardly breathe—the water is that cold. It's as though I have taken a bad tumble down a ski slope and slammed into a wall of powder. I am in shock, still struggling for air.

As I stand there thawing out, watching my friend splash around, and slowly feeling my breath come back to me beneath the sun's warming rays, I look off into the distance and see the white of the mountains mirrored in the stillness of the water, the most picturesque of postcards. I realize as I help her out that nothing is ever so placid or pleasant as it seems. I realize, too, that, although I will never do such a foolhardy thing again in my life, I would not have missed the experience for the world.

ten

Fountains of Life

When you hear the splash
Of the water drops that fall into the stone bowl,
You will feel that all the dust of your mind
Is washed away.

—Zen Tea Master

Fountains have been an important part of my life for as long as I can recall. Not the fountains themselves so much as the feeling associated with them. When I think back over the places I've spent time in, memories of crisp fall mornings in Madison, Wisconsin, wash over me. Listening to the bubbling sculptural fountains on the Capital Square as the vendors hawk their wares at the Farmer's Market, you can't help but feel warm all over.

Then, too, I spent many an evening watching the waters of Chicago's Buckingham Fountain dancing to a myriad of vibrant hues while the Chicago Symphony Orchestra played Sibelius in the background. With a special young lady on your arm, who wouldn't fall in love?

For whatever the reason, fountains remain one of life's many joys. Thankfully, they are becoming increasingly popular, which means they're more widely available today than ever before. They are also simple to set up—simpler by far than creating

a pond, stream, or waterfall. Some are even plug-and-go; you just hook them to a power source and watch the magic.

Despite their simplicity—or perhaps because of it—fountains have the capacity to raise the soul to entrancing heights. And there's a style of fountain that will fit comfortably into any home or landscape. Pre-constructed fountains, such as those designed to resemble an old-fashioned hand pump, work well in a casual setting, while Grecian-style fountains work better in a more stately or elegant setting.

Why such an allure for fountains? Well, they pack a lot of charm into a small space. They propel a stream of water through the air to create a cooling effect. They're great for enjoying close up, which is why you often find them on porches, patios, and decks. And, from a distance, they lend a stately elegance to nearly any setting.

KINDS OF FOUNTAINS

Fountains can stand alone or be attached to a wall. Some are designed to be used in or around pools and ponds, adding even more dramatic effect to the landscape. They range in size from tabletop to slightly smaller than the Empire State Building. Some are elaborate; others are simple. Nearly all take only a few minutes to set up.

OPPOSITE: Fountains come in all sizes and shapes. This one was crafted from copper tubing to form a dramatic ball of continuously flowing water.

You can choose from a wide variety of styles, colors, materials, and sizes for your fountain. But try to choose a fountain in the overall style of your garden or home. You wouldn't want to put a Rococo-style fountain in a Spanish adobe! And a wall fountain made from brick or stone would look awfully funny against a cedar picket fence!

Most fountains today are made of pre-cast concrete. Other popular materials include reconstituted stone and fiberglass, which looks remarkably stone-like. Whether concrete or look-alike, fountains come in numerous colors and surface finishes. Finding just the right one for your home or garden could take some research and more than one trip to your local garden center.

You might also want to run a search of the Internet. Or, if you're looking for a one-of-a-kind gem, ask around at art galleries and specialty shops for local artisans who might be willing to take on a new client.

Wall Fountains

An increasingly popular type of water feature, the wall fountain takes up little space and is ideally suited to small areas. Most are powered by a submersible pump capable of recirculating water from the basin through a delivery pipe up to the spout. Designs are nearly infinite, but most wall fountains feature a jet of water spilling into a small trough or basin.

Plumbing some wall fountains can be complicated, requiring piping behind the wall, so take that into consideration before you buy. Some wall fountains have water lines that run on the surface of the wall and must be disguised with vines or other plants, although complete pre-manufactured kits with a single power cord running from them are becoming increasingly popular. Since the ease and cost of installation varies widely, ask about the installation requirements before buying a wall fountain.

Wall fountains attach in several ways. Stone fountains attach with mortar and are supported with special T-blocks, or decorative braces that act as brackets. Lighter weight fountains, usually made out of synthetic resin, come with mounting hardware.

Freestanding Fountains

Freestanding fountains are popular because they provide a quick, easy focal point for a patio, lawn, or flowerbed. They feature a small, submersible pump housed within the lower pedestal, often in a hollow base just beneath the bowl. Choose a model whose design allows for easy access and cleaning.

Statuary Fountains

Ornamental statuary fountains—fountains whose centerpiece is a statue—can be placed near a pond or pool or in the water feature itself. The decorative statue has a supply pipe projecting from its base. The pipe is connected to a pump via flexible tubing.

As with most heavy landscaping elements, large statues require a secure, level place to sit. If you want to install the fountain in a pond, you can mount it

FOUNTAIN CARE

Fountains in sunny spots tend to have problems with algae. In fact, nearly anything in sunny spots tends to have problems with algae. Luckily, if you're not raising fish or plants in your fountain, you can prevent algae by adding chlorine bleach to the fountain water. Use 2 ounces of bleach for every 10 gallons of water once a month. If you have plants or fish in the fountain bowl, consider using a commercially available algaecide that's safe for both.

on a hollow in-pond pedestal created specifically for that purpose or build your own with mortared bricks or stone. If the statue is small, black plastic storage crates make a quick, easy-to-hide base.

WEATHERPROOFING YOUR FOUNTAIN

Taking good care of your fountain year-round will greatly prolong its life. For outdoor fountains, that means applying a concrete sealer to prevent moisture from getting into the pores and expanding as the water freezes, resulting in cracking.

Also, make sure you drain your fountain before freezing weather sets in. In that way, ice won't form inside the pump, where it could do damage. Ice can also crack basins, so be sure to empty your fountain out with the onset of winter.

Prevent rain, ice, and snow from collecting in the basin by covering your fountain with a sheet of plastic. Tie the plastic down to prevent it from flapping in the wind.

To prevent your fountain's pump from drying out, causing the seals to shrink and preventing the fountain from working properly, overwinter the pump in a bucket of water in a basement or heated garage. It is also important that the cord does not dry out, since cracked cords can cause dangerous shorts.

FOUNTAIN INSTALLATION
WALL FOUNTAIN INSTALLATION

Depending upon the design of your fountain, installation can take anywhere from mere minutes to a day or more, even with professional help. Building a wall fountain can be tricky if you don't plan in advance. Here's what's involved.

For wall fountains, the wall must be sturdy enough to hold the fountain, its basin, and the water that it will contain. Most wood-sided walls are not strong enough, but many stucco and brick walls are. If you're in doubt, check with a local contractor or

Two antique water pumps serve as the business end of a fountain emptying water into a series of pots and urns. A small submersible pump hidden in the lower container powers the fountain.

stone mason regarding the wall's stability. You may need to include a decorative T-block fitted to the wall as a bracket to support the basin.

If the plumbing is to be installed through the wall, you will need to drill appropriate-sized holes (with a power drill) to accommodate your fountain's piping, as well as the electrical cord for the pump. Use a special masonry bit for stone walls. Drill one hole up high (usually just below eye level) for the water outlet and another hole lower for the water intake that will attach to the bowl. Insert piping through each hole and join them behind the wall with two elbow joints and a length of flexible tubing.

INSTALLATION OPTION 1

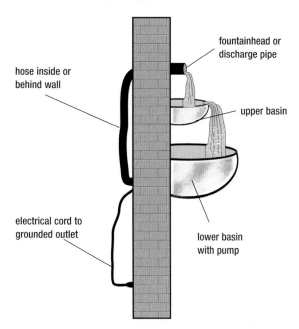

hose inside or behind wall

fountainhead or discharge pipe

upper basin

electrical cord to grounded outlet

lower basin with pump

INSTALLATION OPTION 2

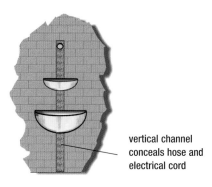

vertical channel conceals hose and electrical cord

A typical wall-mounted fountain includes one or more bowls, a submersed pump, and a hose with a discharge pipe for returning the water to the bowls. The pump's electrical cord can be concealed behind the wall or, where that's impractical, behind a vertical channel of metal or wood glued or screwed onto the face of the wall.

If because of construction the pipe can't be installed through a wall, you'll have to attach it to the surface by chiseling a channel into the surface or, if that's not possible, setting the pipe flush. To hide the exposed pipe, cover it with vines or other plants. You can also disguise the hose and cord with a vertical architectural detail that complements the wall and becomes an integrated part of the fountain, as shown in Installation Option 2 in the diagram.

To attach the fountain to the wall, use mortar and wall plugs. After that's done, connect the pump—if it's not built in—to the intake pipe and plug it into a GFI outlet.

FREESTANDING FOUNTAIN INSTALLATION

Most freestanding fountains come pre-plumbed and are ready to go. Just place the fountain on a level surface, using sand, soil, bits of stone, or wooden wedges as necessary. Then fill the fountain and plug it into a GFI outlet.

STATUARY FOUNTAIN INSTALLATION

Most statuary fountains are designed specifically for either in- or out-of-pond use. Some can be used in both locations. Place your statuary fountain where it's intended to go, and plug it into a GFI outlet.

For a small out-of-pond fountain, use small stones for the base on the edge of the pool or stream. Larger out-of-pond fountains will require a more substantial base, such as a perfectly level stone or concrete pad. With either fountain, place the pump in the pond in order to recirculate water through a flexible hose. You'll need to disguise the hose and the electrical cord with wood chips, plants, or soil.

To position your out-of-pond fountain properly, first test the fountain by hooking up the pump and plugging it in. The spray will vary with the design of the fountain but is usually adjustable. Experiment with both the placement of the fountain and the power of the water flow until you get the effect you're looking for. Most out-of-pond fountains look best when set asymmetrically to one side of the water feature.

In-pond fountains are usually larger than out-of-pond models, which means they usually require a solid foundation on which to be seated. Set small fountains weighing under 30 pounds on a stack of bricks. For larger fountains, you can build a suitable base from concrete, or install a pre-cast concrete pedestal for the foundation. If you're building your own base, be sure to allow a core for any piping that will be connected to the pump. (Most larger fountains are run by an external pump.)

Always use concrete footings for fountains weighing more than 100 pounds. Pour at least 6 inches of reinforced concrete in the ground underneath the fountain before installing the underlayment and the liner. Then build or install the pedestal on this footing.

INDOOR FOUNTAINS

Just as with outdoor fountains, indoor fountains come in all sizes, shapes, styles, and materials. Before investing in one, make sure you know where it's going to go and approximately how large it's going to be. Select a style of fountain that will complement your home's interior.

For large, elaborate fountains, you should probably enlist the aid of a fountain contractor or an architect. For smaller pre-assembled fountains, simply bring the unit home, fill it with water, and plug it in.

Remember, though, that indoor fountains do generate sound. If that sound is going to be annoying in a certain location (say, next to the television set), give a little thought to the idea before putting your money down. If, on the other hand, you'd welcome a little "white noise" (as in the bedroom to help drown out street sounds or—as in our case—the cat scratching at the door to get fed at 5 a.m. each morning), you'll be pleased with the results.

This naturally occurring pond is emblazoned by a large, dramatic fountain, which is powered by a heavy-duty submersible pump. *Photo © Twilight Dragon for Fotolia.*

Not only will you benefit from the beauty and sound of a fountain, but also you'll reap the rewards of all those negative ions helping to cleanse your system while you sleep. Who could ask for anything more?

QUICK CHECKLIST

- Before purchasing a wall fountain, make sure that the wall you're mounting it to is structurally sound.
- Statuary fountains require a sturdy base, whether used in or out of the pool.
- Use indoor fountains where the sound will be most appropriate and appreciated.

SHARK IN SHADES

> Just think of
> the trees:
> they let the birds
> perch and fly,
> with no intention
> to call them
> when they come
> and no longing
> for their return
> when they
> fly away.
> If people's
> hearts can be
> like the trees,
> they will not be
> off the Way.
>
> —Langya

Puerto Vallarta, Mexico. Summer, 1981.

We arrive at the hotel from the cruise ship around 10 a.m.—Harry, Debbie, and I—and as we walk through the open portico past the front desk, I stop before the most beautiful fountain I have ever seen. It is tiled with colorful ceramics and gilded in rare metals. Blue and gold macaws fly through the lobby, stopping occasionally to roost on the top of the fountain or to balance precariously on the edge of the bowl while drinking or chiding a passing tourist.

We head for the back of the building, which opens up onto the pool, meandering snake-like through the property just a few dozen feet from the crashing waves of the Pacific Ocean. We peel down to our suits and slip into the water. A few soft strokes beneath the equally soft Puerto Vallarta sun, and we find ourselves deposited on submerged stools, belly-to-the-bar. We order the house specialty, a Coco Loco, and sail off on a day of off-ship debauchery.

Harry tells me about the time he was in prison in Guadalajara and the ordeals he went through. He had been beaten, starved, stolen from, tortured, and locked away to die. He had been on a case—Harry is a private eye—and ended up on the wrong end of a bad business deal. Debbie, his Gal Friday (actually, he met her on a Tuesday), chimes in whenever he threatens to leave out a particularly salient detail.

By noon, we are feeling pretty relaxed. Debbie suggests lunch, and Harry and I quickly vote her down. We get out of the water and wander over to the beach, where we settle into our lounge chairs just in time for a waiter to bring us more Coco Locos. When we have exhausted them, along with most of the stories Harry has to tell, we decide to take a dip in the sea.

I think as I take my first halting steps into the crashing waves just how warm the water is, perhaps a degree or two warmer than the baths I take back home in Wisconsin. Another wave strikes, this one at our backs, and Debbie goes tumbling head over heels, with me right behind her. I pull myself up from my knees, and the three of us emerge, laughing.

We return to our chairs to dry out when Debbie asks me what I did with my sunglasses. I reach for my face and suddenly realize that they are not where I had left them. Harry makes a comment about some shark swimming around with shades covering his eyes, and I frown.

"Yeah," I tell him. "But not just some shark. The best dressed shark in the whole fucking Pacific. Those were *Porsche* sunglasses!"

eleven

Water Plants

Picture this: You purchase from a salvage yard an antique claw-foot bathtub and transport it to your backyard. You fill it with water and throw in a couple of goldfish. Then you sit back to admire the view.

Huh? Of course, that wouldn't be much fun, because it would always look like a bathtub with a couple of fish in it.

ABOVE: This pond, planted heavily with floating plants and cattails, provides the ideal habitat for goldfish. *Photo © Richard Pross for Fotolia.*

And so it is with ponds, which brings us to the Master Illusionist and the role he plays in turning a man-made object into a thing of indescribable natural beauty. Okay, okay, so it's not actually *natural*, but it's going to be the next closest thing by the time *we're* done with it!

The Master Illusionist is you. The role you play is planting plants. The thing of indescribable natural beauty is a fully landscaped biologically functional and dynamically nifty pond.

Oh, sure, you've done some planting around your pond already, but not enough. After all, does

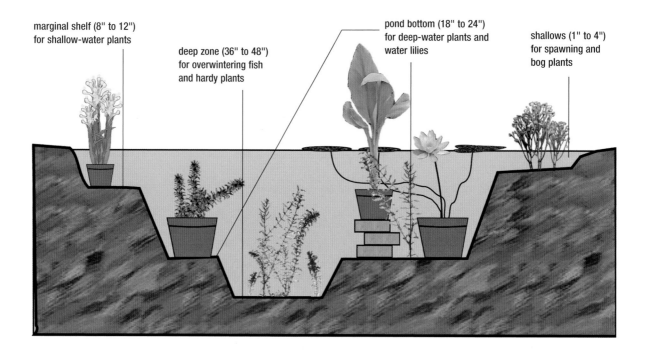

marginal shelf (8" to 12") for shallow-water plants

deep zone (36" to 48") for overwintering fish and hardy plants

pond bottom (18" to 24") for deep-water plants and water lilies

shallows (1" to 4") for spawning and bog plants

nature drop a single seed in a bog for it to sprout in solitary? Does life send forth a sentinel dandelion to bloom in seasonal obscurity? Do worms like fish?

The simple truth of the matter is that plants and fish put the crowning touches on a water feature. They add texture, color, and motion to even the smallest and simplest of ponds and streams.

If you're new to aquaculture, you'll be surprised at just how quickly water plants grow. Bog plants send their roots below the pond surface; exotic water lilies float leisurely by; marginals burst forth from the shallows in a myriad of exotic colors; and fish swim past all of them leisurely, their elegant tails streaming behind them.

PLAN FOR SUCCESS

When laying out your water plants, as in every other aspect of pond building, invest a little time in a plan. You don't need to get elaborate here; in fact, the varieties of water plants you buy may well be

ABOVE: Since not all plants grow at the same water depth, it's important to build various levels into your pond by creating "shelves" at different heights.

subject to whatever water plants your local nurseries carry or what you are comfortable in ordering over the Internet.

There are a couple of considerations to keep in mind with water plants that you don't need to worry about with garden plants. Since most water plants grow relatively fast, make sure you pay attention to the projected height of the plants at maturity. As a general rule, keep the taller growing plants toward the back of the pond and away from your feeding area. You don't want to have to battle the foliage every time you want to get a look at your fish.

Also, pay attention to how aggressive water plants are. Some, such as cattails, can spread amazingly fast. While that might sound like a good thing, plants that can grow 5 to 6 feet tall in a single season and reproduce at an alarming rate could quickly overrun a pond. Either avoid using such plants, or confine their roots to a pot to prevent an imminent takeover.

On the flip side, growing water plants is a relatively painless job. After all, they don't require watering! What they *do* require is planting at the proper depth (often specified on water plant tags; if not, inquire at your local garden center), exposure to the right amount of light (especially for flowering plants), and occasional feeding via water-plant spikes stuck into the planting medium twice a year. See the depth zone diagram and the individual plant information in this chapter for details of planting depths. Make sure that you don't plant them too deep or too shallow for their optimum growth. If you don't have shallow enough terrain in your pond to accommodate some plant species, you can stack bricks beneath the plants to bring them up to the required depth. Although most plants can be rooted directly into the gravel or rock bed of your pond, keeping them in pots allows for easy removal to clean the plants of algae and other debris or to overwinter sensitive tropical plants in a tub in a frost-protected location, such as a basement or garage.

When you choose your pond plants, keep their depth requirements in mind, as well as their visual effect. The shallows (1 to 4 inches deep) are ideal for spawning and bog plants. The marginal shelf (8 to 12 inches deep) is ideal for shallow-water plants. The pond bottom (18 to 24 inches deep) is good for deep-water plants and water lilies. The deep zone (36 to 48 inches) is good for overwintering fish and hardy plants.

TYPES OF WATER PLANTS

Here is a look at the four broad types of water-garden plants, all of which you would likely find in a healthy, natural environment.

FLOATERS

As the name implies, these plants float on top of the water. Their leaves and flowers remain above water, while their roots dangle below. Floaters, which include water lettuce, water hyacinth, and duckweed, provide shade and food for fish and other wildlife. Some species also act as natural water filters.

Most pond owners love floaters because they shade the water, which in turn cuts down on the growth of algae. However, if they spread to the point where they cover more than two-thirds of the pond's surface, they could wind up trapping carbon dioxide and other dangerous gases below. The solution is easy enough. Simply scoop out any excess plants and throw them on the compost pile.

WATER LILIES AND OTHER DEEP-WATER PLANTS

Rooted in pots at the bottom of the pond, water lilies and their look-alike cousins, lotuses, send up leaves that float on the surface. Similar to floaters, these leaves shade the water, lowering temperatures and helping to control algae.

Water lilies come in two basic types: tropical and hardy. Tropical water lilies grow from tubers and are prolific bloomers. Their blossoms are suspended on

Dwarf water lilies growing in an above-ground pond.

stems rising above the water surface. Hardy water lilies grow from rhizomes and are somewhat less showy. Their blossoms are smaller and, for the most part, float on the water's surface. Although tropical water lilies are showier, they can't sustain temperatures much below 60° F, so unless you're willing to provide protection for them when the temperatures begin to drop, stick to hardy lilies.

SUBMERGED PLANTS

Submerged plants, such as water milfoil and hornwort, can also be grown in pots at the bottom of the pond, although their foliage remains completely under water. While they do add small amounts of oxygen to the water, their main allure is in providing cover for fish—particularly young fry— and in absorbing carbon dioxide and minerals, resulting in slower algae growth. They also help filter the water.

Submerged plants are usually sold in bunches of six stems. Plant one bunch about every 3 square feet. Submerged plants do not need soil, which can foul your pond's water; instead, use sand or gravel. Also, you won't need to fertilize submerged plants, since their leaves draw their nutrients directly from the minerals dissolved in the pond. Since some varieties do better than others, mix several different ones to see which grow best for you.

MARGINALS

Marginal water plants take their name from that marginal area between shore and pond. While their roots are submerged, their leaves grow out of the water. Most marginals are shallow-water plants that may be grown in pots or directly in the gravel on shelves at the edge of the pond. Many marginals, such as iris and arrowhead, double as bog plants. In the water, they're best grown in containers that you can lift for grooming and dividing (splitting into smaller plants when they are overgrown), which will prevent them from spreading too quickly and becoming invasive.

Marginal plants are prized mostly as ornamentals. They add color and form to the aquascape and help the water garden blend visually into the rest of the landscape. They also help to filter out some of the impurities in the water. You may want to try putting several plants of one marginal variety in one large container. Don't put several different plants in a single container, as the stronger ones will outgrow and eventually kill off the weaker ones.

When planning for water plants, figure on doing a lot of "winging it." Sure, you can measure the pool's surface area so that you can space your plants evenly. You can make rough sketches of your water garden from various angles and include the location and type of plants. In the end, though, you're going to go out, buy whatever water plants you can find, and *then* figure out where to put them. Unless you're lucky enough to live near a very well-stocked pond supply store or nursery, you often have to settle for whatever you can find.

Regardless, when you begin setting your water plants, try to mix a variety of colors, forms, textures, and bloom times. Include trees and other surrounding plants as backdrops to your water plants to heighten and smooth out the overall dramatic effect of your landscape.

Keep in mind that garden design principles apply equally to water plants. You can use a single large plant as a specimen, but smaller plants in groups of three or more will have the strongest effect and look more natural. Don't overdo things, however. Remember that the focus of your pond is the *water*. Use plants to add to the overall effect, not to divert attention from it.

CONTROLLING INVASIVE SPECIES

Before you buy *any* plant, please find out how well behaved it is. Water-garden plants have a tendency to be invasive in ideal climates. Some states ban certain water-garden species because they have been known to clog natural waterways and even disrupt sewer and storm-drain systems. Invasive plants also can create a maintenance headache; they'll battle you for control, and you'll spend hours pulling them out of the pond.

If you do want to use invasive plants, always put them in pots and be certain that the roots can't escape out of the drainage holes. We usually place landscaping fabric (the stuff used to keep weeds from coming up in the flowerbeds) on the bottom of the pot before planting.

Take into account, too, how your plants and fish are likely to interact. Duckweed, while invasive, is a favorite food for goldfish and koi. The fish like to munch on it between meals, and that helps keep it under control. As for other plants such as water lilies, koi are extremely rambunctious and will often uproot and shred the plants. They do it either for food or for fun, or maybe just because.

Water movement is another element to keep in mind when choosing your water plants. Most floaters and some deep-water aquatics, including water lilies, prefer mostly still water. Other plants, such as watercress and bullrush, thrive in moving water. Others do equally well in either setting.

Although fountains are beautiful, the splashing spray can push floating plants away or keep a plant's leaves constantly wet, which could ultimately kill the plant.

The hardiness of a perennial plant (its ability to survive winter cold) can often be extended by simply lowering the plant's root system below the anticipated depth of the winter ice. If you live where winter temperatures reach −20° F, for example, plants hardy to −10° F may thrive if you set them deeper than normally found in the pond. As spring approaches and the cold snaps are history, move the plants back to their original growing depth.

While plants in natural settings root in the mud on the bottom of the pond, those in garden ponds (except for floaters) thrive best in pots. The potting medium you use for water plants versus garden plants, however, is different.

Since garden soil has a lot of fertilizer, humus, and other organic matter that can decay and foul the water, it's best to use a special water-plant potting medium, which is not soil at all but rather small pebbles. The potting medium won't break down and end up contaminating your pond. Water plants draw their nutrients directly from the water, so this type of potting medium or even aquarium or pea gravel makes an excellent alternative to soil.

POTTING WATER PLANTS

Pot your water plants in the special medium just as you would any house plant. Make sure that you don't pot the plant deeper than it was originally planted. If you're using a lightweight planting medium, moisten the container well after planting and let it stand for an hour or more to give the medium time to absorb the water. Otherwise, when you submerge the pot, the medium will float away. (This isn't necessary if you're using aquarium or pea gravel, both of which are non-porous.) Once the medium is saturated, you can set the pots into place.

Your selection of pots is endless. We prefer those inexpensive black containers in which most nursery stock is sold. If a plastic pot is too tall, it can be cut down to size with sharp scissors, a knife, or a table saw.

You can also purchase special aquatic baskets that have a large, open basket-weave construction designed to allow the roots of a potted plant to

The author placed a submersible stand to accommodate the cattail planting just below the water's surface in the deep end of this pond.

escape the pot and wander out into the pond bottom, which may or may not be a good idea, depending upon how invasive the plant is.

We avoid using clay pots under water, since the clay often has salts and other undesirable elements in it that could leach out into the surroundings. Also, less expensive clay pots can turn to mush under water.

The size of the container you use for your water plants is determined more by common sense and your particular situation than by dictum. For a hardy water lily, for example, you'd normally need a pot that's 16 inches or more in diameter—a huge

investment for a single plant. As an alternative, we put ours in aquatic baskets large enough to hold the main tuber. The roots are then free to spread out as far as they desire.

Marginal plants can do quite well in smaller pots, from 8 to 10 inches in diameter. Tall plants may become top-heavy and tend to tip over, especially in high winds, so add a sturdy stone for ballast in the bottom of the pot before planting.

You can vary the number of plants in a single container based upon your own tastes and a bit of common sense. We regularly group together lilies and other marginals, for example, for the striking effect the plants have in bunches. For water lilies, which tend to send out their leaf and flower stalks in a graceful radiating-spoke pattern, it's best to use a separate pot for each plant. Otherwise, the plants' stalks will intermingle, become entwined, and wind up a jumbled mess.

Of course, you can always forego the use of pots entirely and set your water plants directly into the gravel bottom of your pond, so long as the planting depth is correct and the gravel is thick enough to hold the plant securely. This is an especially natural approach to planting, although not necessarily a practical one. If the need should arise to remove or replace some of your plants, it's far easier simply to lift a pot out of the pond than it is to root around in the bottom.

POTTING TECHNIQUES

Whenever you buy a new plant for replanting, count on two things: One, it's planted in the wrong medium for a fishpond; and two, it's in too small a container. The first thing you'll want to do is to make sure that you have a container that's at least the next size up for the plant than the one it came in. Remove the plant and wash off as much of the gunk, humus, and soil from the roots as possible.

This may require you to poke around inside the root mass some, an endeavor that serves the added purpose of loosening the plant's roots to enable healthy new growth.

Next, take your new pot, fill the bottom with some large gravel or small stones, and top that off with half a pot's worth of water-plant medium. Place your nice clean water plant in the pot ("Green side up, green side up!") and spread the roots out as much as possible. (If you have room for more than one plant, this is the time to add them.) Finally, fill the remainder of the pot with planting medium just up to the base of the plant's crown. Remember, planting a water plant too deep is potentially far worse than planting it too shallow.

Before setting the pot, take a look at your plants and make any adjustments in height or positioning. This is a good time, too, to clip off any damaged or yellow leaves. If a leaf is cracked and bent in half, it will not recover, so remove it.

If you like, you can spread a layer of the same type gravel you use in your pond over the potting medium, depending upon just exactly how anal you are. Otherwise, wet the medium down well, give it time to absorb water, and set into the pond at the correct growing depth.

If you have a very large pond, you may need to get into the water physically in order to set some plants where you want them. So long as you haven't just sprayed your feet with fungicide, feel free to join in the fun. Go barefoot or put on a pair of socks so that you don't puncture the pool lining as you're moving around. And enjoy that refreshing coolness!

PLANTING AT THE RIGHT DEPTH

What if you want to place a plant that requires a depth of 6 inches in a place in the pond that's 12 inches deep? Use patio bricks, stones, or a cedar wooden frame to build a platform of the right height, and then set your potted plants on that. When planting water lilies and other deep-water aquatics, some gardeners believe in placing the plants at the required depth from the start. Others prefer to plant them in shallow water and replant to gradually deeper depths as the plants mature.

Our philosophy is to place the plants at the depth they require and forget about them. It may take longer for the stalks or leaves to reach the water's surface, but the plants will be healthier and fuller by the time they do.

Situating a container in the center of a large water pond is easier if you follow this tip. Choose to use a pot with handles. Run rope through the handles, and set the container near the water's edge. Get a friend to help with one side of the rope while you take the other. Then carefully maneuver the ropes until the pot is centered over the pond. Gently lower it down to the bottom. Release all but one end of the rope and pull it free from the pot.

Now, how you get the pot *out* of the pond is another matter. We'll leave that for you to contemplate.

WATER PLANT MAINTENANCE

As your plants grow, trim off any dead or diseased plant matter. That not only helps the plants look better but also keeps decaying matter out of the pond. Carefully deadhead (cut off) spent flowers to promote continued blooming, prevent disease, and keep the water garden tidy.

Skim out floaters such as duckweed when they begin to cover too much of the surface of the pool. Thin mature marginal plants as required. Remove fallen leaves, grass clippings, and other debris from the pond on a daily basis, or—if you have a skimmer box that does the trick—wash the debris out of the filter pad at least once a week to prevent fouled water.

In time, your plants may become root-bound and crowded in their existing pots. When they do, they'll need division. How can you tell? Check for reduced blooms and crowded crowns in which the older, sturdier foliage prevents new growth from emerging. Watch for signs of dead roots around the crown.

When you need to divide water plants that grow from rhizomes, remove the plants from their pots and break the rhizomes into several pieces. Repot each separate piece with a growing tip.

To divide plants that grow from runners or plantlets, simply break off the "baby" plant, wrap its roots in Spanish moss, and repot in planting medium.

Once established, water garden plants require remarkably little care. They take virtually everything they need for life from the water. Maintain a healthy pond, and your plants will reward you doubly.

If you think fertilizing a heavy-blooming plant is in order, make sure you use a pond-safe aquatic fertilizer. These come in fish-safe, slow-release pellets that you push into the planting medium. Never use non-aquatic fertilizers of any type around your pond or water plants.

Disease in water plants is rare. If it occurs, talk to your local county horticulturist or garden center representative to determine exactly what product you need to combat that specific disease. Make sure that you tell them you have fish in your pond.

THE BEST PLANTS FOR YOU

There are literally thousands of water plants for use in ponds and streams around the world. Some are

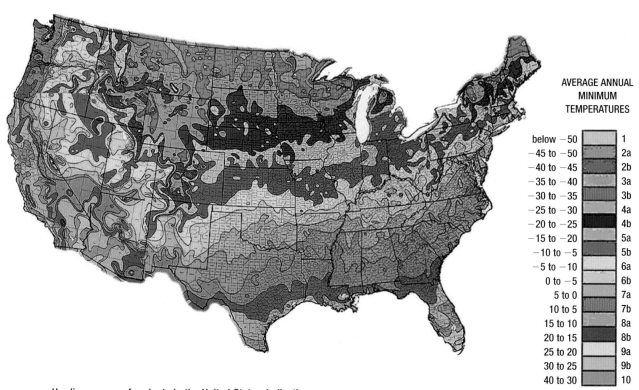

AVERAGE ANNUAL
MINIMUM
TEMPERATURES

below −50		1
−45 to −50		2a
−40 to −45		2b
−35 to −40		3a
−30 to −35		3b
−25 to −30		4a
−20 to −25		4b
−15 to −20		5a
−10 to −5		5b
−5 to −10		6a
0 to −5		6b
5 to 0		7a
10 to 5		7b
15 to 10		8a
20 to 15		8b
25 to 20		9a
30 to 25		9b
40 to 30		10

Hardiness zones for plants in the United States, indicating average minimum temperatures. Match where you live to the color chart to determine your plant hardiness zone.

more suitable than others for particular environments. That's where the selection of plants based upon zones comes in. If a plant is hardy in your zone (check out the Plant Hardiness Zone Chart on page 106 to see the zone in which you live), it should do well for you in your own water garden. Here are a few suggestions from our own personal favorites.

DEEP-WATER PLANTS

Hardy water lilies (Nymphaea spp.). These beauties are able to withstand colder temperatures than their tropical cousins and can over-winter so long as the rhizome remains below ice level. They don't do well when water temperature exceeds 95°F for prolonged periods, but then again what does? Hardy lilies are somewhat less showy than tropical lilies; they don't smell so sweet; and they bloom at night. But they do survive winter! Flower colors are limited to white, pink, yellow, peach, or red, and mature plants bloom from spring through fall, depending on the particular cultivar. Plants grow from 2 to 12 square feet. Plant crowns 8 to 24 inches below the water surface. Plant in calm areas where they will receive full sun

Blue leopardess lily
(Nymphaea spp.).
Photo © Lilyblooms.com

Night-blooming lily
(Nymphaea spp.).
Photo © Lilyblooms.com

for best flowering, although the plants themselves can survive in partial shade. Zones 4 to 10.

Tropical day-blooming water lilies (Nymphaea spp.). These profuse bloomers come in a wide variety of colors—even blue—and have a heavy fragrance and luxurious foliage. They hold their large, showy blossoms up on tall stems several inches above the water and make good cut flowers. Each bloom opens midmorning, closes in late afternoon, and lasts about 4 days. As their name suggests, they bloom during daylight. Some varieties spread up to 5 feet. Plant them with their crowns 4 to 12 inches below the water surface. Day bloomers prefer sun and flourish in hot weather. They must not be in water cooler than 60° F. Bring them indoors during winter in most parts of the country; they are winter hardy only in zones 10 to 11.

Tropical night-blooming water lilies (Nymphaea spp.). Night bloomers share the same characteristics as their day-blooming relatives but open their blossoms in early evening and keep them open through midmorning or longer or until exposed to direct sun. Their evening showiness is highly prized by gardeners who can't be home during the day. Night bloomers often have an even sweeter fragrance than

Hardy water lilies (Nymphaea spp.).
Photo © Erika Walsh for Fotolia.

Dwarf or miniature water lilies (Nymphaea spp.). *Photo courtesy of Hazorea Aquatics, Kibbutz Hazorea, Israel.*

their day-blooming cousins. Plant with their crowns 4 to 12 inches below the water surface. They thrive in intense sun but are highly sensitive to frost and dislike cool weather. Tropical night-blooming water lilies are hardy in zones 10 to 11.

Dwarf or miniature water lilies (Nymphaea spp.). Dwarf species share qualities with other water lilies, but they spread to only 1 to 2 feet. That makes them excellent candidates for small ponds and container gardens. Their flowers are smaller, also, a diminutive 1 to 5 inches across. For their size, they are prolific bloomers, sometimes producing 2 to 3 dozen flowers at one time. The quality of their blooms, though, is less than that of their big cousins. Mini lilies come in fewer colors than full-sized water lilies. Plant dwarfs 5 to 10 inches deep with their crowns 4 to 10 inches below the surface of the water. They are hardy generally in zones 4 to 11, but their hardiness will vary from cultivar to cultivar.

Lotuses (Nelumbo spp.). Lotuses have large, exotic flowers with unusual centers, making them ideal for dried flower arrangements. Blooms often exceed 6 inches across. Unlike water lilies, the flower stalks rise up to 5 feet above floating leaves. Flowers are intensely fragrant, can perfume an entire corner of the garden, and are available in many colors. Miniature varieties of lotuses, including bowl lotuses, are gaining in popularity. They have flower stalks that grow just 1 to 3 feet above the water surface, making them more practical for most ponds. Plant lotuses in full sun with their crowns 2 to 12 inches below the surface of the water. They'll need several weeks with temperatures of 80° F or higher to bloom well. Lotuses are hardy in zones 4 to 11, with their hardiness varying from one cultivar to the next.

SUBMERGED PLANTS

Canadian pondweed (*Potamogeton canadensis*). The diminutive, darkish, red-green fern-like leaves on pondweed's delicate branches create the perfect cover for spawning fish. The foliage also makes a nice meal for fish, especially over winter. Pondweed grows

Lotuses (Nelumbo spp.). *Photo © Lilyblooms.com*

Canadian pondweed (*Potamogeton canadensis*).

quickly. In fact, the plant may need occasional thinning with a pond rake. One of the best and most reliable of the submerged plants, pondweed competes with algae for food. Plant it 6 inches to 5 feet below the water surface, depending on water clarity. It thrives best in full sun but will tolerate some shade. Weight the pot down with small stones in order to keep it on the bottom. Hardy in zones 4 to 10.

Curly pondweed (*Potamogeton crispus*). The narrow, translucent, stalkless leaves of curly pondweed feature wavy edges that resemble seaweed. Each leaf grows to about 3 inches long, but its stems can grow disproportionately up to 14 feet. Its use is therefore usually restricted to larger water gardens. In the spring, the plant develops small, pink-

Curly pondweed (*Potamogeton crispus*).

tinged flowers. Curly pondweed can be invasive in some situations, so you may have to watch it carefully. It does best in a pond with moving water rather than in a still pond. It will tolerate cloudy water. You can plant it as deep as 3 feet. The best site for it is in full sun to partial shade. Curly pondweed is hardy in zones 4 to 10.

Cabomba (*Cabomba caroliniana*). Also called fanwort, cabomba leaves vary with the species. Most have bright green underwater foliage of graceful fans and tiny white flowers in summer. The foliage makes a great spawning area and a safe haven for young fish. Plants do best in cool water up to 30 inches deep. Avoid planting in warmer shallows. Cabomba grows up to 8 inches in length. Plant it in coarse, sandy soil 2 inches deep and submerged under 1 foot of water. It likes filtered light but tolerates part shade to full sun. Plants are hardy in zones 5 to 10, depending on the species.

Cabomba (*Cabomba caroliniana*).

Hornwort (*Ceratophyllum demersum*).

Hornwort (*Ceratophyllum demersum*). Also known as coontail, hornwort is a completely submersed plant commonly seen in lakes with moderate to high nutrient levels. The common names refer to its full, bottle-brush-like growth form and its forked, antler-shaped leaves. Hornwort is used as an oxygen plant for aquatic gardens. In the wild it provides habitat for young fish and other aquatic animals. Waterfowl will eat the seeds and foliage, though it is not a favorite food plant.

Water milfoil (Myriophyllum spp.). Water milfoil has long, trailing stems that grow from 6 to 20 feet long with tufts of fine, feathery foliage in green or

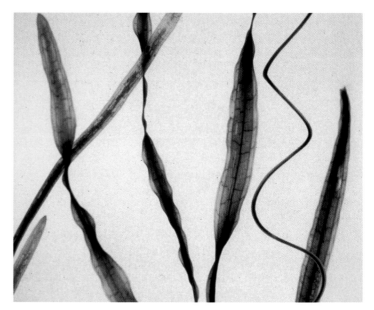

Wild celery (*Vallisneria americana*).

brown. It provides good spawning areas for fish and is a good plant for trapping debris. Its stems extend above the surface with spikes of tiny, pale yellow flowers. Some varieties produce flowers on the water surface. They sway attractively in moving water. Water milfoil does well in shallow water or small ponds. Plant it 12 to 30 inches below the water surface in full sun to partial shade or filtered light. It is hardy in zones 4 to 11, depending upon the species. Caution, very invasive.

Water milfoil
(Myriophyllum spp.).

Wild celery (*Vallisneria americana*). Also known as eelgrass and tape grass and sometimes confused with ribbon grass, which is similar, wild celery has attractive, ribbon-like leaves that reach 1 to 3 feet in length. The leaves sway in moving water. 'Spiralis' is a dwarf cultivar that grows to only 8 inches in height and is suitable for small ponds and containers. Wild celery is tolerant of warm water, and it will spread to form a pleasant carpet across the surface. It's an excellent source of food, shelter, and shade for fish. The plants produce greenish flowers all season long, and they are an ideal natural filter for the garden pool. Plant wild celery in water that is 12 to 24 inches deep. It grows in full shade to full sun and is hardy in zones 4 to 11.

MARGINAL PLANTS

Parrot's feather (*Myriophyllum aquaticum*. Also listed as *M. proserpinacoides*). This plant's pink

Parrot's feather
(*Myriophyllum aquaticum*).

stems rise above silvery blue or lime-green foliage. Its flowers are insignificant. Leaves are sparse under water. However, about 6 inches above the surface, they grow into feathery whorls. Parrot's feather is good for trailing over the side of a container garden or alongside a waterfall. It is a fast-growing marginal plant and may need to be thinned occasionally to keep it in check. To survive cold winters, plants must be under ice. Plant their crowns 4 to 10 inches below the water surface. Parrot's feather likes full sun but tolerates partial shade. It is hardy in zones 3 to 11. Caution: Invasive. Banned in some states.

Iris (Iris spp.). *Photo © Lilyblooms.com*

Iris (Iris spp.). The marginal species of this popular garden plant include a cultivar of wild blue flag (*I. sinfonietta*, with attractive blue, bearded flowers); rabbitear iris (*I. laevigata*, blue-purple or white with broad-petaled, beardless flowers); Louisiana iris (*I. fulva*, red to orange beardless blossoms); and Japanese water iris (*I. ensata*, also called *I. kaempferi*, with white, blue, purple, reddish purple, and lavender-pink beardless blooms). Another variety, yellow flag iris (*I. pseudacorus*, beardless), is especially easy to grow. *I. laevigata* 'Variegata' is popular for its striped leaves. All of these iris varieties make excellent marginal growers. Plant iris rhizomes (the fleshy, root-like portion) from 2 to 4 inches below the water surface in full sun to light shade. Iris are hardy perennials in zones 2 to 10, depending upon the species.

Arrowhead (Sagittaria spp.). This marginal is named for its arrowhead-shaped leaves that rise up 1 to 2 feet above the surface of the water on slender stems. Because of their legginess, the plant may tend to lean some. Three species are popular as garden-pool marginals: *S. sagittifolia*, *S. latifolia*, and *S. japonica*. Arrowhead blooms later than most other marginals, with white flowers emerging in summer. It is a North American native plant, an easy grower that does not transplant well. It prefers bog-like conditions. Plant its roots 1 to 5 inches beneath the water surface in full sun to partial shade. Plants are hardy in zones 4 to 10.

Marsh marigold (*Caltha palustris*). One of the most popular of marginals, marsh marigolds feature bright golden spring flowers that bloom above heart-shaped, shiny, dark green leaves for a month or more. The plants rise about 1 foot above the water and spread about 1 foot across.

Arrowhead (Sagittaria spp.).

Marsh marigold (*Caltha palustris*).
Photo © Martin Dzumela for Fotolia.

They go dormant by midsummer. Grow them near other marginals to ensure that the bare spots they leave during dormancy are hidden by neighboring foliage. Marsh marigolds are a good choice to plant in damp spots near a stream, and they grow well in bog gardens. They are native to North America. Plant them in full sun with the crowns no deeper than 2 inches below the surface of the water. Plants are hardy in zones 4 to 10.

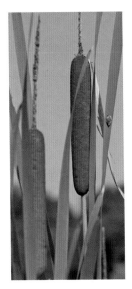

Cattail (Typha spp.).
Photo © Lilyblooms.com.

Cattail (Typha spp.). The familiar brown flower heads of cattails are borne in late summer through early fall. Many species are too invasive to grow in garden pools except in pots, but there are some that can be planted without fear. For large water gardens, there's *T. latifolia. T. laxmannii* is suitable for gardens of medium size. The miniature cattail, *T. minima*, does fine in small garden ponds. Cattail plants can grow up to 6 feet tall or taller, depending on the species and growing conditions. Plant them so that their crowns are up to 6 inches below the water surface. The plants grow best in full sun to partial shade. Cattails are hardy in zones 2 to 10, depending upon the species.

Canna (*Canna flaccida*). These magnificent bloomers send up stalks with brilliantly colored, electric flowers from 5 to 6 inches across. They grow in up to 4 inches of water and reach a height of 4 to 6 feet, making them ideal for strong backdrop plants or a splash of color mixed in with your cattails. Bulbs are readily available and inexpensive; cannas can be treated as annuals in most locales. The plants are hardy in zones 9 to 11, although we have overwintered our pond cannas in zone 8.

Canna (*Canna flaccida*). Photo © EyeMark for Fotolia.

Pickerelweed (*Pontederia cordata*). Photo © Lilyblooms.com.

plants grow happily in up to 10 inches of water and are hardy in zones 5 to 11.

Umbrella palm (*Cyperus involucratus*). Umbrella-like fronds emanate from a single tall stalk on this clumping plant. In summer, insignificant white flowers appear. Umbrella palms make a good source of filtered shade for the water feature. They grow to around 5 feet in height and are hardy in zones 9 to 11.

Dwarf umbrella palm (*Cyperus alternifolius* 'Nana'). These are similar to their full-sized cousins, except they grow to only 2 feet in height and are hardy in zones 9 to 11.

Umbrella palm (*Cyperus involucratus*). Photo © Lilyblooms.com.

Dwarf umbrella palm (*Cyperus alternifolius* 'Nana'). Photo © Lilyblooms.com.

Pickerelweed (*Pontederia cordata*). The spade-shaped leaves of this plant reach 24 to 30 inches in height and are punctuated with spikes of vivid purple flowers, resembling the flower heads of grape hyacinth. The flower heads grow to 5 inches in length, providing a splashy show of color throughout late spring and early summer. The

Horsetail (*Equisetum*).

FLOATING PLANTS

Water lettuce (*Pistia stratiotes*). This plant's deeply creased, lime-green leaves form heads vaguely resembling lettuce. Water lettuce spreads by plantlets that break off from the mother plant, making them ideal for most water gardens. Mature plants can stretch 6 inches across and form a colony several feet wide by summer's end. Growing it is prohibited in some states because it can become a nuisance. Easy to grow in most climates, water lettuce can be tricky in cool water and low humidity. It prefers warm water and is thus an excellent selection in shallow ponds and containers. Plant it in partial shade for the best color and growth, although it will tolerate full sun. Treat water lettuce as an annual in most parts of the country, since it is hardy only in zones 9 to 10.

Horsetail (*Equisetum* spp.). This is a genus of very primitive vascular plants. As with ferns and club mosses, relatives of the living horsetails thrived in the Carboniferous period (when they contributed to coal deposits). They have whorls of small scale-like leaves around a hollow, green jointed stem that carries on photosynthesis. They reproduce via spores and are hardy to zone 5. Be careful to confine your plantings to the pond, however, since unrestrained horsetail can quickly overtake a lawn or garden!

Water lettuce (*Pistia stratiotes*). *Photo © Lilyblooms.com.*

Duckweed (Lemna spp.). This is a vigorous plant with thin, tiny, angular, or clover-like leaves that hang just below the water surface. It is a prized source of food for goldfish and koi. Duckweed shades the water surface well, and it tends to thin out slightly in summer's hottest weather. Ivy-leaf duckweed (*L. trisulca*) is the smallest leafed and least invasive. Skim out excess plants in small ponds as needed. Avoid other varieties. *L. minor*, for example, is extremely prolific and is found in stagnant natural ponds everywhere. Thick duckweed (*L. gibba*) and greater duckweed (*Spirodela polyrrhiza*) are also very invasive. Duckweed has a broad range of hardiness, growing well in zones 2 to 11.

Water hyacinth (*Eichhornia crassipes*). Photo © Lilyblooms.com.

Water hyacinth (*Eichhornia crassipes*). Water hyacinth produces lovely blue midsummer blossoms on short, 6- to 8-inch spikes that grow above leathery, rounded leaves. It spreads rapidly, is invasive in warm parts of the country, and has been banned from many states. It is killed at the first frost. Its trailing roots make good spawning grounds for fish and a nice salad for koi. It is outstanding as a vegetative filter. Water hyacinth likes full sun and is treated as an annual in most parts of the country. It is winter hardy only in zones 9 to 10.

Duckweed (Lemna spp.).

Frogbit (*Hydrocharis morsus-ranae*).

Fairy moss (Azolla spp.) Also called water fern, this is one of the most widely available floaters. Its tiny fronds, about a half-inch across, spread rapidly and form dense, pale green clusters that fish love to graze upon. Fronds turn red in summer. Fairy moss can be invasive, so use it only in ponds where it's possible to control by netting. Although it is hardy to zone 7, it will die if the water freezes. In colder areas, save some in a jar filled with water and soil, and reintroduce it to the pool the

Fairy moss (Azolla spp.).

following spring. *A. caroliniana* is the most commonly available variety. It grows in sun to partial shade and is hardy in zones 7 to 10.

Salvinia (*Salvinia rotundifolia*). Sometimes called water or butterfly fern, the leaves of these tiny plants form layers of ruffles along the length of the stems. The small, floating leaves are pale green or purplish brown and covered with fine silk-like hairs. Salvinia grows in large, floating colonies and can become invasive. Thin it regularly by netting. Plan on a heavy thinning early in the summer because salvinia thrives especially well in hot, sunny conditions and can quickly grow out of control. In most regions, water gardeners use salvinia as an annual because it is hardy only in zones 10 to 11.

Salvinia (*Salvinia rotundifolia*).

Frogbit (*Hydrocharis morsus-ranae*). Its tiny flowers, measuring about a half-inch across, resemble small, white water lilies. Frogbit leaves are kidney-shaped, veined, shiny, and about 1 inch across. The foliage dies back in autumn and the plants survive as dormant buds on the bottom. Growth begins again early the following summer. Frogbit spreads by runners, but its growth is restrained. It likes calm, shallow water about 1 foot deep, and it may root in mud. You can over-winter the buds in a jar filled with water and soil, replanting

PLANTS AND GOLDFISH

We've read a lot of nonsense about how tough goldfish are on water plants. They munch on them, uproot them, tear them to shreds, devour them. Uh-huh. Only if your fish are cross-bred with Bossie the Cow.

In our experience, goldfish are relatively benign when it comes to plants. They enjoy swimming around in them, rooting around for food beneath their canopies, and taking in the extra oxygen the plants give off. But destroy them? Hardly.

We have a large number of water plants both in our ponds and in our aquarium. While it's true that koi are incurable green grazers, none of our goldfish—and we have everything from common goldfish rescued from the "feeder" tank at the local pet store to fancy Orandas—have ever shown more than a mild interest in our plants.

Are you adding plants to a koi pond? Get ready to replace them soon. Are you adding plants to a goldfish pond? Not to worry!

don't try forcing a round peg into a square hole (or a marsh pickerel into a water lettuce). Each plant has its own needs and place in the garden, and if you honor them the way you would your favorite grandmother's last wish, you'll have success beyond your wildest dreams.

Of course, as with all living things, plants die—often for inexplicable reasons. When they do, try to determine if you did something wrong so you can keep from making the mistake again.

Remember that the world of plants—as in the larger ecosystem—is constantly changing, evolving, and adapting. In time, you'll find little volunteer plants coming up where you least expect them (and might not want them, but that's another story!). When that day comes, you'll know you've created a modern-day emulation of Mother Nature at her best.

Water plants are a critical element in helping turn an antique bathtub into a natural work of art. By mixing textures, forms, and colors the way you would elsewhere in your garden, you can bring an entirely new element of joy into your life. And, hey, you know those fish that we're going to add next? Well, they'll thank you for it. *Guaranteed!*

them in spring. This plant likes full sun but is treated as an annual in cold areas, since it is hardly only in zones 7 to 10.

As you can see, there are a lot more readily available water plants than you might ever have thought. In truth, there are far more still that we haven't touched upon because either they're not easily obtainable or they're more difficult to grow in an artificial environment.

What's most important of all to remember when introducing water plants into your aqua-scaping is that you must meet the plants' needs first;

QUICK CHECKLIST

- Develop a plan for your water plants, keeping in mind their different habits and requirements.
- Try to incorporate all four types of water plants—floaters, deep-water, submerged, and marginal.
- Plant invasive species in pots to prevent them from taking over your pond.
- Plant water plants in special media or gravel instead of garden soil to keep your pond clean.

A DAY IN THE LIFE

Clambering up the
Cold Mountain path,
The Cold Mountain
trail goes on
and on:
The long gorge
choked with scree
and boulders,
The wide creek, the
mist-blurred grass.
The moss is
slippery, though
there's been
no rain.
The pine sings, but
there's no wind.
Who can leap the
world's ties
And sit with
me among the
white clouds?

—Han-shan

Sokol Summer Camp, Willow Springs, Illinois. Summer, 1958.

We have been here for 3 days, now, and my shyness remains unabated. I do not want to go canoeing unless I can be in a canoe with my cousin. I do not want to turn out for archery class because I will be required to interrelate with others. I do not want to go to the Recreation Hall to pick up my leather-working kit because I will need to speak to a counselor before making my selection.

But I do like the lake.

It is not overly large so far as lakes go, although to a young boy it is sprawling. Later, we would hear tales about boys from camp—strong, strapping, athletic boys with plenty of muscle tone already built into their lithe young bodies—who had actually entered the water on our side of the lake and swum completely across it to the opposite side, where a Girl Scout troop holds summer bivouacs. But I never believed it for a moment.

So, after being taught pretty much how to swim, or at any rate how not to drown within the first 30 seconds, I begin exploring the out-of-bounds area, which, of course, is strictly forbidden. It happens by accident, when I dive underwater and swim just as far and as fast as I can in order to see how long I can hold my breath without turning blue.

When I come up, panting and gasping for precious air, I find myself beyond the floats demarking the swimming area, and I feel the water plants that sprout from the lake bottom clutching at my legs. I look quickly back toward the beach, toward the lifeguard, who is flirting mercilessly with some camp counselor and has not yet seen me, and I take a few steps toward shore, where instead of neatly combed sand and a few shells I see something leap. I move closer, and it leaps again, and before you know it, I have captured a frog.

It is small, and it is dumb (obviously), but it is nonetheless a living, breathing frog, and sure enough, I hold it. I cup it in my hands to keep it alive, for there is little value to a child of 10 in catching a live frog only to have the damned thing die before reaching its destination, and I set off to search for Dale.

But the frog, it turns out, is not so dumb as it looks, and by the time I am back in bounds and calling for my cousin, there is nothing cupped between my two small hands at all except air.

Undeterred, I regale him with stories of the wild things I have seen far beyond the ropes and buoys, perhaps 4 or 5 feet beyond. Later that afternoon, while the rest of the camp is in lockdown, Dale and I sneak down to the lake. It seems strange suddenly, so void of traffic. No screaming, no yelling, no laughing, but nevertheless plenty of sounds. Crickets and croakers and toads and cicada. They are all hard at work, doing whatever it is they believe they should be doing, with Dale and I hot on their trail.

We spy a red-eared turtle sunning on a partly submerged log and, after brainstorming for what seems like forever, decide that the best way to capture it is for Dale to approach it from the lake while I wait on shore. In that way, should the turtle spook before my cousin can reach it, it will jump off the log and swim right toward me, where I will swoop down upon it and, with all the agility of youth, pluck it from the water to have and to hold as a cherished treasure forever.

Dale slips silently into the water (he is the older and stronger of us and, according to him, the stealthier) and gradually maneuvers to within what appears from my vantage point to be mere inches of the turtle. Suddenly Dale leaps up and grabs at the beast, which naturally has been watching him approach all the time and has by now slipped off the log and into the water; he grabs instead a mass of slowly rotting fallen wood. Not one to shirk my responsibilities, I wait for the turtle to come to me, and when it does not, I take a step or two into the water before placing all of my weight on a submerged rock covered with algae.

My feet go out from under me, and I land on my butt in 2 feet of this slimy, cold (colder somehow than it is when we swim in it) witch's brew of life. I say something appropriately cynical along the lines of "Oh, shit," and clamor to my feet before working my way back toward shore.

Dale eventually joins me, and, undeterred, we make our way farther along, looking for more turtles. By the time it is 5:30 or so and the sun is beginning to wane, we decide to surrender our quest and return to camp.

By that night, our heroic feats have echoed across the land. Everyone in camp knows of our valiant explorations. At mess, we are toasted by one and all, pretty much, topped off by none other than the Director of Camping, herself, Mavis Maplebottom, who stands up to speak.

She clears her throat. She gestures toward Dale and me. She makes a brief but stirring announcement during which she addresses those malignant few brain-dead societal dropouts who have not yet heard of our laudatory exploratory sojourn, capping off her remarks with the annunciation of a suitable reward:

If we ever do it again, we will be assigned to permanent latrine duty for the rest of our pathetic little lives.

I look at Dale. Dale looks at me.

We do not do it again.

twelve

Border Plants

God has no religion.

—Mahatma Gandhi

By now, you're probably beginning to feel pretty smug. You've built your own pond, set up a pump and filter, added a few rocks and stones for that natural look, placed your water plants, and lighted the entire affair ... but something is still missing. Something isn't right. Your pond doesn't look like ... well, *nature.*

The reason? The transition!

Transition literally means a transfer or changeover. When we're talking about ponds, transition is the changeover from your pond to your landscape.

Picture a woodland, with its trees, grasses, ferns, wildflowers, rocks, weeds, and birds.

Now picture somebody building a 5-foot-square woodland setting in the center of a putting green. From here to there, nothing but neatly shorn lawn, and there—right in the middle—25 square feet of woodland.

Would it look natural? Of course not. In nature, woodlands come about *gradually.* One moment, you find yourself in a field of prairie grass as you come across a tree and then some shrubs and a few more trees and a few more shrubs. As you continue on your way, you encounter some rocks, a boulder or two, a few wildflowers, more trees, more shrubs. Finally, when you look up, you discover that you have wandered into a thicket. Not from one step to the next, but gradually, over the course of a few dozen (or even hundred) steps.

That's transition—transition from field to forest. *That's* what your pond is missing. So ...

Take a few steps back and look at your water feature. Ask yourself what's wrong. I'm betting you're going to say that, as wonderful as it all looks together, it doesn't "flow" into the entire landscape. In other words, there's no transition.

How do you create a transition from a natural-looking pond or stream to a neatly shorn lawn, trimmed evergreens, and a two-story Williamsburg with a silver Beemer in the driveway? You make it *gradually,* beginning with border plants.

LIST OF BORDER PLANTS

Border plants are those plants surrounding the border—or exterior—of your water feature. You've created a work of art that mimics nature in nearly every way. Now you need to finish the job. Instead of stopping what you've done at the banks of your stream, you need to continue your planting and landscaping away from the waterway.

OPPOSITE: Orange Asiatic lilies at the edge of a pond.

Spreading yew
(*Taxus* × *media* 'Everlow').

Columbine (Aquilegia spp.).

Bleeding heart
(Dicentra spp.).

Violet (Viola spp.).

Starting at the water's edge, you need to reach outward to plant and landscape the perimeter of your water feature. Remember to concentrate the heaviest number of plants nearest the water, just as you would most likely see in nature, and then gradually allow them to thin in numbers as your eye radiates outward from the pond.

What kinds of plants make good border accents? That pretty much depends upon what you hope to accomplish. If you want an all-natural water feature, try to use those plants that you'd find growing naturally in your vicinity. Since we have few waterways in our neck of the woods (and fewer plants in general due to the harsh environment), we had to improvise. Here are a few of our favorite border plants.

Spreading yew (*Taxus* × *media* 'Everlow'). This emerald green evergreen is a slow-growing spreading plant ideal for rock gardens, pond edging, and anywhere you'd like to see color all year long. It is hardy to zone 4.

Columbine (Aquilegia spp.). A delicate, graceful spring-flowering plant with light blue-green foliage that looks good throughout the growing season. Hardy to zone 3.

Bleeding heart (Dicentra spp.). This shade-loving flowering plants grows to 15 inches and blooms in dramatic pendulous droplets throughout spring and summer. Hardy to zone 2.

Violet (Viola spp.). This robust, spreading, low-growing plant produces beautiful vibrant blooms all summer and fall. Grows well in full sun to partial shade and makes an excellent stream bank flower. Hardy to zone 4.

Millet (*Panicum miliaceum L.*). Introduced into the United States from Europe during the 18th century, this grain plant was grown first along the eastern seaboard and later introduced into the Dakotas, where it was grown on considerable acreage. It makes a stunning grass-like introduction to the stream and pond area and develops large brownish-red bract-like seed heads. A free re-seeder. Hardy as an annual; does not accept frost.

Blue fescue (*Festuca glauca*). An elegant, thin, easily clumping non-invasive grass that features blue-green coloring, an insignificant white seed head summer through fall, and a height of 8 to 10 inches. It makes an excellent plant in full sun to part shade and is hardy to zone 5.

Bullrush (Scirpus spp.). A moisture-loving clumping plant that spreads slowly outward and upward as it ages. It features a brilliant deep green coloring and interesting seed heads held upon individual stalks. This is one of a large number of hardy rush plants that grow easily in moist soil. Hardy to zone 5.

Liriope (*Liriope muscari*). Evergreen or semi-evergreen broadleaf plant resembling thick-leaved grass. It reaches a height of 12 to 18 inches and spreads slowly. Grows from sun to shade. Its flowers are variable in color, depending on the variety. Hardy to zone 6.

Scotch moss (*Sagina subulata*). A wonderfully attractive low-growing moss that adds a great sense of texture and drama to the pond and stream bank. It features a brilliant light green color and sometimes insignificant white flowers. Difficult to overwinter in heavy snow areas or when allowed to dry out, but otherwise hardy to zone 4.

Millet (*Panicum miliaceum*).

Blue fescue (*Festuca glauca*).

Bullrush (Scirpus spp.).

Lirope (*Lirope muscari*).

Scottish moss (*Sagina subulata*).

Baby tears (*Helxine soleirolii*).

Nandina (*Nandina domestica*).

Potentilla (*Potentilla fruticosa*).

Hawthorn (*Crataegus crusgalli*).

Chinese arborvitae
(*Platycladus orientalis*; formerly
Thuja orientalis).

Baby tears (*Helxine soleirolii*). This moss-like creeping plant features tiny, round leaves that form above mats of fleshy stems. The plant spreads quickly, grows on nearly anything, and makes a versatile ground cover, especially around rocks, ponds, and streams. Grows to 6 inches and likes to be well watered. Hardy to zone 8.

Nandina (*Nandina domestica*). A delicate looking shrub with light green foliage tinged with red, this plant makes a good background shrub or an interesting specimen. It flowers and spreads readily via seed—sometimes to the point of becoming a pest. Hardy to zone 6.

Potentilla (*Potentilla fruticosa*). This fine-leaved plant features bright yellow flowers set against dark green leathery-looking leaves, making it a stunning plant around water. Likes moisture, but will tolerate some drought. Hardy to zone 4.

Hawthorn (*Crataegus crusgalli*). Also known as cockspur, this slow-growing tree (which eventually reaches 20 to 30 feet) features dark green leathery leaves and white, pink, or red flowers from late spring through fall, making it a showy plant used in limited numbers or as a specimen. It thrives in moist areas but can also tolerate some drought. Tolerating full sun to partial shade, it is hardy to zone 2.

Chinese arborvitae (*Platycladus orientalis*, formerly *Thuja orientalis*) This evergreen tree prefers well-draining soil and moderate moisture, although it is easily tolerant of other conditions. The brilliant lime-green/golden foliage of some varieties, such as 'Golden Globe,' stands in marked contrast to the rest of the garden. For a more dramatic look, prune off the foliage at the base to expose the beautiful reddish brown bark and trunk. This is a slow-growing tree, to 8 feet, although without pruning, it could grow taller in time. Hardy to zone 5.

Daylily (Hemerocallis spp.). A wide range of species populate this family, which is marked by tall, thick, grass-like foliage coming before spikes of slowly opening flowers. Some varieties bloom for 2 weeks in spring while others bloom continually throughout summer. For best blooms, plant in full sun, although the foliage can tolerate partial shade. These plants make for dramatic additions to any garden or pond area where added height is required. Hardy from zones 3 to 9, depending upon the variety.

Lilies (Lilium spp.) There are over 100 species of lilies, which grow from bulbs. Depending on the kind, they flower from early June through September. True lilies have stiff stems with relatively narrow, straplike leaves. Large, showy flowers develop at the tip of each stem. They may be trumpet shaped, bowl shaped, or bell shaped. They are available in a variety of heights and colors and are not difficult to grow. Hardy from zones 3 to 5.

Cyclamen (*Cyclamen hederifolium*). A most welcome sight during the depths of winter, cyclamen offer beautifully shaped, often variegated green/white leaves with brilliant wax-like flowers in various shades of white and red. They bloom prolifically, even during periods of frost. The leaves tend to be round to kidney-shaped and can be plain dark green or strongly patterned with silver tracings or pewter-colored with a silvery overlay. Hardy to zone 4.

Armeria (Armeria spp.). Small, evergreen, grass-like foliage serves as a backdrop for brilliant pink flowers in summer. Delightful in pockets between rocks or on walls. Hardy to zone 2.

Daylily (Hemerocallis spp.).

Asiatic lilies (Lilium spp.).

Cyclamen
(*Cyclamen hederifolium*).

Armeria (Armeria spp.).

Northern maidenhair fern (*Adiantum pedatum*).

Northern maidenhair fern (*Adiantum pedatum*). An airy fern with fan-shaped fronds held on thin black stipes. Delicate pale green fronds emerge in early spring and turn deep blue-green as summer progresses. It grows in tight clumps that spread to form broad patches. They look delicate but are good, tough additions to the pondscape. They produce more fronds all summer and are hardy to zone 5 and in containers.

Blue Atlas cedar (*Cedrus libani atlantica*). These dramatic and elegant evergreens are mostly blue with a hint of green. They grow in an upright, spiral habit. They can grow to 100 feet, although they are such slow growers that they make good garden and water feature specimens for many years. Hardy to zone 6.

As we were forced to build nearly everything up from solid bedrock, we brought in a ton of soil and shredded pine bark in which to set our plantings. Our new motto quickly became: *If you can't dig down, build up!*

We backfilled against our raised streambed to make it look more natural, and we did the same against the backside of our largest pond. In order to disguise the front side, we planted the area heavily with evergreen shrubs and capped off the edge with flat rocks and stones interspersed with mondo grass and baby tears growing in moss balls.

The point is that an entire world of plants awaits your selection. From one nursery alone, we could replant our entire waterway with completely different plants—never using the same species twice. That's how wide a selection is available to us.

Oh, and about never planting the same thing twice? Don't take that advice seriously. Nature seldom drops a single seed to sprout and take hold. More likely, she scatters groups of seeds in specific

Blue Atlas cedar (*Cedrus libani atlantica*).

areas so that you might have a stand of wild grass to one side, some shrubs off in the distance, and a few trees and wildflowers in yet a third location.

Don't feel shy about experimenting. If you think something will look good in one spot and it turns out not to be so, take it out. Just so long as you keep the roots moist when the plants are out of the ground, they rarely object to being "field tested." When you come across exactly the plants that work best for you, you'll know it, and all that extra effort will have finally paid off.

One other thing to note: nature isn't at her prime a hundred percent of the time. As some plants come into bloom, others die out. As some open new leaves, others begin showing their age. Don't let that bother you. It's simply another aspect of nature at work.

You *can* hold your plants' "down time" to a minimum and increase your bloom time by mixing a wide variety of species that bloom at different times of year. Be careful, though, to use plants that require basically the same water conditions. You don't want to put a succulent next to a fern or a desert willow beside a carpet rose.

PLANTING RIGHT

Tons of articles—and books, as well—have been written about how to plant things properly. While I don't want to belabor the point, there are a couple of very important things you should know before you set about planting or transplanting anything in order to increase your chances for success. After all, if you're going to go through all the time and expense of acquiring new plants and putting them in the ground, you might as well take a few seconds to make sure you do it properly.

Most of the plants you buy come in plastic containers. To remove small plants without damaging them, squeeze all around the container in order to

OVERWINTERING YOUR PLANTS

To use plants that are not winter hardy in your growing zone, try putting the plants in pots and setting the pots in the ground. Place some Spanish moss around the lips of the pots to disguise them. Then, when the weather turns bad, you can lift the plants, pots and all, out of the ground to over-winter in your home. Set the pots back outside the following spring, and no one will ever be the wiser.

loosen the soil from the container walls. Place your hand across the top of the pot with the plant's stalk between your thumb and your fingers, and turn the pot over. Shake it sharply until the plant falls out into your hand. For larger potted shrubs and trees, shake the plant out onto its side on the ground. While the plant is out of the pot, examine the root system. It should look white and vigorous. You should see a combination of thick roots and finer feeder roots.

Now comes the part everybody fears. Taking your fingers or a sharp knife, poke holes into the root ball and pulls some of the roots free. You want to open up the plant's root ball to encourage new growth. Otherwise, the roots might tend to keep growing in circles, as they did in the round container, and the plant's growth could be stunted.

Once you've loosened up the roots, set the plant in the hole you've already dug for it—about one and a half times the size of the original root ball. Make sure the crown of the plant (the part where the plant's main stem meets the soil) is set no deeper than it was in the pot. Covering the crown with soil could damage or even kill the plant. Spread the roots out in

SAVING MONEY ON GROUNDCOVERS

In case you have not yet deduced it, we use baby tears a *lot* around our ponds. They're quick growing, stay low to the ground, act as a natural groundcover, and disguise a multiplicity of sins. We use so many baby tears, in fact, that we decided to plant them all around our garden—beneath shrubs and tall flowers, in bare spots within the landscape, wherever we can find the room.

Now, whenever we find a need for baby tears around the pond, such as when we add new plants or rock features, we simply dig up a clump of them from elsewhere in the garden and transplant them to where we want them. The plants that we removed will grow back soon enough, and we have a nearly endless supply of free groundcover.

Food for thought!

the hole and begin backfilling with fresh potting or garden soil. You can use a general-purpose potting soil for most plants, although acid-loving plants such as azalea, camellia, blueberry, etc., should have soil mixed with peat moss or other organic material to increase the soil's acidity.

Once the hole is backfilled, make sure you tamp the new soil down firmly. This is very important. Some gardeners are hesitant to apply too much pressure to the soil for fear of damaging the plant's roots; failing to tamp down well could result in trapped air pockets that could end up drying out the roots and killing the plant.

After you've tamped the soil down firmly, cover with wood chips, pine needles, stone, or some other type of mulch to hold the moisture in and water well with a dilute fertilizer solution or mulch tea,

being careful not to wash the soil away from the plant. The mulch will help the soil retain moisture, even during periods of drought.

SETTING UP AN AUTOMATIC WATERING SYSTEM

If your water feature is relatively small and your plantings are few, you may not need to concern yourself with watering. Breaking out the hose a couple times a week can be therapeutic.

If, on the other hand, you have a large water feature with dozens or even hundreds of plants spread out over a large area, you're going to need to set up an automated watering system. The good news is that it's easier than you might have thought.

Watering systems come in two basic sizes. One uses half-inch plastic or PVC lines to deliver the water where you want it to go. Not surprisingly, this is referred to as a half-inch system. This is the type of system that most homes use to water their lawn, shrubs, and trees.

The second system uses quarter-inch plastic lines to deliver the water. In a stroke of unmitigated genius, the creators called it a quarter-inch system (see the diagram of the watering system for an overview). A typical ¼-inch watering system includes some sort of valve control for turning the system on and off, a timer to automate the process, a filter to keep suspended impurities from clogging up the drippers and spray heads, a length of ½-inch tubing to carry the water roughly where you want it, and barbed connectors for running ¼-inch tubing from the ½-inch tube to the spray heads and drippers, placed where you want them. The ¼-inch tubing is more flexible and easier to disguise than the larger ½-inch tubing yet offers plenty of pressure to water your plants.

A half-inch system uses relatively expensive pop-up sprinkler heads and bubblers to deliver a lot

A typical ¼-inch watering system. The ¼-inch tubing is more flexible and easier to disguise than the larger ½-inch tubing, yet offers plenty of pressure to water your plants.

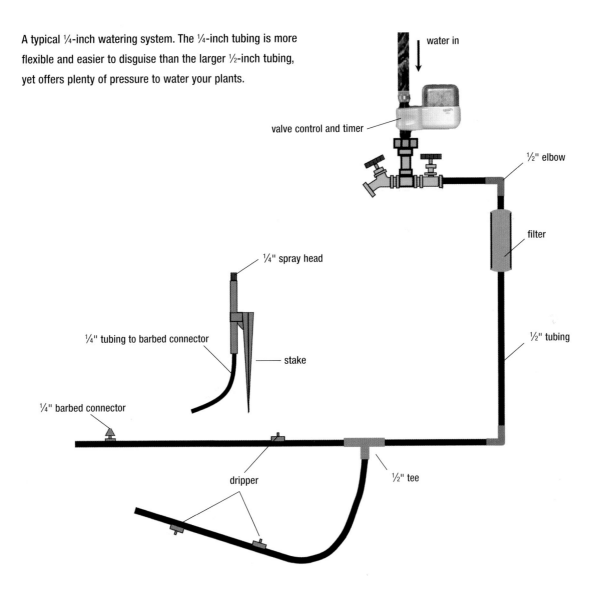

water in

valve control and timer

½" elbow

filter

¼" spray head

¼" tubing to barbed connector

stake

½" tubing

¼" barbed connector

dripper

½" tee

of water in a short period of time wherever you need it most, which is usually on the lawn. While this type of system works well for most landscaping needs, you're going to want to install a quarter-inch system around your pond because it's quick, easy, efficient, less costly, and less noticeable than its larger cousin.

To install a quarter-inch system, take stock of your watering needs. We installed three separate systems in order to service our three major ponds.

One operates off a standard hose bib connected to the back of the house. The others (on either side of the house) come from a water line we ran from the front hose bib and buried alongside the house.

We attached an electronic timer to each water source and hooked up a half-inch black landscaping hose to the bibs. We buried the half-inch lines in horseshoe configurations around our plantings, capping off their ends. Then we tapped into the lines with quarter-inch barbed connectors. To those, we hooked quarter-inch lines. At the end of the quarter-inch lines, we installed quarter-inch drippers or sprinklers, depending upon the water requirements of the plants in each specific area. We repeated the process until all of the plants in our system were covered.

Now, whenever the timers come on (you can set them for time, frequency, and duration), water is pumped into the half-inch lines, where it radiates out through the quarter-inch lines to the plants. We disguised the quarter-inch lines with moss, bark, baby tears, or whatever else was available. Regardless of the weather, our plants are protected from drying out, all automatically.

If all this work sounds intimidating, relax. You can purchase just about everything you need to set up a quarter-inch watering system in a single kit. We chose to purchase our system piecemeal simply because no kit was large enough to handle all of our requirements. But several different sized kits are available, and one may be just right for you. Some kits even include timers, and most are fairly affordable. They also come with detailed installation instructions.

We're secure in the knowledge that all of our plants are healthy. Our water features look great. Best of all, we're no longer slaves to watering!

QUICK CHECKLIST

- Create a gradual transition from your water feature to your yard for a more natural look.
- Choose native plant species to enhance the natural look.
- Use flowering plants sparingly to avoid detracting from the overall effect.
- Place your plantings on a timed quarter-inch sprinkler system for convenience and consistency in watering.
- If you can't dig your plants into the ground, build the ground up with fill dirt and mulch and place the plants in the raised mounds.

NOTHING IS AS IT SEEMS

Unfettered at last,
a traveling monk,
I pass the old
Zen barrier.
Mine is a traceless
stream-and-cloud life.
Of these mountains,
which shall be
my home?

—Manan

Steamboat Springs, Colorado. July, 1988.

Stein is a former Norwegian Olympic Team ski racer who works concrete during the summer and teaches skiing during the winter. On precisely one of those winter days, while cruising down the face of Mt. Werner, he catches an edge and blows out his anterior cruciate ligament—the dreaded ACL.

Following his operation, he rehabilitates for several weeks. Long before the rehab period is up, he stops by my home to ask if I want to go hiking with him over the Continental Divide.

Now, I am no weakling, and I am no stranger to hiking, but the thought of hiking with a man who is recovering from knee surgery makes me queasy. What if he can't do it? What if he slips, falls, and re-injures himself miles from civilization? What do I do then?

But Stein is nothing if not persistent—stubborn, if you're a Norsky—so the next day, we drive to a parking area where the trailhead leading up and over the demarcation separating the eastern slope of the Rocky Mountains from the west begins. He tells me he has taken this hike numerous times, once carrying his 3-month-old son in a sling over his back. The round trip takes 4 hours.

Stein brings with him a backpack and a hiking stick, and I have dressed myself in Ralph Lauren Polo shorts and a white long-sleeved shirt. We both wear hiking boots that, within minutes, are carrying us up into the woods and toward the mountaintop.

Three hours later, I am beginning to tire. Stein outdistances me by a good 50 yards or more and stops to allow me to catch up. I imagine that we are quite near the Divide, the very top of the mountain overlooking the scenic Yampa Valley, and that the trip back down will go much faster. I imagine wrong.

After 5 hours, we break out of the woods and upon a meadow where we encounter a light dusting of snow. A few hundred yards farther deposits us on the shores of a shimmering lake. The clouds, billowing white-and-gold, reflect off the azure blue of the water as I find a place to sit. I do so casually, as if I am not really tired at all. Let's face it. I am a good 10 years younger than Stein, and it would not do to let this man with the giant ego know that he has worn me out.

As I struggle to catch my breath, my partner scurries around the area like a crazed squirrel scavenging nuts before winter. He returns with a handful of firewood, and soon the coffee pot, nested precariously on the edge of a flat rock, chirps at us softly as we begin feasting on French bread and cheese. We finish off with green apples and a granola bar.

An hour after arriving, sated and dulled, we put out the fire, and as Stein slips his pack onto his back, I ready myself for the journey home.

"No, no," he tells me. "We are not there yet." He points to a snowfield a few hundred yards away. "There. There is the Divide. "

Incredulously, I follow his finger toward the east and sigh. Within moments, my feet take their first few halting steps upward until we find ourselves in calf-deep snow. Then thigh-deep. I wonder if the snow will not grow so deep that we will be forced to turn back.

Remarkably, the snow begins to shallow, and the hiking grows easier. We make a wide loop around several huge boulders craning their necks at us and eventually find ourselves back in among the trees. Finally, we are heading downhill.

Seven hours after our journey began, we break onto the parking area. I am ready to collapse and I don't care who knows it. Stein turns to me as he slips the pack off his back and throws it into the car.

"That was some 4-hour hike," I tell him.

"Yah, well, we take longer at the lake than I planned. I am an old man," he says, grinning, "not young like you. You have to make allowances."

I smile as he pulls a small object from his pocket and holds it out to me.

"What's this?" I ask, taking a dark colored stone into my palm. It is round and smooth as if polished by a jeweler.

"A little remembrance of your first hike over the Continental Divide."

"Hey, thanks," I say. "But tell me, when we got to the lake, I thought we'd reached the Divide—and it was still higher up. Just where exactly *did* we cross it?"

Stein slips into the seat of the car and opens the passenger door. I slide in next to him and buckle my belt. He shrugs. "Who can say exactly where a line is. On a map, it is easy to find. But in nature, nothing is as it seems...."

thirteen

Stocking Your Pond

It has been a long time in coming, but we have finally arrived at the place that first prompted us to begin our journey into water culture so many years ago. We have finally arrived at the fish.

Fish are one of life's simpler joys. I say simpler because they exist in the wild with few problems and little intervention by humans. Nature provides for the well-being of fish via a sprawling and complex

ABOVE: A man-made pond with a school of medium-sized koi. *Photo by Neezam for Fotolia.*

ecologically balanced micro-system. So perfectly balanced is that system that few predators outside of human beings are a substantial threat to them.

We've all seen how humans have disrupted this delicate balance with devastating results: fish die-offs in the Atlantic Ocean, kill-offs in the Straits of Alaska, genetic mutations in the Great Lakes. Wherever humankind has meddled, either unwittingly or otherwise, fish—and other animals as well, of course—have paid the ultimate price.

Now we ask not only to meddle in nature, but also to recreate it. We dare to turn our eyes toward

A closeup view of the author's small pond planted with horsetail toward the rear, featuring several types of floating plants, including water hyacinth and duckwort.

the skies and say, "Oh, Lord of the Universe, Who hath created such wondrous and matchless things, give *us* a shot at it!"

And that's exactly the role we take on when we build a fishpond.

So, if I were to ask you what a fishpond is, and you were to reply, "A fishpond is a place of beauty where plants and fish and water come together," I would advise you to forget about stocking your pond with fish. You do not have a clear enough understanding of the journey upon which you are embarking.

If, on the other hand, I asked you the same question, and you replied, "A fishpond is a place imitative of nature, where all things must function in harmony and balance, toward which goal the pond keeper must be prepared to work as long and as hard as it takes," I would not only advise you to stock your pond with fish, but also recommend what colors.

The difference between the two responses is one of (a) setting up a fishpond and walking away from it while hoping for the best, and (b) setting up a fishpond while diligently working to maintain its health and balance. Only by doing the latter can you hope to have a healthy, *happy* colony of fish to entertain and amuse you for as long as you desire.

Happy? Yes, fish can feel happy, and they can definitely be amusing. They can reach out in an effort to relate to you. In doing so, they can offer a harmonious link to the nature of a world that is foreign and even deadly to us—the world of underwater life.

Perhaps that is the greatest allure that fish hold for us—their ability to live in what to us is a hostile environment. We look at them and marvel. They have no lungs, and yet they breathe. They have no stomach, and yet they eat. They have no arms and legs, and yet they move.

What fish *don't* have is the ability to control their own environment. That's where we come in.

REQUIREMENTS

Most fish (there are always exceptions, but rarely for pond keepers) require several things in order to survive in their environment. They need a high oxygen level in the water. They need sunlight and shade. They need an ambient temperature between 40° F and 90° F, depending upon the species. They need food, vitamins, minerals, and all of the other supplements that most living things need for survival and that they obtain through various complex mechanisms.

Most fish *won't* survive, or at least remain healthy, with certain other elements in their environment. These include high ammonia levels, high or low pH levels, and high nitrite, nitrate, chlorine, and chloramines levels, not to mention a whole host of other toxic chemicals.

Thankfully, there are some early warning signs for the observant aquaculturist that things are not as they should be. The first sign is a fish floating belly up. I don't say that to be flip, but a dead fish is absolutely the first and surest sign that you need to take some drastic steps and take them fast! Unless the fish died of disease or old age, which for a goldfish means from two to three *decades,* there is something wrong with the makeup of your water. You need to do an immediate 50% water change (make sure that the temperature of the new water is close to that of the old) and begin testing for signs of high ammonia or nitrate levels, followed by chlorine, chloramines, and a high or low pH.

Most likely, if the fish died suddenly and without any warning, the culprit is ammonia. Go back and read the information about pumps and filters (Chapter 7), and check your own system to make sure that it measures up.

Swimming near the surface of the water, gasping for air, is another sure sign that fish are unhealthy. They are attempting to ingest enough oxygen through their mouths to make up for what they cannot process through their gills. That could mean that your pond's water is low on dissolved oxygen. It could also be a sign that nitrate or ammonia poisoning has damaged the fish's gills to the point where they are no longer able to function properly. In either case, an immediate 50% water change and additional testing is required.

A third sign that fish are unhealthy is their failure to answer the dinner bell. Fish are ravenous feeders. Get in the habit of talking to them whenever you feed them—preferably in the same spot each time so that they get used to coming to you. This is an excellent opportunity to observe the fish up close to make sure that they all appear healthy. If, come feeding time, all but one or two show up for lunch, there's a good possibility that the missing fish are ill. Again, a 50% water change and further testing are indicated.

There are other diseases and problems that can affect your pond fish, and we'll go into them in Chapter 15. But, for now, keep in mind that, if you monitor your pond regularly and test for harmful imbalances at least every other day depending upon the size of your pond (small ponds and containers require a closer watch), you should rarely have to worry about such things.

THE HISTORY OF GOLDFISH

Goldfish have been sought after, appreciated, and bred by many different cultures throughout history. Once considered by many fish keepers to be "junk" or "pest" fish, they have today risen to an exalted place in society. Not surprisingly, goldfish enthusiasts pursue their hobbies with a devotion rivaling those of any other aficionados.

If you still think of goldfish primarily as small feeder fish or the unwilling prizes for hapless winners at the local county fair, you're in for a surprise. The variety of fish available today is astounding. The exalted history and development of these fish is similarly nothing less than remarkable.

The first mentions of goldfish are found in ancient Chinese records during the Tsin Dynasty, circa 300 A.D.; early cultivation of these fish reaches back close to 1,000 years, when crucian carp were first domesticated for their docility and durability. The carp were bred for the courtyard ponds of the Sung Dynasty.

The elongated, flat-sided carp were a long way from the exotic varieties of goldfish available today. As breeders worked with ponds throughout the East, the fish began to develop different colors and patterns. From their simple carp ancestors came new and exciting varieties with double tails, long flowing fins, and protruding eyes. By carefully selecting and breeding these fish, new hybrids were created, and the Chinese today lay claim to the exalted hobby of goldfish keeping.

Since the fish were originally kept in ponds or tubs, they were bred for colorful or distinctive traits that were most easily observed from above, rather than from the side, as is true with aquarium fish. Goldfish became so popular during the Ming Dynasty that people began keeping the fish in clay pots in their homes.

The Japanese discovered the joys of raising goldfish in 1500. Today's hobbyists have the work of the Chinese and Japanese to thank for varieties such as the Fantail, the Veiltail, the Globe-Eye, and the various transparent-scaled varieties currently available. Many of these varieties trace their heritage back to the late 16th and early 17th centuries.

As trade flourished with the English, Portuguese, French, and Dutch during the 18th century, goldfish became popular pets and fashionable gifts in England and around the continent. In 1870, goldfish were introduced to America, where the first goldfish farm was established in Maryland in 1889.

The first goldfish show was held in Osaka, Japan, in 1862, and the British Aquarists Association in London organized the first Western show in 1926.

Although most aquarists realize the wide variety of goldfish available, the exact recorded number of recognized varieties varies between 100 and 300.

Interestingly, if the most exotic goldfish breeds available were left to breed at will in natural ponds, they would revert back to their wild ancestry within a few short generations.

Goldfish today come in all sizes, shapes, colors, and conformations. They differ in types of scales, body structure, eyes, fins, tails, head growth, and colors. Although the term "goldfish" was once self-descriptive, today it's more a general catch-all, since most modern-day goldfish are anything but gold. They may be solid colored or marked in various combinations of red, white, gold, blue, chocolate, black, pale yellow, and olive green. Most goldfish change colors and even markings throughout their life span, with the brown fish you have one year developing into a deep red, or your solid white fish developing into a white-red one the next.

These colors vary even more depending upon the fish's scale type. The scales may be metallic, glimmering in the sunlight; matte, with a nonreflective, flat, or skin-like appearance; or nacreous, with a combination of both metallic and matte scales. Calico, which denotes a goldfish with three or more colors on its body, is considered part of the nacreous group.

Because the more exotic egg-shaped fish swim more slowly and react less aggressively than their more streamlined single-tailed cousins, a pond keeper needs to choose common fish mates carefully, combining only similar body types and levels of aggression in the same pond.

An important factor in determining the compatibility among the different varieties of goldfish is body type. The single-tail, flat-bodied goldfish are among the hardiest and therefore the most commonly used in outdoor ponds. The second type, which has a round or egg-shaped body, is divided into two groups, those with dorsal fins and those without.

GOLDFISH TYPES

Common Goldfish. Of all the flat-bodied goldfish, the Common Goldfish is considered the hardiest of all. With its long, sleek body, it remains closest to its wild carp cousin. The fins and tail of the common goldfish are not especially long, but they are functional. The fish are fast swimmers and extremely competitive when it comes to feeding. As young fry, they tend to be a dull blue-gray in color, turning to a metallic orange as they mature.

Saraso Comets.

Common Goldfish.

Comet. Of the hundreds of different varieties of goldfish, the only one developed in the United States is the Comet. It features longer flowing fins and tail and a more streamlined body than its Common Goldfish cousin, yet it retains the hardiness for which goldfish are known. The Comet is also an aggressive swimmer and feeder.

Tancho Singletail. The only differences between the Comet and the Japanese-developed Tancho Singletail are the bright red cap and silvery-white body that set the Tancho apart.

Saraso Comet. The Japanese-developed Saraso Comet is red and white, as opposed to the all-red U.S. Comet.

Shubunkin. Shubunkins, both the Bristol and the London variety, are variations in color on the common goldfish. What makes this breed of fish distinguishable is its nacreous scales. It is primarily bred for its beautiful patches of red, orange, yellow, sky blue, violet, brown, or black, often scattered across a field of blue.

Shubunkins.

Wakins.

Wakin. Wakins are the common goldfish of Japan. These fish are bluish in color when young, turning a deep red as they mature. They're similar in conformation to the common goldfish except that they have a double tail fin. Nevertheless, Wakins swim fast enough to be kept with single-tailed fish.

Jikin. A very old race of goldfish, the Jikin, also called the peacock tail or butterfly tail, is as pleasing to view from above as from the side. The color on the fins is solid red astride a solid white body.

Fantail.

Fantail. Round-bodied (sometimes called egg-shaped) goldfish can be found in an unbelievable variety of different tail lengths and sizes, body shapes, eye types, and head shapes. The most commonly seen variety of this type is the Fantail. More Fantails are purchased each year than any other double-tail breed. It features long, flowing fins and a lack of head growth.

Calico Fantail.

Calico Fantail. As with other types of fancy goldfish, Fantails come in numerous colors and patterns. One of the more popular is the Calico Fantail, which is, outside of its coloration, virtually identical to other Fantails.

Ryukin. Ryukins, round-bodied fish with a highly developed shoulder hump, are also popular with aquarists. Hardy and colorful, they make good fish for beginning fish keepers. The Ryukin is known in Japan as *Onaga,* which means long-tailed. Telescope-eyed Ryukins are commonly called Demekins.

Veiltail. Graceful Veiltails are among the most exquisitely beautiful of all goldfish. They feature flowing, square-cut, double tails along with delicate

Ryukin.

Veiltails.

ornamental of fish, well deserving of its popularity among breeders.

Oranda. Many goldfish enthusiasts consider Orandas to be their favorites. Their full bodies, flowing fins, rounded head growth, and inquisitive nature add up to an unusual and appealing fish. They, too, require exceptionally clean water to keep their head growth and fins in good condition.

Red-Cap Oranda. An offshoot of the Oranda is the Red-Cap Oranda, which features as its most prominent decoration a red cap. Besides that, they are virtually identical to most other Orandas.

Oranda.

dorsal fins. Veiltails are difficult to keep, requiring special care that is best suited to experienced hobbyists. The fish's long fins are especially susceptible to ammonia damage. They require extremely clean water with little current, a lot of room for their fins, and very little in the way of tank ornaments or plants. Many breeds of goldfish, including Orandas, Telescopes, Moors, and Pearlscales, owe their own lovely finnage to the Veiltail. The Veiltail is one of the hardest fancy goldfish to breed true to type, and it is very difficult to produce good quality specimens conforming to all of the breed's standards. It is nonetheless one of the most graceful and

Red-Cap Orandas.

Pearlscale.

Moor.

Pearlscale. Perhaps no other round-bodied gold-fish are as eye-catching as the Pearlscale. Their overly plump bodies and distinctive scales are well worth a second look. Good quality Pearlscales feature a hard raised area, usually white, in the center of each scale. The Pearlscale's tail is square-cut, similar to a Veiltail's, but considerably shorter.

Globe-Eyes.

Telescope.

Telescope and Globe-Eye. At first glance, the bulging eyes of the Telescope and Globe-Eye fish are quite shocking, but take a closer look and you will discover a friendly, comical face. The shape of the eyes varies from fish to fish. The Telescope has many variations in eye type, color, fins, and scale types. These fish can be found with nacreous, metallic, pearl, or matte scales, making them popular with a wide range of breeders. One of the most commonly seen forms of this type is the solid black matte variety, the **Moor**. Moors are often called Black Moors, but since all Moors are black, the name Moor is sufficient.

Black Moor.

Exotics. Less is certainly more for the hobbyists who favor the Exotic goldfish. These round-bodied fish are missing something conspicuous—a dorsal fin. Exotics exhibit an assortment of unique traits, which makes these fish even more interesting. It also makes them less efficient swimmers, so tank and pond mates must be chosen with care.

Pompon.

Ranchu.

Lionhead and Ranchu. Lionheads and Ranchus are two very popular dorsalless breeds of goldfish. They are similar in appearance in many ways: both are missing dorsal fins and both have elaborate head growth. They differ in that the Ranchu's back displays a sharp downward angle near its double tail. The Lionhead's back is straighter, although it still curves down slightly toward its butterfly tail. The Lionhead's head growth is also different from an Oranda's. Usually, the Oranda's growth is limited to the top of the head, while the Lionhead's growth covers its entire face.

Hanafusa.

Pompon. Another dorsalless fish features a couple of "extras." The short, round, boxy Pompon's nasal septum or narial flaps are enlarged and folded so that they resemble the fluffy tops of a child's knitted cap. Older Pompons will also sport a small head growth. Several other breeds of goldfish also have pompons, including Orandas, Lionheads, and **Hanafusa** (Pompons with dorsal fins).

Lionhead.

Celestial. Celestials, according to Chinese legend, were the jewel of one particular emperor because their gaze was constantly upward toward the heavens...and, of course, toward the emperor. Celestials' upturned eyes are encased in a hard covering. Because of their conformation, they eat only floating food and must be tank and pond mates with similarly docile fish.

Celestial.

COMMONLY KEPT POND FISH

Although there are literally hundreds of different species of goldfish—and thousands of fish altogether—only a few are generally kept in ponds, because of their attractiveness and their adaptability. Here are the more commonly stocked fish.

- **Red Comets.** A relatively new introduction to the world of fishponds, Red Comets boast long, elegant fins and a single long, swaying tail. The United States' only contribution to the species, Comets feed at all levels of the pond from bottom to surface and are winter hardy, tolerating water temperatures down to 34° F and as warm as 95° F, although neither extreme is desirable.

- **Fantails.** Wider in body structure than Red Comets, Fantails have a more egg-shaped body and an even larger double tail. Their scales can appear metallic or pearly. They can tolerate water temperatures of only 55° F to 70° F, so you must monitor your pond carefully or avoid using them if your climate is uncooperative. Being sensitive to prolonged low temperatures, they are not suitable for cold-climate ponds.

- **Shubunkins.** Often called Calico goldfish, Shubunkins are popular and easy to care for. They come in a wide variety of colors, including blue. Two varieties are commonly available. These are the London, which have a calico pattern on a striking blue background, and the Bristol, which have the same pattern as Londons but with pearly scales and a large, forked tail with rounded ends. Shubunkins grow to 10 inches or more and are hardy, tolerating water temperatures between 39° F and 85° F.

- **Koi.** Although some koi can be costly, not all of them are expensive. They commonly grow up to 3 feet in length, can weigh more than 20 pounds, and live to be 100 years or more. They are voracious grazers, eating nearly constantly. They nibble on algae, pond plants, roots, and nearly anything else they can find. They require a large pond with a good filtration system to dispose of their prolific waste. They are playful, rambunctious, and powerful and can knock over underwater pots. They are also prolific jumpers and should be watched closely, especially when newly introduced to an environment. Koi have been known to live for several hours out of water, so, if you find one that has jumped out, wet your hands, pick it up carefully, and slowly introduce it back into the pond.

  Koi do not do well in small ponds of less than 100 gallons, since they are extremely sensitive to water chemistry fluctuations. They feed at all levels and breed easily. They prefer cool water temperatures of 39° F to 68° F, making them ideal for most backyard ponds.

- **Common goldfish.** Usually orange-red, white, or spotted, common goldfish feed at all water levels. Although many resources claim that they grow to a maximum of 10 inches in length, we have some that are considerably larger. An extremely hardy fish, they tolerate water as cool as 38° F and as warm as 95° F, although neither extreme is recommended for long periods.

Bubble-Eye.

Bubble-Eye. A fish demanding even more careful scrutiny is the Bubble-Eye. This unique fish has a large, fluid-filled sac, or bubble, located beneath each eye. The bubbles wobble as the cigar-shaped dorsalless fish swims from side to side. The sacs can vary in size and thickness. Take care to keep this fish's environment free of any objects that could puncture or harm the fluid-filled sacs, and avoid strong currents in the tank or pond. To move the fish, avoid netting or hand-scooping; instead, guide the fish gently into a plastic bag or bowl.

THE HISTORY OF KOI

Nishikigoi, or koi, are the national fish of Japan. Hundreds of years ago, according to legend, the farmers in the mountain village of Yamakoshi noticed a red carp swimming among the black carp that they raised to supplement their diet of rice and vegetables. Through years of selective breeding, Japanese fish keepers succeeded in creating the hundreds of unique varieties of koi that we see on the market today.

Broadly divided into two main types, koi are considered to be either common or butterfly, depending primarily on the shape and length of their tails and fins.

Common koi are those without overly fancy tails or fins. They most resemble in shape their genetic ancestors. They have been bred over the years to a wide range of colors and patterns, with each one having its own name, its own characteristics, and its own devoted following.

Butterfly koi are those with long, flowing tails and fins, which when viewed from above resemble the delicate, lacy wings of butterflies. These fish have been bred apart from common koi in order to produce increasingly exotic looking fish. Like the common koi, butterfly koi have an intriguing history. About 12 years ago, the breeders at Blue Ridge Fish Hatchery noticed an ad in a pet industry trade magazine from a New York City firm offering long-finned koi for sale. The ad piqued the breeders' interest, and they bought a dozen of them. The long-finned koi were uniformly unattractive, mostly resembling their ancestral carp but with longer fins and tails.

Through careful and patient cross-breeding with common koi, the breeders eventually managed to produce a new koi type—a fish of extreme beauty, with vibrant color and long fins and tails. Some of them had long fins with a luminous metallic glow

Butterfly Koi.
Photo © Roger Fattig, Fattig Farms, www.fattigfish.com

Tancho Koi. *Photo © Carolyn Weise, Ecological Laboratories.*

that could be described as pearlescent. Wyatt LeFever, then-president of Blue Ridge, explained, "We were admiring them in a small pool when my son Randy said, 'They remind me of butterflies.' Hence the name. We realized we had some diamonds in the rough. We were pretty excited about their commercial possibilities."

By selecting the best of the butterfly koi and interbreeding them, they created even more beautiful butterfly koi. Their commercial possibilities began to look very good indeed. With further selective breeding, Blue Ridge created a koi that, unlike regular koi, was beautiful when viewed from the sides as well as the top. They swam with grace and regal bearing. Said LeFever, "What a beautiful pond fish they would make! Due to their hybrid vigor they are stronger, more hardy, and more disease resistant than either common goldfish or regular koi."

While butterfly koi are undoubtedly more exotic looking than common koi, their introduction to breeders around the world has failed to dampen the enthusiasm for common koi.

In keeping with their Japanese heritage, the common Tancho Koi, which sports a large red circle on the top of its head, is considered in Japan to be a symbol of the rising sun, found in the Japanese flag, and has become a very coveted koi, both in and out of Japan. Even today, koi breeders from the United States and Israel (the two other major koi breeding countries in the world) procure their initial inventory from Japan in order to be able to claim a genuine Japanese heritage, which is important in breeding koi for show.

Understandably, most water gardeners today aren't into showing koi. Rather, they are nature enthusiasts who are not exactly crazy about spending thousands of dollars on a fish only to watch a blue heron come swooping down from the sky to scoop up a *very* expensive meal.

There are some things that make one koi more valuable than the other. And the most important factor in valuing a koi is its size. Very much like a sumo wrestler, the bigger the koi, the more valuable it is. Therefore, when buying baby koi, look for the ones with the largest heads, assuming that a big head eventually begets a big body.

Conformation, or overall body shape, also plays a role in valuing a koi. The most valuable shape is best described as "torpedo-like." If you find a koi that looks as if it could be shot out of the forward tube of a WWII submarine, grab it. It's a winner!

Finally, skin quality, color intensity, and clarity also count big time. Experts check very closely in order to spot any blemishes or flaws in the skin of the fish. They consider color intensity, balance, and clarity of the pattern on the koi, seeking fish with clearly marked color delineations.

GENERAL KOI CATEGORIES

There are three commonly accepted general categories of koi throughout the world. These include, from bottom to top, pond quality, ornamental quality, and show quality.

- **Pond quality koi** (the most common and the least expensive). These include fish sold by local pet shops and some breeders. Pond koi are usually locally bred, have mixed bloodlines, have no papers that distinguish them, and are not suitable for competition. They are, however, very inexpensive and can be every bit as enjoyable as keeping ornamental or show quality koi.

- **Ornamental quality koi** (the next most common and moderately expensive). These are a higher quality fish than those labeled pond quality. Most will have been bred from good quality parents, have good bloodlines, good conformation, and a beautiful color. The differences between ornamental and show koi are found in the pattern, the body conformation, the skin quality, and the evenness of color. In other words, most ornamental koi have unbalanced patterns with "flaws" in their skin, coloring, and shape.

- **Show quality koi** (the least common and the most expensive). These koi are expected to have good bloodlines, good body conformation, shiny and unflawed skin, sharp edges, and balance in their patterns. Experts consider bloodline to be such an important factor that they almost take for granted that show quality koi have come from show quality parents.

Most pond fish owners stock their ponds with koi that are of the pond or ornamental variety, for obvious reasons. Fewer than 1% of all koi owners own or care about owning show quality koi, making this variety of koi that much rarer and driving the prices even higher.

KOI TYPES

Nearly 95% of all koi in the world fall into a handful of basic Japanese categories. Three of these categories are collectively known as *Gosanke* (in Japanese, "three families"). The Big Three are composed of Kohaku, Sanke, and Showa. All three breeds are shown regularly in koi shows around the world.

The **Kohaku** is a uniquely beautiful white koi with red markings. Just as with fingerprints, no two are ever alike. Various sub-categories of Kohaku refer to differing patterns of red on white. When people talk about koi, Kohaku is inevitably at the top of the list.

One of the primary concerns in valuing any koi, including the Kohaku, is the intensity of their color and the degree of contrast, in this case, red vs. white. The more clear-cut and stark the contrast, the more valuable the Kohaku is considered. In fact, there's even a Japanese name for the crispness of the pattern's edge. It's called *kiwa*. Back in the early 1900s, a new variety of koi emerged. It added some unique black markings to the red and white of the Kohaku. This new breed is called the **Sanke** or **Sanshoku**. This category constitutes the second of the three families.

Then, during the 1930s, a third new breed was developed and introduced into the market. It features red and white markings contrasted against a

Sanke, or Sanshoku, Koi. *Photo © Carolyn Weise, Ecological Laboratories.*

jet-black base. The new breed is known as **Showa**. In keeping with tradition, its color intensity, clarity, and crispness of pattern all play major roles in the valuation of the breed. Showa represents the third member of the Gosanke, or Big Three.

The fourth major category is the most popular in America. It's known as **Yamabuki-Ogon**, which means "metallic." The name refers to a bright, metallic sheen that characterizes this category of koi. They are singular in color, meaning they are "without pattern," and they can be jet-black, green, red, yellow, blue, or gold, which makes them unique among koi.

Another category is known as the **Kawarigoi**, which translated means "changing," or "different"

Showa Koi. *Photo © www.usakoi.com.*

Yamabuki-Ogon Koi. *Photo © www.usakoi.com.*

KOI FACTS

The tusks on either side of a koi's mouth are not there merely for ornament. They have evolved over the years as an aid to helping the fish root around in the mud. Originally bottom feeders, koi still enjoy digging around the pond in search of roots, insects, crustaceans, and whatever else they can find, although they are intelligent and adaptable enough to know to come to the surface during feeding time.

Feeding your koi floating food will encourage them, as well as your other fish, to come topside to eat, giving you an excellent opportunity to observe them up close and to watch for signs of parasites, injuries, and disease.

koi. Into this category fall all the varieties both named and unnamed that either have unstable characteristics or do not fit any other recognized category.

As you may well imagine, this category contains literally hundreds of different examples and provides an all-inclusive category for anything new that might come along. Ranging from spectacular to bizarre, the Kawarigoi are what Westerners would consider mutts or strays, even though numerous champions have come from this category, as well as from the others.

GETTING READY

Once you've decided upon what fish you want to use in your pond, make sure that you prepare the water for them properly. Check it for water quality. Inexpensive, easy-to-use test kits are available at building supply centers, pet shops, garden centers, and over the Internet.

If your water is high in ammonia, chlorine, or chloramines, buy a product such as AmQuel to neutralize the chemicals. Just follow the prescribed dosage. You can use the additive to neutralize undesirable compounds when starting up your pond or whenever you do a routine water change.

Also check your pond's pH. If it's much beyond the 7.0 range in either direction, add some Neutral Regulator to bring the pH back to an acceptable level, somewhere between 6.8 and 7.2.

Remember that, as a general rule, the smaller the pond, the more fluctuations in water chemistry you're going to have, meaning the more tolerant your fish must be. Water heats and cools with ambient (surrounding) temperatures, making small ponds of 50 to 100 gallons fluctuate more wildly, from the cool of morning to the heat of late afternoon.

Small ponds are also much more susceptible to chemical spikes than are large ponds. Half of a well-aerated whiskey barrel, for example, is adequate for 8 to 10 small goldfish, which are relatively complacent about temperature and chemical fluctuations, whereas such a home would be death for a single koi.

A pond that is 3 feet deep holding several hundred gallons or more, on the other hand, can house fish with a narrow tolerance for temperature and chemical change. That makes larger ponds ideal for raising koi, which need plenty of space to roam and water at least 2 feet deep, even though koi often spend much of their time at the pond's surface—another bonus for keeping koi in the pond.

WHAT TO LOOK FOR IN CHOOSING FISH

When picking out new fish for your pond, try to find young, healthy fish from 3 to 5 inches in length. They should have bright eyes, a sturdy body, fully extended fins and tails, and a lively inquisitive habit. They should have no damaged or missing scales and show no unnatural spotting or lesions. You can easily detect all these things simply by watching the fish swim around the tank for a while.

You might also look for what I call the curiosity factor. Take your finger, place it near the glass (never tap on the glass, because the magnified sound could injure the fish), and move it slowly from side to side. See which fish's eyes you catch, and watch how curious that fish is. If you find one that's particularly interested in following your finger around the tank, count on the fact that it's (a) more intelligent than mosquito larvae, and (b) going to be more fun to relate to than your Aunt Edna.

Just remember that, no matter how many fish you buy, don't place small fish in with substantially larger koi, who relish just about anything that will fit into their mouths! That's one good reason to have a second small pond or fish container up and running—to serve as a nursery for small fry until they're large enough to join the gang.

We use a wine barrel for raising small goldfish to the point where they can be moved to a larger pond and released with the koi. The barrel can also be pressed into service as a hospital tank for our fish, if necessary. We've fitted the barrel with a mechanical-biological filter, two aeration stones, a fountain, and some water lilies to keep conditions relatively stable. Even with all that hardware, it's interesting to note that the barrel is *still* not suitable for even the smallest of koi, whose demands are much greater than those of most goldfish—and greater than the barrel can supply.

BUYING YOUR FISH

When you go to buy your fish, you'll probably receive them in a small plastic bag half-filled with water. Get the fish home as soon as possible. Those bags hold only so much oxygen, you know. (How would you like to take a long trip somewhere with a plastic bag over your head?)

Once you get the fish home, make several quarter-inch slits with a small knife in the upper half of the bag, and float the sealed bag in the pond for 15 minutes. That will allow for both the slow equalization of temperatures between pond and bag and the mixing of some pond water into the bag.

If you're adding new fish to an existing colony, or if you have any suspicions whatsoever about the health of the fish you've just bought, consider quarantining them for 10 days to 2 weeks in a small aquarium. In that way, if they show any signs of disease or parasites, they will be segregated from your main school, and you'll have an easier time observing and treating them without running the risk of infecting the others.

After floating the bag for 15 minutes, acclimate the fish to the pond by adding three or four handfuls of pond water to the bag every 5 minutes. Repeat several times. When the time is right to release the fish into their new environment, open the bag and gently turn it on its side, allowing the fish to swim out of the bag and into their new home on their own.

If your fish are hardy (hardiness varies, even among goldfish, although the single-tailed varieties are far and away the most durable), they can overwinter in your pond, so long as there's enough open water at all times for oxygen to enter and carbon dioxide to escape. Usually, the area below a waterfall will remain open—another good reason for installing at least one spillway in your pond. If necessary, an electric water heater will also help keep a section of the pond surface thawed.

HOW MANY ARE TOO MANY?

Remember not to place too many fish into your pond, which could result in deteriorated water quality, stress, and disease. To find the number of fish your garden pool can safely accommodate, figure the total surface area of the water feature in which fish will be present. (Surface area is determined by multiplying the length of your pond by its width.) Don't include in your calculations areas filled with marginal plants, but do include areas covered by floating plants.

As a rule of thumb, provide each inch of fish with from 6 to 12 square surface inches of water. Koi, as you might have already supposed, require more space—*much* more. For them, plan on 20 square *feet* for every fish, regardless of size. If you're unsure of your calculations, always err on the side of too much, rather than too little, space per fish. Use the box opposite to help when stocking your pond.

OUT-AND-ABOUT PREDATORS

It's sad to say, but low oxygen and excessive chemical levels aren't your fishes' only nemeses; other things attack fish, as well. And they do so with much more cunning.

One summer's morning, after going outside to check on our ponds and feed our fish, we noticed that some potted water lilies in the lower pond had been knocked over. Upon closer inspection, we found some of the leaves shredded and some of the rocks on the spillway upset. We also found absolutely no sign of the 13 small goldfish that had been inhabiting the pond, only a couple of glimmering scales on the top of the pond wall.

Raccoons are notorious water scavengers. They love rooting around shallow streams and ponds in search of a good meal. Since they're omnivorous, fish make an excellent target—what's that saying about shooting 'em in a barrel? The same holds true in a pond.

Well, a few nights later, they raided our barrel, as well, and stole all but one fish. We had thought that, since the barrel was relatively deep and had a flat stone ledge under which the fish could go for protection, they were safe. But the predators

ROCK REFUGE

A raised rock on the bottom of the pond serves more than one purpose. Besides offering fish protection for predators, it provides a place for skittish fish to hang out.

We bought a small silver koi measuring about 4 inches a couple of months ago. We brought him home and introduced him into a pond just above our large holding pond. The water that flows from the one pond into another barely skims the surface, perhaps one-quarter inch in depth. We were confident that the koi wouldn't go over the falls.

Naturally, he went over the falls, and we found him—somewhat traumatized—swimming around the big pond with our monster goldfish the next morning. He soon took to hiding out in the skimmer box during the day and coming out to forage for food toward evening. Then he discovered a medium-sized stone near the base of the falls. The stone forms a natural "tunnel" as it sits on the bottom, and Casper darts for cover nearly every time he catches sight of us, which is a bit disheartening.

Recently, we introduced two small koi into the same pond. It took them exactly 2 days to locate Casper and his rock home, and now all three koi hang out together, coming and going whenever they please, which is just fine with us. Not only are they safe from predators, but also they're secure while they grow. In time, they'll no longer be able to fit under the rock, and we'll have three healthy, hardy (albeit socially maladjusted) koi ready to train to eat from our hands!

apparently clung to the barrel's lip, swirling their razor-sharp claws around until they hit their mark. The one fish that was somehow spared we named Miracle and immediately moved him—as traumatized as he was—to a deeper pond with a larger rock ledge under which our fish can hide for as long as they want.

We have since realized that a wide variety of wildlife, while fun to see hanging around the pond, can wreak havoc with fish. Ever since those first two attacks, we have critter-proofed all of our water features, making sure that the shallower ones have plenty of deep rock ledges under which the fish can go for protection. As for the wine barrel, we fitted it with a slatted wooden top that we place over the opening every evening so that nothing can get in.

Although the Great Coon Attack of 2004 was the single greatest loss of fish in our fish-keeping history, it may not be the last. We were in a nursery, selecting water plants, when we ran into an elderly couple who kept a pond. We started talking to them and relayed our story about our run-ins with raccoons. Well, did they have *our* story beat.

They told us that they had come home one afternoon, gone out back to visit their pond, and noticed

Heron.

on top of the garage a single perched bird. Not a dove, not a robin, but a Great Blue Heron. Well, naturally, they were ecstatic! What a magnificent treat, having so majestic an animal share their environment. They were even happier when it returned the next morning and kept coming back daily.

One day the couple walked out to their pond and happened to catch sight of the bird just as it was leaving, its majestic wings spanning more than 4 feet. It did not leave hungry. In fact, it had emptied the pond of their prized koi!

What other raiders of the dark might you have to worry about? I'm pretty sure opossum will eat fish, if they can catch them. Cats might try snagging one now and again, if the cats are not declawed. Some species of diving waterfowl might find happy hunting between the shores of your waterway.

Of course, you can chase away potential predators or scare them off with a loud cap pistol or a whistle, if and when you find them. But it's best to provide your fish with some means of escape from a direct attack, such as a large flat piece of flagstone raised 4 (or 5 or 6, as necessary) inches off the pond floor and placed in the deepest part of the pool. In that way, if something does reach in or dive in or do whatever it does in the wild to catch its food, the fish—with their amazing quickness and instinct for survival—will be able to duck out of reach and remain there until the coast is clear.

INTRODUCING OTHER POND CRITTERS

Fortunately, not all visitors to your pond are going to be predators. And, if you're like me, you'll eventually come to the conclusion that fish are not enough. When I visit my pond, I am not merely a fish keeper. I am an 8-year-old child scouring the banks of a local watering hole, rooting around for tadpoles, crayfish, frogs, turtles, and whatever else I might possibly find living in such a rich environment. And that's just fine, to a degree. All of these critters make wonderful new additions to the landscape, some more than others. Some are predatory and shouldn't be mixed together or with your fish unless you plan on making a habit out of providing dinner for everybody. Otherwise, you'll want to spend a little time thinking about what you introduce to your pond *before* you introduce it.

TADPOLES

Tadpoles, as you already know, are the post-egg, pre-metamorphosis stage of frogs and toads. Oh, yes, toads come from eggs that hatch into tadpoles, too. When you go to your local nature center with net in hand and plastic bags in pocket, remember that, unless you're an expert on reptilians, there's no guarantee of what you're bringing home.

One year, we netted several hundred tadpoles that we assumed were frogs. Since they were barely ¹⁄₁₆ inch in diameter, we placed them in a lighted, well-aerated, filtered aquarium. We fed them a mixture of ground kelp (you can use the kelp from kelp capsules, available at your health food store) and peas.

To make a long story short, each tiny tadpole grew and thrived and finally matured into a tiny toad, which we subsequently released in an unstocked pond out back. As soon as they possibly could, every one of them rewarded us by climbing out of the pond and disappearing forever.

Well, "every one" isn't exactly correct. At least once each year, we still stumble across a toad or two while digging around in the grass alongside the stream. After the initial shock of the discovery subsides, we feel a warm glow inside. Don't ask me why.

A couple more things about toads. They don't cause warts—ever. That means not under any circumstances. They do secrete a toxic substance from their skin as a means of warding off predators,

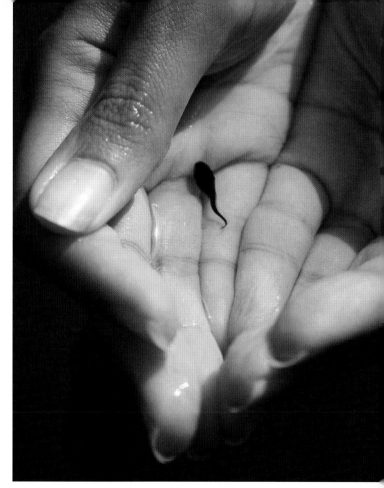

Tadpole.

including inquisitive dogs and cats. They also urinate for the same purpose. Beyond those minor annoyances, toads are among the best insect eaters in nature, gobbling up literally anything that moves that they can fit between their oversized lips. Toads and frogs are compatible with fish.

A word of caution about tadpoles. If you plan on introducing them to your pond, make sure they're too large for your fish to eat, or they'll disappear in a hurry. You can sometimes find larger frog tadpoles in a pet shop or over the Internet. We bought three of them from a pet shop once. All three matured into healthy little frogs. Two immediately hit the road, while the third—which turned out to be a genuine bullfrog—hung out the rest of the summer. He came to recognize our voices, and he would serenade us with his distinctive *garr-rump, garr-rump, garr-rump* each evening, whenever we called his name. Honest to God.

CRAYFISH

Crayfish are among nature's most fascinating creatures. They extract oxygen from the water, as do fish, and are pretty much omnivorous, meaning they'll eat anything they can get their little claws on, which includes fish! I've seen a crayfish in an aquarium go about the task of picking up excess food from the bottom of the tank and devouring it. I've seen the

Turtle.

Snails help keep the pond clean.

same crayfish with a fish clamped to death in one of its claws, slowly and methodically picking it to pieces.

The only time crayfish are not a threat to fish is when the fish are large enough to be a threat to the *crayfish*. Either way, it's a lose-lose situation for fishponds.

TURTLES

We recently showed our ponds to a contractor who was laying some ceramic tile for us, and he asked us if we kept turtles in our ponds. I told him that we didn't, because they would eat the fish. He didn't believe me, saying that he had an aquarium in which he kept several prized angelfish along with two turtles. I told him that he wouldn't have them long. The very next day, he came by, shaking his head. "I can't believe it happened," he said, "just like you said. Those turtles are history!"

Turtles *do* make enjoyable pets, albeit not with fish. These colorful amphibians are intelligent, trainable, and just plain fun to watch. They're also extremely inquisitive and, so long as they don't feel threatened, will explore their surroundings both day and night. They, too, are omnivorous, eating anything they can fit into their mouths or shred apart with their claws. They're also tremendously talented escape artists; so, unless you have vertical glass walls taller by far than the turtles they're containing, plan on their getting out.

SNAILS

If you have a pond, you're going to have snails. Enough said. I don't know how or why, but it never fails. Most of the water snails that find their way into your pond will be small and relatively insignificant. That means they're not going to be much fun to watch, and they're not going to eat much algae—which is one of the main reasons for keeping snails in the first place.

That, however, doesn't mean that you can't enjoy snails. Pick up some of the larger water varieties available at pet shops and through the Internet. A few species are winter-hardy, and some grow to several inches or larger in diameter. Now, *their* appetite for algae is enormous! Snails live in peaceful communion with all but the most aggressive of fish.

A HAPPY MEDIUM

Introducing frogs, toads, and snails to your fishpond is one of the nicer things about having a pond in the first place. You'll soon find these natural cohabitants mixing comfortably, just as they would in any natural pond or lake.

Expect, too, to find Mother Nature discovering how nice it is to have a new pond in the neighborhood, as well. It won't take long before you'll see birds landing on the stones and drinking water from the pond, while others will discover that your pond's waterfalls and spillways make a great place to shower.

How much more enjoyable it is to sit out by the pond in the evenings, listening to a bullfrog croak and the birds chatter, watching a toad stalk a caterpillar, and marveling at the sight of your fish swimming around in lazy circles in your pond.

Once you've seen to it that conditions are right for your fish and other pond inhabitants; that the oxygen level of the water is high; that the biological, chemical, mechanical, and UV filters are working properly; and that no dangerous levels of toxic chemicals exist, you'll be off and running. Just remember to vary the diets of your fish and remove excess food before it has a chance to decay. Your other pond inhabitants will feed themselves quite nicely, thank you.

Taking care of business—it's as important a part of pond keeping as it is anything in life. Take care of your pond's business from the start, and

Frog.

you can rest assured that its inhabitants will live in harmony within their own environment, the environment that *you* created and that *you* oversee, for years and even decades to come.

QUICK CHECKLIST

- Remember that fish require sunshine, shade, proper temperature, the right pH, a balanced diet, and clean, well-oxygenated water for healthy growth.
- Check your pond water regularly and make frequent partial water changes to keep things clean.
- Choose the type of fish best suited for your environment.
- When introducing new fish into your pond, float them in a plastic bag to acclimate them before releasing them slowly into their new home.
- Feed your fish a widely varying diet for healthier, happier fish.
- Choose your other pond inhabitants carefully, remembering that some of them look upon fish as prey ... and vice versa.

THE FISHERMAN'S PRIZE

In studying
ourselves, we find
the harmony that
is our total
existence.
We do not
make harmony.
We do not achieve
it or gain it.
It is there all
the time.
Here we are,
in the midst of
this perfect way,
and our practice
is simply to
realize it
And then to
actualize it in our
everyday life.

—Maezumi Roshi

Sturgeon Bay, Wisconsin. Summer, 1964.

We arrive sometime in early morning, shivering, and take a small boat out to the concrete wing of the hydroelectric dam. I have fished here often. My father has fished here more. He does so by loading his reel with 40-pound test line equipped with weighted treble-hooks.

After casting a weighted hook into the swirling sea of churning water, he waits until something wide and muscular comes along and brushes against the line. My father yanks hard on the rod, snapping the hook into action. As he does, he snags the fish on the jaw or the belly or the tail, after which he bulls it to shore. He quickly looks around and cuts the line before pulling the fish up and into the boat, which is tied to a rock. He hopes that no one from the Department of Natural Resources will come out to check his illegal harvest.

This day, however, my father is not with us. We are only my uncle, my cousin, and I, and I am fishing with an open-face spinning reel and 12-pound test line. It is not something with which I expect to snag and land a giant sturgeon, but then again, that is not my idea of fishing.

I pull back on my rod tip, whip my arm forward, and listen to the hum of the line as the baited hook whistles through the air toward its goal. I do this several times before I finally feel a light tug and quickly set the hook. I land a striped bass, weighing perhaps a pound and a half; and my uncle—who does not like fishing with treble-hook sinkers any more than I do, smiles. "Son-of-a-bitch, that's gonna taste good on the skillet tonight!"

Another few casts, another few misses, and finally I decide to try a different location, so I cast as far out into the open water as I can manage. I watch as the bait, a giant nightcrawler, disappears beneath the foam. My uncle shakes his head, knowing damned well that the stripers are closer in, toward the shallows, up against the concrete wing of the dam, and I can only imagine that he wonders just how great an idiot his nephew is.

After allowing the crawler to settle to the bottom, I begin reeling in steadily, hoping for a bite, when my line snags on something, a log or a rock or the bumper from a '52 Ford pickup or God knows what. I curse softly and wonder just why it is that I had to cast out into no-man's land in the first place. I pressure the line cautiously, hoping to pop the snagged hook free so that I will not have to tie a new leader, sinker, and hook onto it, but to no avail.

Suddenly, as I pull back against the snag, I feel something strange. I feel pressure. I feel *movement,* as if the snag is pulling back. At first, I think it is the swirling of the water against the tautened monofilament, which can give the illusion that a fish is on the other end. In time, I realize that it is no current, no swirling water, no movement whatsoever that I feel except that of my quarry.

I think briefly about calling out for help and look over to my uncle, who snatches a quick glance at me before looking away. He looks back.

"Snag?" he yells.

I shrug. "I don't think so."

"Well, take your time. Don't bull him, or you'll break the line."

Yeah, I think to myself. Twelve-pound test. You're Goddamn right I'll break the line.

I continue the contest, straining against the line just enough to move the fish closer to shore and loosening the clutch so that it is set soft enough to allow him to turn and run whenever he wants to. It is one big game of cat-and-mouse. An hour and a half later, my arms throbbing, my face sweating, my back aching, I *finally* feel the fish give up some ground. *Major* ground. I reel in, and I feel a sudden tug, but only for a second, and then I feel the pressure go slack as I reel in some more. And more. When I look up, I see that my uncle and my cousin have put their rods down and come over to watch. My uncle has a long-handled landing net ready. When he finally spies what is on the end of the line, he sets the net down and whistles.

"Careful," he says. "Don't bull him."

I nod, my adrenaline racing, my pulse pounding. As I bring the fish to shore, Dale reaches down and snags the beast by the gills. Slowly, he pulls it up onto the gravel, and the monster looks at me—5-feet-something of pure armored prehistoric might. Two giant tusks hang ominously from each corner of its mouth, which appears wide enough to swallow a turkey, roasting pan and all. The hook with crawler still attached hangs from one lip.

The fish slaps its tail weakly, and its breath comes in quick short pants. I have done it. What no one else in my family has ever done. I have done it without even trying. I have caught and landed a giant freshwater sturgeon, more than 5 feet of prehistoric beast weighing in the neighborhood of 65 or 75 pounds, and I have done it using 12-pound test line.

My uncle grabs the fish by the gills and pulls it higher up away from the water. He turns to me and smiles. "Well, by God, you've managed to do at 16 years of age what your old man hasn't done in 30 years of trying. You caught a sturgeon legally!"

I grin. "Yeah," I say. "I guess I did."

He looks at the fish. I look at the fish. Dale looks at the fish.

"Well," my uncle says again. "What do you want to do with it?"

I think for just a moment, think about how proud my father will be when I bring home a sturgeon of this size, one that I landed all on my own, one that I caught ... in the *mouth*. I think about it for just a moment. I look deeply into the fish's eyes, which are rolling slowly from one person to the next, and I reach down. I try in vain to get the hook from the fish's plated jaw. My uncle reaches into his back pocket and pulls out a pair of pliers. Holding the line taut, I separate the hook from the fish and, straddling the beast, work him slowly down toward the water. I get him into it, a couple inches' worth, then a couple inches more, until his gills are covered. I am about to try to take him in both hands and move him out farther into the water when, with a giant slap of his tail and a rush of power like I have never seen in any living creature before or since, the water spits up the ghost, and the sturgeon is gone.

fourteen

Feeding Your Fish

There is hardly any aspect of fish keeping more widely misunderstood than feeding your fish. Within this seemingly innocent enough endeavor lie more misconceptions and outright falsehoods than any other area of concern the pond keeper is likely to encounter.

Among the controversies: Goldfish and koi will die from overfeeding. Feeding your fish more than they can eat in 5 minutes is detrimental to

ABOVE: Koi feeding.

their health. Fish need high-quality commercially manufactured fish food. Fish need fish flakes. Fish need fish pellets. Fish need dried peas. Fish need food high in protein. Fish need food high in carbohydrates.

Obviously, not all of these oft-espoused dicta can be correct. So, let me try to clear some of the mud from the feeding controversy. It all begins with fish in the wild.

FISH ARE OMNIVORES

Have you ever noticed how many fish in the wild make a habit of eating fish flakes or dried peas?

Have you ever watched wild fish feed for 5 minutes and then stop? (*Oops, that's it! Gotta run, my time is up!*) Have you ever seen them pass up a meal because it was or wasn't high in protein?

If you're a fisherman, you already know that different types of food appeal to different types of fish. Catfish like bread dough. No, wait, make that corn meal. No, no, that's night crawlers. Well, now that I think of it, I've caught my share of catfish on artificial lures, as well. Hmm, maybe we'll get back to catfish later. Let's try this:

If you're a *fly* fisherman, you know that different types of flies are preferable to different types of fish at different times of year. Trout, for example, will gorge themselves on midges, but only during naturally occurring hatches. If you try to get them to strike at a midge at any other time, their naturally cautious nature will kick in, and you're going to go home empty handed.

Similarly, bass devour tadpoles during hatching season, but once the tadpoles turn to frogs and become too smart to try to swim past those gaping mouths, the fish turn their attention to minnows, bugs, worms, and just about anything else that moves—and a few things, such as roots and leaves, that don't.

Wait a minute. In that respect, they're pretty much like those catfish I mentioned earlier. And, for that matter, catfish are like salmon. And salmon are like sharks. And sharks are like crappies. And crappies, like carp.

The bottom line is that nearly all fish everywhere are omnivores. They may have certain predilections toward one type of meal or another, but in a pinch, they'll make do with whatever crosses their path. That's because fish are incredibly flexible when it comes to selecting a menu. We once purchased two tropical algae-eaters, or *Plecostomus,* for our aquarium. The guy who sold them to us said that they eat only algae. *Period.* That was fine with us,

since we had bought them to keep the green slime off the aquarium walls, anyway.

Two weeks later, they were dead. They had cleaned up all of the algae and, without a food supply (unlike most fish, plecos can live only a few days without food), they died. After they had done such an admirable job on our aquarium, we rewarded them with our own stupidity.

Since replacing the plecos a couple of years ago, we have come to learn firsthand not only that the fish must eat regularly, but also that they will eat, besides algae, mosquito larvae; bloodworms; fish flakes; blanched cucumber slices; lettuce; blanched cabbage; chopped spinach; and even ground raw turkey. *In between,* they eat algae. We also learned that, in eating a varied diet, they are healthier than any plecos you'll find in a store. We currently have two, one of each sex, and both have grown about four times their initial size. The male is nearly 9 inches long!

Needless to say, if we feed the plecos a delectable potpourri of varying consumables, we feed the same diet to the fancy goldfish, the Orandas and the Fantails and the Ryunkins that share their tank. And if we trust that diet for our fancy goldfish, we certainly trust it for our pond fish.

How have our goldfish and koi responded to so eclectic a feast?

Before we began varying their diets, we lost a fancy goldfish to bladder bloat—which is nearly always fatal (and certainly has always been for us)—four or five times a year. You've probably seen or heard about the disease. Once a fish gets this bloat, it has difficulty swimming upright. It will roll over on its side or go belly up, even when on the bottom of the tank. Our fishes' bladder bloat problem got so serious that, at one point, we thought about giving the aquarium away.

Then I read somewhere about a pond keeper who feeds her koi ground worms, wheat germ, black

Zen and the Art of Pond Building

FEEDING TIME: A VARIED DIET

It's more difficult to give your fish a variety of food at each feeding than it is to pick up a can of fish flakes and throw a pinch or two onto the water twice a day. It's more difficult, but it's absolutely necessary if you want to avoid exposing your fish to ill health, disease, and ultimately death.

To make the task easier, we take some old ice cube trays, fill them with homemade fish food, and freeze them. We place the cubes in a plastic bag, and whenever we need chopped black beans or spinach or turkey, we pop a couple of frozen cubes into a warm cup of water. When they're defrosted, we feed them to the fish.

Just remember when making your own fish food that you should use only pure food free from any chemical additives, including table salt. Chop the food up into small enough pieces for the fish to fit into their mouths. (Large fish will eat small food, too—only more of it!) Before freezing the food, blanch firm fruit and vegetables such as cucumbers, lettuce stalks, apples, and cabbage leaves. The rest can be used raw.

Here's a normal week's diet for our goldfish and koi:
- Blanched chopped vegetables; ground turkey or chicken; chopped cooked black beans; chopped cooked green peas; chopped cooked shrimp and clams; fresh orange; dry wheat germ; earthworms; Cheerios (don't ask me why, but fish love them!); and frozen bloodworms, mosquito larvae, and brine shrimp (the only fish food we purchase from the pet shop).
- We buy dried kelp, or seaweed, from the Oriental section of our local health food store, rehydrate it, and add a few leaves of that in with their food every now and then. We also keep a worm box handy for two purposes: to create invaluable mulch for our gardening (we throw all of our raw fruit and vegetable waste in it), and to provide us with a highly nutritious food for our fish.
- About a year ago, we introduced a few nightcrawlers (purchased from a bait shop) into the bucket. We keep the contents damp, and we cover the stuff with a light layer of sphagnum moss so that it doesn't look like anything more than an unplanted flower pot. But is it ever! Today, when we pull back the top layer, we find thousands, possibly even tens of thousands, of worms busily engaged in turning the plant wastes into top-quality mulch. We use the mulch on our plants, and we feed the worms to the fish as an occasional treat. Since the worms eat only human-grade vegetation, they are not only healthy, but also healthy for the fish!

The results of all of this food foolery? Well, we haven't lost a fish to bladder bloat—or, for that matter, any other disease—since we switched diets from commercial fish food to homemade over a year ago. And I doubt that we ever will.

beans, and even halved oranges, rind and all! (She swears they savor them as a treat!) Her fish are as healthy as, well, koi.

We began experimenting. So far, the only rule of thumb we've found regarding fish and what they should or shouldn't eat is this: mix it up. Never feed them the same two things in a row. Alternate between high-protein food and carbohydrates. If you use commercial food, make sure the analysis includes a minimum of 35% protein and a maximum of 10% ash. If you make your own, be creative!

WHEN AND HOW TO FEED

Avoid overfeeding your fish, especially in summer. Even though they're most active during the warmer months, fish begin munching more on water plants and roots. If you overfeed them, the excess food will go to waste, resulting in the production of ammonia, nitrites, and nitrates. Don't feed your fish unless they appear to be ravenous. The best time to feed is in the afternoons until an hour or so before sundown.

Get in the habit of feeding your fish in the same spot and at the same time each day. In that way, all of the fish will be there, waiting for a handout, when you show up, and more of the food you feed them will get eaten.

Also, don't worry if you notice a sudden influx of insects hanging around your pond beginning in late spring. Insects just naturally hatch out in swarms, and many of them are beneficial to the environment. All are part of your pond's ecological system. Diving beetles and dragonflies, for example, feast on mosquito larvae, while fish feed indiscriminately on nearly *everything*.

So far as overfeeding being the scourge of fish-pond owners, forget it. It's not overfeeding and overeating that are harmful to fish. It's overfeeding and allowing the excess food to turn into toxic ammonia, nitrites, and nitrates. *That* can be deadly. Just make sure your fish eat what you give them, or scoop out the excess within a few hours. Also, check your filter box regularly and remove excess food that has gotten caught up in the filter media. It, too, will change to toxins if you allow it to decay.

QUICK CHECKLIST

- If you feed your fish commercially processed food, supplement it with fresh fruit, vegetables, and ground meat.
- Feed your fish in the same place and at the same time each day—once a day when the water is cool and twice a day as the water warms and the fish become more active.
- Stop feeding your fish entirely when the water temperature drops below 45° F.
- Feed your fish a varied diet for healthier, happier fish.
- Avoid overfeeding your fish so as not to produce toxic ammonia.
- Remove excess food from pond and the filter media often.

THE CHARTER

Something has
existed before
heaven and earth;
Shapeless and
silent in its origin,
Yet the master of
every image
and form,
It can never
wither with the
passing of time.

—Bankei

El Sirata Motel, St. Petersburg, Florida. Summer, 1962.

It is an exciting night. I hardly sleep at all, or at least it seems as if I lie in bed awake all night long. The next morning, around 5:30, I pile out of the car with my father, uncle, and cousin, and Dale and I race down the dock overlooking Long John Pass and up to the boat—it would be a sacrilege to call it a ship—where we mingle with two dozen or so other people before we are finally invited aboard. As the last of the people load and the hands slip the ropes free from the moorings, I tremble at the sound of the engine firing up. Low, slow, deep, guttural, like an airplane idling on the tarmac before takeoff. Slowly, we begin drifting away from the pier, out into the open water of the causeway, where the engine shifts into high gear and we launch ourselves out to sea.

"If either of you kids feels sick," my father tells us for the fifth time since we boarded, "just go below and lie down, understand?"

We tell him for the fifth time that we understand, and by now I am beginning to worry that we may indeed get sick. Sometimes, the more you hear something, the more likely it becomes that it really could happen. Apparently, kids getting sick onboard a boat in the middle of the Gulf of Mexico is one of them.

We continue out to sea, to where the grouper and the sea bass and the red fish and all of the other prey the area has to offer congregate, we say goodbye to the last remaining vestiges of land. Before long, we have passed the point of no return. We have traveled hundreds or even thousands of miles from civilization if not more, I don't know.

"Don't forget, kids," my father says. He is holding a paper cup filled with steaming coffee. He stops to take a sip before continuing. "If you start to feel seasick, just go below and lie down. There's no shame in getting seasick."

We tell him once again that we will, and we watch as he opens the door to the cabin and makes his way to the hold to take a short nap. We watch him disappear before we make the rounds of the deck for the twelfth time, stopping periodically to check out the other passengers. Someone offers me half a ham sandwich, which I politely refuse, even though I am beginning to grow hungry. We peer through the glass window leading to the cabin, the cockpit where all the real action takes place, and see the glowing green dials and the large wheel and several men milling about, laughing and drinking coffee from paper cups, just like my father.

Finally we hear the engine go soft, and then we hear it stop, and the crew scurries out on deck and begins handing out the tackle. The air crackles with anticipation. When I receive my rod, already rigged for action and ready for fish, I can barely stand it.

"Now, you don't need to cast with these babies," one of the crew tells me. "You just hold it out away from the boat and release this clasp on the side of the reel here, see? Let the weight of the line take your bait about halfway down to here, see?"

I see plenty. I understand. I am no idiot. I look around for my father, who is nowhere to be found. I turn to my uncle and say, "Uncle Joe, where's my dad?"

My uncle does not look up. He is smitten by the sea and the daunting task before him.

"Someone should go wake him up," I say. "He's going to miss everything."

My uncle makes an adjustment to the reel before turning toward me. "Uhh, better not bother him right now."

"What?" I say. "Why not?"

"Well, he's not feeling too good."

I stand, dumbfounded. "*Dad* isn't? What's the matter with him?"

"I think," my uncle says, "he's seasick."

fifteen

Fish Diseases

No matter what you do, no matter how hard you try to avoid it, if you have fish in your pond, sooner or later they're going to get sick. Not necessarily all of them, and not necessarily all at the same time, but eventually they will get sick.

There are many reasons for disease among fish. An airborne pathogen can find its way to your pond or pool. A fungal disease might be introduced on a newly added plant. A newly introduced fish may be

ABOVE: Koi in a pond.

harboring a harmful bacterium that has yet to show its might. A fish might be predisposed to illness. For whatever the reasons, when your fish become sick, you need to act fast.

Whenever possible, remove the sick fish from the community and segregate it in a tub or hospital tank for easier treatment and to avoid possible contamination of the other fish. Beyond that, treatment usually varies from one malady to the other. Remember, though, that not all fish will survive. For whatever the reason—from genetic predisposition to secondary infections or various other complications—some fish will recover faster and better than others, while some won't pull through at all. Look at it as part of the natural cycle, Darwin's Law. The strong survive while the weak perish. Not all fish can be strong.

Fish maladies come in four different types: bacterial, fungal, physical (from an injury or a pre-existing genetic defect), and parasitic. Luckily, suitable treatments are available at pet shops and pond-supply stores or over the Internet for nearly all of the health-related problems you're likely to experience.

A word of caution: when considering treatment of your fish, we recommend that you *not* use the "old-fashioned salt bath" as your primary modality, even though it has been touted by some sources as the most time-tested cure-all in the fish world. One source claims that salt cures ick, fungus, velvet, tail rot, and other malignancies. Experts, the same source says, swear by it. We have a slightly different take. We swear *at* it. We have used salt baths for all sorts of fish ailments for years, and we haven't experienced a single success. We obviously no longer use them as the primary cure for any disease or malady, although we recognize the value that increased salt levels can play in helping fish to overcome disease when used in conjunction with an appropriate medication.

USING SALT WITH SICK FISH

To use salt as a conjunctive healer, make sure that you use the proper type of salt. This includes aquarium salt, rock salt, pickling salt, and sea or solar salt. Sea salt is especially beneficial in that it provides important minerals to the fish. You can find it in large bags at your home improvement center.

Never—I repeat, *never*—use table salt in your pond. It can be deadly to the fish due to the anti-caking agents and the iodine added to the salt by manufacturers.

When you use salt in conjunction with other medications, choose a low concentration of 0.1%, or approximately 1 teaspoon per gallon (1 tablespoon per 3 gallons) of water. This concentration is low enough to be safe for fish, plants, and most invertebrates. You can increase the concentration to 0.3%, applied over a 12-hour period. Add 0.1%, wait 4 hours, and repeat two more times.

Although some pond owners advise using higher concentrations of up to 0.9%, I wouldn't recommend doing so for more than short periods, as in a quick dip or bath. If fish or plants are kept in a high salt concentration longer, they will die. Never subject young or weakened fish to high salt concentrations for *any* length of time.

When adding salt to an existing pond or tank, dissolve it first in water. If you add undissolved salt that comes in contact with the fish's skin, serious burns could result.

Remember when using salt that what you put into the water—just as with many chemical additives—stays in the water. Evaporation merely concentrates it. That's why you should always use salt treatments in a hospital tank or tub so that you can dispose of the water when the treatment is completed. Otherwise, you'll need to purchase a salt testing kit to monitor the concentration of the salt in your pond and make frequent partial water changes to gradually remove excess salt from the water once the fish are healthy.

FISH DISEASES AND REMEDIES

Here are some of the more common diseases and problems that fishpond owners encounter.

Constipation, indigestion (not contagious). A fish suffering from constipation or indigestion is usually lethargic and will often rest at the bottom of the pond. Its abdomen may be extended. The problem is usually the result of a disagreeable diet. The first step toward cure is to stop feeding for 2 or 3 days until the fish begins to move around normally. Beware of the fact that the problem, being food-related, is likely to recur unless you change your fishes' diet (see Chapter 14).

Swim bladder bloat (not contagious). A problem with a fish's swim bladder is easy to diagnose. The fish can't swim properly. Usually, it will swim on its side or even upside-down. It is a serious and often a fatal problem over time. Swim bladder may be related to constipation or indigestion, or the fish may have received a bladder injury after running into something. We have lost more fish to bladder bloat than to any other malady. Worse still, once a fish has experienced bladder bloat, it is likely to suffer recurring bouts. Treat by changing diet. Since we began varying what we feed our fish, we haven't had a single case of bladder bloat (see Chapter 14).

Dropsy, kidney bloat (not contagious). Sometimes called pine-cone disease, the symptoms of this \disease include a bloated belly and scales that stick out, similar to a pine cone. As with bladder bloat and kidney bloat, this disease is often recurrent. If possible, move the fish to a hospital tank or a small well-aerated tub. Treat with Fungus Clear by Jungle Laboratories.

Tumors (rarely contagious). The telltale signs of tumors include lumps, bumps, or protrusions. They occasionally look like a large blister or wart. Rarely fatal, they can be removed surgically by a veterinarian.

Pop eye (not contagious). As the name implies, this disease manifests through the formation of abnormally swollen eyes that protrude from the fish. Usually striking common goldfish, Comets, and Shubunkins, it is rarely fatal. If possible, move the fish to a hospital tank or a small well-aerated tub. Treat with tetracycline tablets.

Fish lice (highly contagious). Impossible to misdiagnose, fish lice are round, disk-shaped parasites that clamp onto a host fish and refuse to let go. The infected fish will often rub up against objects in an effort to scrape the pests off. The lice suck blood from the fish through the skin and scales. Lice may also transmit other microscopic diseases. If possible, move the fish *immediately* to a hospital tank or a small well-aerated tub to prevent contamination of healthy fish and watch for problems with the remaining school. Treat with Masoten, Dylox, Nequvon, or Parasite Clear by Jungle Laboratories.

Anchor worm (highly contagious). Another parasitic invader, anchor worm burrows into the scales of the fish, creating a red, agitated area around white worms. Sometimes the worms can grow quite long. If possible, move the fish *immediately* to a hospital tank or a small well-aerated tub. Treat with Parasite Clear by Jungle Laboratories.

Leeches (highly contagious). Yet another serious parasite, leeches are relatively uncommon among goldfish, which is of little solace to you if your fish contract them. These small worm-like creatures are difficult to eradicate. If possible, move the fish *immediately* to a hospital tank or a small well-aerated tub. Treat with Parasite Clear by Jungle Laboratories.

Skin fluke, gill fluke (highly contagious). This parasite attacks the gills or skin of the fish, causing swollen pink and red splotches. Affected fish will often come to the surface, gulping air. The gills may exude a pus-like fluid. The flukes themselves are microscopic and multiply rapidly. If possible, move the fish *immediately* to a hospital tank or a small well-aerated tub. Treat with tetracycline or Parasite Clear by Jungle Laboratories.

Furunculosis (contagious). This is a bacterial infection that can go unnoticed for some time before spreading rapidly among the school. The bacteria infect the flesh below the scales, appearing as raised bumps. The bumps eventually rupture, creating large bleeding ulcers. Because the bacteria are microscopic, the entire pond should be treated with tetracycline. Also, consult a veterinarian for any more current treatments.

Ulcers (highly contagious). An internal infection that produces large, red boils and dark reddening at the base of the fins, ulcers tend to eat depressions into the fish's body. If possible, move the fish *immediately* to a hospital tank or a small well-aerated tub. Switch to a medicated food, and consult a veterinarian for current treatments.

Ick (highly contagious). This is a common parasitic disease that appears as white spots that grow on the body and fins. Ick multiplies quickly and, if not treated, results in death. If possible, move the fish *immediately* to a hospital tank or a small well-aerated tub. Treat with Parasite Clear by Jungle Laboratories. Also, treat the pond and remaining fish as a preventative action.

Velvet (highly contagious). This is a fungal disease distinguished by a fuzzy yellow- or golden-colored spot. If possible, move the fish *immediately* to a hospital tank or a small well-aerated tub. Treat them with Fungus Clear by Jungle Laboratories. Also, treat the pond and remaining fish as a preventative action.

Fungus (highly contagious). This appears most often as a fuzzy growth on any part of the fish. It's different from velvet in that it is white or light gray and easier to spot. Treatment is mandatory, or infected fish will die. If possible, move the fish *immediately* to a hospital tank or a small well-aerated tub. Treat with Fungus Clear by Jungle Laboratories. Also, treat the pond and remaining fish as a preventative action.

Body slime fungus (highly contagious). This is a deadly affliction that can kill your fish in 48 hours, so treatment must be immediate. The disease appears as a protective slime coating that begins to peel off, as if the fish were shedding its skin. If possible, move the fish *immediately* to a hospital tank or a small well-aerated tub. Treat with Fungus Clear by Jungle Laboratories. Also, treat the pond and remaining fish as a preventative action. One word of caution: Oranda and Lionhead goldfish develop a white film covering their heads in spring or summer as a natural process of continuing hood growth. Be careful that you don't mistake that normal growth for body slime fungus.

Mouth fungus, mouth rot (contagious). This is distinguished by the usual white cotton-like growth on the mouth, occasionally spreading outward toward the gills. It's caused by a bacteria known as *Flexibacter*. The disease can be fatal. If possible, move the fish *immediately* to a hospital tank or a small well-aerated tub. Treat with Fungus Clear by Jungle Laboratories. Watch the remaining school closely for any additional outbreaks.

Fin rot, tail rot (contagious). This pernicious disease is easy to diagnose because the flesh is gradually eaten away on the tail or fin. There may also be redness at the base of the area. In time, the entire fin or tail will become shredded. If possible, move the fish *immediately* to a hospital tank or a small well-aerated tub. Treat with tetracycline tablets or Fungus Clear by Jungle Laboratories. Watch the remaining school closely for any additional outbreaks.

Fin congestion, hemorrhagic septicemia (contagious). This common disease usually attacks long-finned breeds. It is easily diagnosed because of the red blotches that appear on the trailing edges of the fins. These blotches, or hemorrhages, are bright red in color and are differentiated from the normal appearance of red veins running through a fish's tail. The disease begins at the outer edge of the fin or tail and moves inward, as with fin rot. If possible, move the fish *immediately* to a hospital tank or a small well-aerated tub. Treat with tetracycline, penicillin, or Fungus Clear by Jungle Laboratories. Also, treat the pond and remaining fish as a preventative action.

FOLLOWING TREATMENT

After treating your fish precisely as described with the proper medication, you can reintroduce it back into the pond, but I would suggest making a 50% partial water change to the pond first. A water change will dilute any remaining pathogens or diseases, allowing the fishes' own immune system to resist future attacks. Remember that fish are inclined to be healthy; disease is the exception rather than the rule.

That's another reason for providing your fish with the best water conditions possible.

A happy fish is a healthy fish, and a healthy fish is prone to remain that way. Avoid stressing your fish through poor water quality, and you're likely to have to turn to the use of medical treatments only rarely.

QUICK CHECKLIST

- Your fish are susceptible to four different types of maladies: bacterial, fungal, physical, and parasitic, and each one must be diagnosed and treated accordingly.
- When a fish gets sick, act quickly to remove it from the pond to a hospital tank or well-aerated tub whenever possible in order to prevent infecting the rest of your fish and to make observation and treatment more efficient.
- Since fungal and bacterial diseases can spread rapidly, it's a good idea to keep a supply of antibiotics and fungicides around the home for when you need them.
- You can often purchase bacterial, fungal, and parasitic medications in bulk over the Internet or on e-Bay for less money than you can buy smaller aquarium-sized packages from your local pet store.

A GATOR FOR BREAKFAST

> That the self advances and confirms the ten thousand things is called delusion; That the ten thousand things advance and confirm the self is called enlightenment.
>
> —Dogen Zenji

Tampa, Florida. Summer, 1977.

I am on a golf course built by Johnny Weismuller or Johnny Bench or someone named Johnny, I don't know. All I know about golf courses is that someone famous always designs them and sticks their name on them and makes a lot of money from them. I know that, and I know that they require an awful lot of water to keep grass so short from burning out. Oh, yes, and I know one other thing about golf courses: I don't golf.

Nevertheless, I am staying here, at Innisbrook, which has only recently opened its doors and is looking for the kind of publicity that writers such as I can give them. While I did not bring with me the golf clubs that I do not yet own, I did bring my fishing rod and reel. On this particular evening, an hour or so before I need to shower and dress to meet the resort's management team for dinner so that they can tell me about all of the wonders that only a place such as Innisbrook has to offer, I grab my rod. I head out along the fairway or whatever it's called and up to a small water hazard. There I spy the unmistakable telltale ring that marks a fish rising to the surface to take in an insect.

Where there are fish eating insects, there are fish eating minnows. I tie a Rapala silver minnow onto the end of my line, bring my rod back, and cast out to where I saw the fish rise. Naturally, as is always the case in fishing, nothing happens.

I cast over and over again with similar results. I have one strike, but I am slow to respond, and the fish gets away. I am torn between calling it a day and watching the wild peacocks strutting along the lawn when suddenly I feel it. I rear back on the rod, and inside of 2 or 3 minutes, I pull in the most beautiful looking smallmouth bass I have seen all day. It will make a wonderful breakfast, I reason; so, after looking around to make sure no one is watching, I slip my prize onto a stringer, tie the stringer off on some reeds, and lower him back into the water where I will retrieve him in the morning.

After showering and shaving and dressing and dinner and coming back to my suite and collapsing, I sleep the sleep of the dead. The next day, as I prepare to goad my toothbrush into action, I recall the stringer and the bass on the end of it.

I throw on my clothes and pull a comb through my hair before slipping through the sliding glass doors, across the lawn, and down to the pond. I breathe a sigh of relief to see that the stringer is still there.

I bend down to untie it from the reeds and pull it out of the water; I find the most beautiful *head* of a smallmouth bass I have seen all day. I hold the stringer up high, staring in utter amazement, before a flash of sunlight catches my eye. I look off in the distance, toward the island squatting low in the middle of the pond, as a 5-foot gator crawls up out of the water and plops down in the sun.

I look again at the stringer and back to the gator, and I swear I hear him belch.

sixteen

Pond Maintenance

There's a unique joy that unfolds when you walk out the back door, past your pond, and see crystal clear water, healthy plants, and frisky fish. It's a feeling like, "Yeah, I did something really great out here. I did it right."

That's exactly the way it should be. After all, a well-executed pond should be virtually carefree.

ABOVE: The serene setting of this naturally occurring pond is spiced up by a large fountain powered by a submersible pump. *Photo © Vulcan57 for Fotolia.*

Oh, sure, you'll have to feed the fish and take some time to test the water and, when necessary, treat it. Unless you have a very large water feature, you'll spend about an hour or less each week feeding, grooming plants, cleaning filter media, monitoring water quality, and making partial water changes. As a rough estimate of the time you'll need to budget for pond maintenance, plan on 30 minutes a week per thousand gallons of water. That's not so bad.

But if you should find that caring for your water garden is taking way more of your time than that, you may have a fundamental problem in design

This dramatic man-made pond at the Casablanca Resort Casino in Mesquite, Nevada, features a series of spillways over a 10-foot-wide ledge. The large boulders and mature palm and pine trees fit the large scale of the dramatic setting.

or construction or in the ecological balance of plants, fish, and water. It's always better to correct the basic problem instead of spending hours each week fixing its side effects. You'll save time and money in the long run. If you can't determine the cause of the underlying problem, consider consulting with a professional water-garden designer.

One thing you'll nearly *never* have to do is completely empty and clean your water feature. Frequent emptying and cleaning can upset the pond's fragile ecological balance. Think about all those good bacteria in your pond, the ones that

gobble up ammonia and nitrites and take months to establish. Think about them getting rinsed down the gutter along with the carnauba car wax and potato peelings! At most, water gardens need a thorough cleaning only once every 4 or 5 years.

Assuming your pond is trouble-free, you'll find that most of your work will take place in spring and again in fall, with just a little periodic grooming in between. During the rest of the time, the pond is yours to sit back and enjoy.

MAINTAINING A BALANCED ECOSYSTEM

Well-designed ponds don't require much maintenance time because they are part of a carefully balanced ecosystem. Both wild waterways and garden ponds are composed of a complex network of checks and balances that help to maintain a healthy environment.

If your pond suffers from foul-smelling water, dying fish, green or gray coloring, or stunted or diseased plants, your pond's ecosystem is out of balance, and it's time for you to take the necessary steps to return it to optimum operating condition.

AVOIDING POND OVERLOAD

For starters, make sure that your pond contains plants, fish, and other pond life in proper balance. If you overload the pond with too many fish, for example, you're likely to have problems. If you find yourself with too many plants or fish, give the excess to friends or neighbors. They'll thank you for them, and your pond will be better off.

Also, keep your pond well aerated. You can never have too much oxygen in your water. Besides helping to clear up that stagnant-water smell, oxygen encourages healthy plant and fish growth and helps in the battle against algae.

Provide enough floating plants to shade, cool, and filter the water. Floating plants also compete with algae for the same nutrients, so a healthy colony of water hyacinth and duckweed will help hold algae to a minimum.

Submerged plants also act as filters, in addition to providing fish with extra food, shelter, and spawning areas. Fish, in turn, control mosquitoes by consuming their larvae. They also help control algae. Snails are great pond assets, too, since algae are their favorite food.

Stock fish and plants in appropriate proportions to each other and to the size of your pond. Experiment until you achieve the right balance. As a rule, a 6- by 8-foot pond can sustain up to 16 fish of 5 inches in length. It can also accommodate a dozen water snails such as great pond or ramshorn snails along with a couple dozen bunches of submerged plants.

TESTING YOUR WATER REGULARLY

In order to anticipate changes to your ecosystem, you'll need to test your water frequently. Test kits are inexpensive and widely available. Make sure you have a kit that will test for ammonia, nitrite, and nitrate levels. Test the water whenever you first fill your new pond and periodically thereafter, more often if you suspect you have a problem.

If you *do* discover a chemical problem, make a partial water change immediately. Regular partial changes will help hold ammonia and nitrite levels down via the process of dilution.

Snails eat algae, so they are a great asset in a pond.

KEEPING YOUR POND FILLED

If your pond loses water due to evaporation or splashing from waterfalls and spillways, refill it. A loss of an inch or more below its normal water level could create unhealthy concentrations of salts and other minerals that are left behind. A low water level could also expose the liner to the damaging ultraviolet rays of the sun. When you add water, fill the pond with just a trickle from the hose to allow fish and other pond life to adapt to any changes in temperature and pH. If the hose water is substantially colder than the pond water, add it in increments over a period of time, especially in smaller ponds. That will allow the fish to acclimate to the new water without going into shock.

For similar reasons, do not make water changes of more than 30% to 50% at any given time. If you need to change out more water than that, do so over a period of 2 or 3 days.

MAKING FREQUENT WATER CHANGES

I know, I know. We've already stressed this point, but we haven't stressed it enough. Listen to this.

A friend we know who has a medium-sized pond of around 400 gallons balks at making water changes. His wife claims the changes are stressful on the fish. He claims his water looks fine. Of course, he can't understand why he lost eight fish last year or why he's medicating another half dozen in an aquarium in the house right now. But we understand. His water is high in ammonia, nitrites, and nitrates.

And why wouldn't it be?

Think of a pond along the same lines as the Dead Sea. In most natural bodies of water, old water flows out and new water flows in, continually flushing the pond with uncontaminated, oxygenated, healthy water. In the Dead Sea, new water comes in whenever it rains, but the old water never flows out. The sea loses water through evaporation, leaving behind all of the salts, minerals, and chemicals in increasingly high concentrations. Over the years, that concentration has resulted in a body of water in which virtually nothing can survive.

Unless you make frequent water changes to your own "Dead Sea," you're doing the same thing to your pond that nature is doing to that land-locked lake. Why on earth would you ever expect anything to be able to live in *that* kind of environment?

How do you know when it is time to make a complete water change? You should probably consider doing so when the results of your tests show that the nitrate levels are more than 40 ppm (parts per million). I know that doesn't sound like much, but remember that in nature, nitrate levels in water rarely exceed 1 ppm! Assuming you have no measurable quantities of nitrites or ammonia in your water (if you do, make a water change *immediately*), a high nitrate level of 40 to 60 ppm is a good indicator of the need for a drastic water change. If your biological filter is working properly, it will rid your pond of ammonia and nitrites, but the nitrates stay behind, gradually building up to potentially toxic levels. Get my drift?

On the flip side, if you have 20 to 40 ppm of nitrates and *no* measurable amounts of ammonia and nitrites in the water, you can rest assured that your biological filter is working properly. Now all you need to do is give it a little "nudge" to reduce the level of those nitrates.

High nitrate levels, though, accompanied by high ammonia and nitrite levels, mean that your biological filter isn't keeping up with the amount of ammonia being produced—ammonia that converts into nitrites and, ultimately, nitrates.

If you have a tremendous number of plants in your pond, they should be able to absorb the nitrates and convert them into oxygen—*theoretically*.

But, even though we have plants galore in our main pond, they're nowhere near enough to do the trick. We still get nitrate readings regularly hovering in the 20- to 40-ppm range, so we still make regular partial water changes.

Just remember that topping off your pond as the water evaporates does not qualify as a partial water change, since the evaporating water leaves behind the concentrated nitrates and other chemicals. In order to reduce the percentage of nitrates in your water, you must remove some of the existing water (and the nitrates, along with it) and replace it with fresh water.

What's the best way to remove water from your pond? That depends upon your pond. We don't have a drain in any of our ponds, so we use a garden hose. We place the hose beneath the water's surface, turn on the spigot, and, once the water begins running into the pond, turn it off again. We disconnect the hose from the spigot, and out comes the water via suction. If you have smaller fish in your pond, make sure before using this method that you tape some netting to the end of the hose to keep those particularly nosey fish from getting sucked up and deposited on your begonias!

Once we've drained 10% to 20% from the pond (we put the drained water on our plants—they love nitrates, which are an integral part of commercial fertilizer), we hook the hose back up to the spigot and reverse the process. Just make sure to run the new water into the pond slowly. At this point, it's a good idea to add some AmQuel to neutralize any chlorine, chloramines, and ammonia in the new water.

CHECKING FOR AERATION

Make sure you check your pond's aeration system from time to time to be certain that it's working properly. You can visually inspect the obvious:

A natural pond is given a spectacular focal point with the addition of a pump-powered fountain. *Photo © Tammy Mobley for Fotolia.*

waterfalls, spillways, and fountains. For underwater sources of aeration, such as aerating stones, pull the stone up to the surface to see that it hasn't become clogged and that it's still functioning properly. If the stone *is* clogged, replace it with a new one.

Fountains also periodically become clogged, with either debris or algae. If yours seems to be running a little slow, turn it off, remove the fountainhead, and run a round bristle brush down the up-tube. Rinse the tube and the motor of any debris, clean out the head, and reinstall it before turning the pump back on.

If that fails to do the trick, check the intake valve of the pump itself. It can pick up leaves, grass clippings, insects, and other debris and become clogged. Remove the screen from the intake valve pipe and clean the screen under running water. If possible, run a round brush through the intake pipe

One of the author's ponds features a small fountain, several low-wattage outdoor lights, and strategically placed plants and rocks to simulate a more natural effect. Aerated water provides oxygen, which encourages healthy plant and fish growth.

as far as it will go. Then put everything together and plug the fountain in.

Keeping your fountain in top running condition is the best way to ensure its long life. When the fountain is part of a larger water feature, such as a fishpond, it's even more important to keep it clean and running efficiently.

CONTROLLING ALGAE

Nothing takes the joy out of pond keeping like massive swarms of algae. Not only does it make the water look green and murky, but it also chokes out other plants and places an unnecessary strain on your fish.

Luckily, not every kind of algae is bad for ponds. The smooth algae that grows on the pond liner and on rocks is actually beneficial. It works as a passive vegetative filter, removing nutrients that feed other, less desirable, algae.

Filamentous and tufted algae (sometimes called blanketweed or string algae), on the other hand, are invasive and need to be removed. It grows in long, dark green, ropey colonies.

All garden ponds experience excess algae from time to time, most noticeably when the pond is new and also in springtime, when the pond is still struggling to reestablish its ecological balance. As your floating plants and marginals grow and begin to shade the water, they compete with the algae for light and nutrients, helping to clear out the algae. Using a properly sized UV water-clarifying filter will help in the battle, as well, while it helps to protect your fish from harmful bacteria, viruses, and fungi.

Fish often enjoy a light lunch of algae, nibbling on it from time to time. Snails, too, which you can purchase from any supplier or over the Internet, are also voracious algae-eaters.

Remember that, since algae grow rapidly in warm, stagnant water, you'll need to keep your pond filled and circulating, particularly in hot weather, since deep ponds remain cooler longer than shallow pools.

Filamentous algae, which look like floating seaweed, should be removed from the surface of the water by hand or with a rake. If they form on rocks or waterfalls, turn off the pump and let the algae dry before scraping or brushing them off. If that fails to do the trick, you can sprinkle wet algae with non-iodized salt, such as natural sea salt or pickling salt. Allow the salt to sit for several hours before brushing it, and the algae, away. Sea salt is non-toxic to freshwater fish when used in moderation.

Finally, use algaecides as a last resort. Contrary to what their labels may say, they can stunt good plant growth and stress your fish.

REMOVING DEBRIS FROM THE POND

This may sound like a no-brainer, but you'd be amazed at how many people think "out of sight" means "out of mind." Once debris sinks to the bottom of the pond, they tend to want to leave it there. Bad idea, because waterlogged debris quickly begins to rot, giving off toxic ammonia in the process. And we all know what *that* means!

Make it a point to skim leaves, flower petals, and other floating plant material from the pond's surface before it has a chance to sink to the bottom. Remove sunken debris with a long-handled net or a wet-dry vacuum. Make sure to stay well clear of curious fish, though.

You can help yourself with maintenance by removing dead or dying leaves of marginal plants *before* they fall into the water. For problem tree leaves in autumn, you can cover the pond with bird netting until the leaves have stopped falling.

EVALUATING YOUR FILTRATION SYSTEM

If your biological, mechanical, or chemical filter isn't keeping your pond as clean and clear as you'd like, try using more than one type. Consider adding a UV filter and possibly some additional water plants. Two or more different types of filters nearly always work better than one. Rest assured: There *is* a proper balance to be struck when using filters. Sometimes, you get lucky right from the start. Other times, you have to experiment before getting just the right combination of filter systems for your specific conditions.

CLEANING YOUR POND

Although cleaning a pond is a chore you'll rarely need to do, the time might come when it's necessary to shut the pond down by draining most of the water out and physically entering the pond to clean out the muck, thin out the water plants, and so forth. Cleaning can also reduce certain kinds of algae and other pond problems, at least for a while.

Under most circumstances, you shouldn't have to clean a pond more often than once every 3 to 5 years, even less often with large ponds of a thousand gallons or more. If the pond is in balance, and if you've done a good job of keeping the pond floor clear of leaves and other foreign debris, the naturally occurring fish wastes that settle there should quickly decompose and become part of the pond environment. Little in the way of large waste products should remain.

If you *do* have to clean your pond, try to do so in late spring or early summer, after danger of frost, in order to give newly placed plants a chance to recover before winter sets in.

To clean a pond, drain about half the water so that you can more easily net the fish. Remove them to a safe place for holding. Make sure that their temporary home has plenty of oxygen (from a pump and aerator stone, for example) and that you cover the container so that the fish can't jump out.

Continue draining the pond, using a submersible pump or a siphon hose. If it's a small pond, you can bail the water out by hand.

Once you get down to within an inch or two of the bottom, stop draining and check for any beneficial snails, tadpoles, water insects, plant rhizomes, etc., and transfer them with a net to a bucket of water for reintroduction to the pond later.

Next, remove your water plants, placing them in a bucket of water or rapping their roots in wet newspaper and setting them in a shady place. Then bail out the remaining pond water, being careful not to damage the liner. Use a plastic dustpan and a soft-bristled brush to remove the mud. Once the pond is empty of all but rocks and gravel, take the hose and spray the pond down, stirring up any remaining debris. Drain the pond again with a pump or siphon. Repeat the washing and rinsing routine until the water is clear.

Fill the freshly cleaned pond to about a quarter of its capacity. Reintroduce the plants, dividing any overcrowded tubers or rhizomes into two or three smaller clumps. Set filter boxes and pumps in place, and then fill the pond the rest of the way. Treat the water with AmQuel for chlorine, chloramines, and ammonia. If you like, you can add some bentonite clay, which is a great natural water conditioner filled with beneficial minerals useful for both plants and fish. Don't worry if the water appears cloudy; the clay will settle within a few hours.

Finally, reintroduce your fish and other critters to their newly invigorated environment, making sure to add water from the pond to the holding tank *gradually,* giving the fish time to acclimate to temperature and chemical differences. Test your new pond water for pH, ammonia, and nitrates. If everything looks good, place the holding tank within the pond, allowing the fish to swim out on their own. If that's not feasible, carefully net each fish individually and reintroduce them to the pond one at a time.

WINTER MAINTENANCE

If you live in a region blessed by mild winters, maintaining your pond during the cold months involves little more effort than during any other time of year. In colder climates, however, you're going to have to make plans to protect the pond and its residents from the ravages of freezing temperatures and that scourge of pond keepers everywhere, *ice.*

First, the water feature. Ponds constructed of brick, masonry, tile, concrete, or other porous material can crack when subjected to freezing and thawing. If there's any danger of a water feature freezing solid, you'll need to drain it, using a pump or a siphon hose, or heat it. You'll also need to drain fountains and ponds made from rigid liner. Ponds made from

The author's upper pond features several flat rocks placed in a series to provide for a small waterfall, beneath which the koi congregate in search of food.

flexible liner or natural clay-lined ponds don't need to be drained.

As an alternative to draining your pond, you can install a stock tank deicer to keep it from freezing. They're available over the Internet or from most farm and feed stores. Be careful to avoid having the heater touch the lining of the pond, though, as it might burn a hole through it.

In climates where winter temperatures rarely drop lower than −10°F, use an air pump and aerating stone to keep the water moving enough to prevent freezing. If your pond is equipped with a waterfall or spillway, you probably won't have to worry about the surface freezing over.

Although deeper ponds are less likely to freeze solid than shallower ponds, we have a 50-gallon wine barrel fitted with a fountain spray and a couple of aerator stones. The barrel hasn't frozen over yet, despite temperatures down into the lower teens or lower. Most of the time, if you use common sense, keep an eye on the water surface, and do whatever else is required to keep at least 30% of the surface free from ice, your pond and the fish within it should fare just fine.

Remember that as water temperatures drop, fish become less active. Most pond owners stop feeding their fish entirely when temperatures reach 40° F. Fish don't need food when they go semi-dormant. After all, fish in nature stop eating at those temperatures, too, except under rare circumstances. And none of *them* are any the worse for it! Overfeeding in winter is just one more way of guaranteeing toxic levels of ammonia and nitrites in your pond. Without the biologically friendly activity of the summer pond to counteract them, you'll only be asking for trouble.

ENJOY, ENJOY

With just a little extra work, you'll soon find that your pond in winter is every bit as beautiful as it is in summer. What it surrenders in the form of tall grasses blowing in the breeze and bountiful flowers opening to a canopy of colors it will make up for in the everyday allure of winter—mist rising from the surface, ice forming on a spillway, steam evaporating off the rocks in the mid-morning sun.

True, there's a little more work to preparing a pond in a cold climate for winter, especially if you have to move tropical plants to the house or garage to keep them from freezing. But, with a little thoughtful care and an eye toward keeping the pond surface open, you'll find your waterway as exciting an addition to your environment in the dead of winter as you do during the heat of summer.

QUICK CHECKLIST

- Keep your water feature in balance by combining plants, fish, and other types of aquatic life in the proper proportion.
- Keep your pond filled, and avoid making total water changes for a healthy, biologically balanced pond.
- Keep aerobic algae in check through the use of filtration, shade, competitive water plants, and snails.
- During winter, make sure that at least 30% of your pond's surface remains open.

RUNNING WILD

On a cruise ship through Alaska's Inside Passage. Early fall, 1984.

I'm off on a cruise, doing research for a travel piece for the *Milwaukee Journal* on cruising to Alaska or some such nonsense and having a pretty good time. I enjoy cruising, even cold-weather cruising. It's tougher to come home with a tan, but it's easy to come home with a new outlook on life.

Already, along the way to Ketchikan, I have stood, leaning against the rail, and watched grizzlies and brown bear fishing off the Canadian coast, gold eagles perched in tall Alaskan pines along the waterway, and porpoises leaping across the ship's bow as we lumber slowly along on our way north.

That evening, after watching a floorshow and visiting the lounge for a nightcap, I decide to turn in early. We will be in port around 10 a.m., and I want to be sure that I'm awake in plenty of time to enjoy a leisurely breakfast—one of life's grandest moments aboard ship—before embarking for shore.

I lay my clothes out for the next day, slip into my bunk, and drain the snifter of Remy by my bedside. I am soon snoozing, dreaming about the sights and sounds of the day, when suddenly another sound enters my world, a horrendous crash that jolts me out of bed. I reach my foot down for the deck, which has somehow managed to disappear. When I finally find it again, I slip out of my bunk and scurry up, hurrying to throw on some pants and a coat before flinging wide the door to my stateroom.

"What is it?" I ask a parka-clad woman scurrying down the hall. *We have hit something—an iceberg, just like the Titanic, and we are all going to die,* I'm thinking. A man runs past her in the opposite direction. Oh, my God.

"What's wrong?" I ask again.

"It's calving," the woman says. "I don't want to miss it!" Before I can ask her just what the hell calving is and whether or not it is dangerous to one's health, she's gone.

Suspecting that nothing observed first-hand is worth knowing at all, I hurry into my shoes, slam the door behind me, and scurry up the steps leading to the main deck. There I emerge into the crisp cold of the early morning light just in time to see the ship's bow bouncing slowly up and down. But the motors are silent; we are at rest.

I pick a position on the rail next to a man with a thick red beard, an Irishman or a Scotsman or something to that effect, and stare out to sea. His eyes are trained behind a pair of glasses pointed at an iceberg, a monolith standing 70 or 80 feet tall. Just staring at it. Finally I ask him what's happening.

"My son, life is happening, and we're here to witness it."

He never breaks his gaze, and I think for a moment about looking for a more lucent mind to plumb when suddenly I feel a tremor. My knees begin to shake. The deck rattles beneath my feet. A giant crack of thunder breaks the stillness of the early morning, and the monolith begins to shift. The iceberg's tip begins to tremble—slowly, oh, so very slowly—until a mighty *kerr-ack* echoes across the surface of the water and the calf begins to pick up speed. Finally, it plunges down the face of the berg like a young child down a waterslide, and when it reaches the sea, it disappears in a thunderous cloud of spray. The water washes over us, and I wipe it from my face, amazed at how powerful a force has just been released upon nature.

"My God," I say to the man next to me. "That was ... fantastic!"

He takes his eyes slowly down from his glasses, sets them against the rail, and turns to face me for the first time. "No," he says. "That was simply God attempting to imitate Nature."

seventeen

Troubleshooting

> Nothing in the cry of cicadas suggests they are about to die.
>
> —Basho

Inevitably, pond-keeping problems will arise. This chapter will help you solve them.

LIST OF PROBLEMS AND SOLUTIONS

Problem: The pond's location is uneven.
Solution: Either dig out the high spots or, if that's not possible, build up the low spots with sand; check for level before settling the molded pond or covering with liner.

Problem: After the pond is complete, the liner shows.
Solution: Make sure the pond is completely filled with water. If that doesn't solve the problem, try turning excess pond lining underneath itself along the length of the bank or disguise the exposed liner with Spanish moss planted with baby tears or other groundcover plants. Also set rocks and stones along the bank and place spreading yews or similar evergreen plants alongside the edge of the liner. That will provide a quick cosmetic fix and help protect the liner from deterioration due to ultraviolet rays.

OPPOSITE: This man-made pond features a wide spillway and fencing to prevent small children and animals from entering the water. *Photo © Martina Bock for Fotolia.*

Problem: Fish are dying.
Solution: Test the water for quality. If you find high levels of ammonia, nitrites, nitrates, chlorine, and chloramines, do an immediate partial water change of between 30% and 40%. Then add AmQuel to neutralize the ammonia, chlorine, and chloramines, and test the water again. Keep an eye on the water quality over the next few weeks. If the toxic chemicals return, search for the problem. Make sure you're not overcrowding the pond (see Chapter 13).

Fish can also die because of a lack of oxygen in the water. Install a fountain or a pump with an air stone for additional aeration and make a partial water change. Follow up with AmQuel to make sure that excess ammonia isn't attacking the fishes' gills.

Disease is another possible reason for dying fish. Remove any fish that appear to be sluggish or have clamped fins or that show abnormal marks such as blotches and patches, or ragged fins or tail. Remove fish that keep to themselves in a far corner of the pond or that do not swim normally. Once you determine whether the problem is bacterial, fungal, or parasitic, you can medicate the fish. Keep a close watch over your other fish, as some diseases and parasites are contagious. If the problem is serious, consult with a veterinarian or fish specialist.

Problem: The pond is muddy following a heavy rain.
Solution: Although muddy water is rarely a problem for fish, it's annoying for pond owners. It is most likely caused by erosion around your pond's banks. Cover any exposed soil with plants, rocks or stones, or mulch to alleviate the problem.

Problem: The water level drops and the pond leaks.
Solution: All water features lose some water to evaporation. Just how much is normal evaporation depends upon your particular pond and environment. If the pond loses more than a quarter-inch a day, the loss may be from water splashing out of the waterfalls or sneaking out along a stream bank. If those possibilities are eliminated and the pond continues losing water, the pond could have a leak. Move the fish to a well-oxygenated holding tank and drain the pond to locate the leak. You should be able to feel it easily—it's at the spot where the pointed object is sticking through the lining. Remove the offending object and use a pond repair kit as instructed to seal the wound. Allow the patch to dry before refilling the pond.

Problem: A submersible pump quits operating after just a few months.
Solution: A good quality water-garden pump should last for several years. If it stops, unplug it and check to see that debris or algae haven't clogged the blades. Clean the pre-filter or water intake manifold throughout the season. Place the pump on a rock or stone above the bottom of the pond to avoid picking up silt and debris. Plug the pump in and see if it works. If not, check the warranty or take the pump back to wherever you purchased it for a replacement.

Problem: The water has a disagreeable odor.
Solution: Bad odors from your pond nearly always mean that anaerobic bacteria (those that do not use oxygen) are at an unacceptably high level. This could be caused by lack of oxygen in the water, or a dead and decaying fish or excess fish food. To correct the problem, make a partial water change, clean the bottom of the pond, and increase aeration by adding a pump and air stone, a fountain, or a waterfall. Minimize feed for your fish. Finally, check your filtration system. You may need to add a biological filter or a UV filter of the right size, if you don't already have one installed (see Chapter 7).

Problem: Portions of some water plants brown out and die off, although the plants are still alive.
Solution: Some dieback and loss of leaves is normal in any pond. Simply snip away yellow and brown leaves to keep the plants healthy and the water free of debris.

Problem: Falling leaves in autumn pollute the pond.
Solution: Use a long-handled net to remove fallen leaves on a daily basis. If your pond is situated directly below a deciduous tree, you may stretch netting over the pond to catch the leaves until the fall is over. Anchor the netting along the bank with bricks or stones.

If you have a larger pond, you may have to remove the debris with a soft plastic rake. You can also invest in a pool sweep, which attaches to a garden hose and uses the water pressure to pick up debris and silt from the pond bottom. It's available from pond supply houses and over the Internet.

Problem: My fish don't seem hungry.
Solution: Fish become especially lethargic in cold water. During the cold period, stop feeding them entirely, and resume again when the water

temperature reaches 48° to 50° F. Also, don't over-feed your fish, which could result in ammonia and nitrite spikes. Feed once a day at the same time and location within the pond. The best time is in the afternoon to within an hour of sunset.

Problem: I have too many fish and need to get rid of some. No one I know keeps fish. What do you suggest?

Solution: You can check with your county agricultural agent to see if there's some place that would welcome your fish. If not, you might place an ad in the local paper or call around to different pet shops. So long as the fish are healthy, you should be able to find them a home somewhere.

Problem: I need to divide my water-garden plants, but they're so root-bound, I can't get them apart.

Solution: Try breaking the root ball apart with a pruning fork. If that doesn't work, slice through the roots with a sharp knife. Try not to squeeze the stalk of the plants while working on them, as that could kill the plants. Always handle plants by their leaves, branches, or roots.

Problem: Fish in a small tub die off within a few weeks.

Solution: There could be too much current in the tub. Fish need a place where they can relax quietly on the bottom instead of constantly struggling against a current. To rectify the problem, reduce the current by adjusting the flow on the pump and/or fountain up-tube.

Dying fish may also be caused by high ammonia or nitrite levels, which is a frequent problem, especially in small ponds and containers. Test the water quality in the tub, and install a biological filter. Make frequent partial water changes, and add AmQuel or Neutral Regulator whenever replacing water.

The spillway in this pond (on the left) empties into a small holding pool planted with cattails, which act as a natural vegetative filter, before the water empties out the right side of the pool and down a man-made stream leading to a larger lower pond. The healthy plants are one result of a healthy, balanced pond.

BORN FREE

St. George, Utah. Summer, 2000.

We take our two turtles—the ones that have developed a fondness for sushi-on-the-fin—and under cover of darkness walk them down to the golf course where we plan on releasing them into the pond. We do this at night because we can't help but think there must be something illegal or at least inherently unethical about releasing one of nature's own creations back into nature.

It is after 11 p.m., and no one else is around. As we work beneath the lights from the parking lot, we perform a little ceremony. "May the God of turtles watch after you always and bring for you only the best of life's watery offerings."

We place Christian, the larger of our two red ears, on the manicured lawn and wish him luck. He covers the 5 furlongs to the water in record time. Next, we place Slater on the lawn. He takes a step or two toward the water and stops. We pick him up and place him nearer the water's edge, thinking that perhaps he doesn't know where he is, how close he is to freedom and not merely to another pre-cast black plastic tub filled with tap juice.

When after several minutes he pokes his head out of his shell, a minor miracle occurs. Christian, faced with a body of water that must seem by comparison like the Gulf of Mexico, comes swimming back toward shore. With his shell barely covered, he lifts up his head, and Slater, I swear, catches sight of him, before turning and walking toward his pond mate, walking that painfully slow lumbering walk that only turtles can walk. Before long, he is lost to his brother and the sea.

That is all to the story that there is to tell. Or, rather, that's all there would be to tell if not for the flood of 2004. As we watch the Virgin River rise and the banks begin to collapse into it, houses and all, a peculiar event unfolds at the golf course. The river overruns its banks there, too, and in doing so erodes away the small peninsula that separates it from the pond, the home of Christian and Slater, until river and pond become one.

We stand on the hillside behind our house, overlooking this whole bloody mess, and watch as logs and timbers and roofs and other debris wash lazily along on their way out of Utah and into Nevada. The next evening, we see a newscast out of Las Vegas, and a young girl smiles for the camera. She is on vacation with her family at Lake Mead, and her dog has retrieved a turtle for her from the shore. She holds it up for the camera—it is Christian, I'm sure—before releasing it with some flair back into the lake. I shout out, "Hey! Don't forget Slater!"

eighteen

To Your Health!

ABOVE: Girl meditating near pond.
Photo © Piotr Sikora for Fotolia.

We live in a world where air pollution is the single most powerful threat to our health and well-being. Studies point out a direct link between urban air pollution—especially particulate pollution created by combustion-powered vehicles and power generation plants—and cardiovascular and pulmonary diseases. Long-term exposure to particulates, those tiny beasts smaller than 10 microns across (a human hair, by comparison, is 70 microns wide), has been shown to increase human illness and death rates from lung cancer, chronic obstructive pulmonary disease, and emphysema. Exposure to other airborne pollutants, including sulfur dioxide (SO_2), nitrogen dioxide (NO_2), and ozone (O_3), also plays a role in diseases such as asthma, bronchitis, and various respiratory infections.

Darning needle.

European researchers investigating the risks of long-term exposure to traffic pollution discovered that people living near major roads (and therefore, one assumes, to major traffic flow) are more likely to die from cardiopulmonary disease or lung cancer than their rural counterparts, simply because they are exposed to more harmful airborne particulates.[1]

AIR POLLUTION LINKED TO HEART DAMAGE

In addition to lung damage, medical researchers are finding a greater link between air pollution and cardiovascular health—heart disease! In the March 6, 2002, *Journal of the American Medical Association* (*JAMA*), researchers reported on long-term health data for half a million people to compare increases in air pollution levels with incidence of death. They discovered that when air pollution levels suddenly increase, so too do deaths from asthma, pneumonia, and emphysema.[2] They also found an unexpected increase in the number of deaths related to heart attacks and stroke. Most surprising was the finding that when air pollution levels rise, so do deaths from *all* causes, not only those related to the heart and lungs.

The reason is not that difficult to understand, once you begin rooting around in the science of human physiology. Air pollution causes oxidative stress that, in turn, triggers an inflammatory response in the lungs. Such inflammation leads to the release of chemicals that impair heart function and blood pressure.

One study in Vancouver, British Columbia, found that exposure to high levels of air pollution stimulates bone marrow to release leukocytes and platelets. These are the killers that accumulate in pulmonary capillaries and that can result in heart attack or stroke.

DIABETICS AND ELDERLY AT INCREASED RISK

That's not the only bad news linking air pollution to disease. The medical journal *Epidemiology* recently examined Medicare records and hospital admissions in several U. S. cities. It was found that, between 1988 and 1994, people suffering from diabetes were *twice* as likely as others to be admitted to a hospital with a cardiovascular problem caused by airborne particulate pollution.[3] It was also found that persons 75 years of age and older face a higher risk of cardiovascular injury than persons who have not been exposed to particulate pollution. Children are even more susceptible than adults. This is serious stuff.

AIR POLLUTION AND DNA MUTATIONS

As sobering as this information is, it may not be the worst news about the effects of air pollution. Canadian studies conducted in 2002 showed that animals exposed to the polluted air generated from a nearby steel mill actually suffered *genetic* damage and produced fewer offspring than their unexposed counterparts. Their damaged DNA was passed on to offspring by the fathers; females may also be susceptible. The obvious implication is that steel workers, who are mostly male, may be at extra risk of incurring similar DNA damage.

In another study, researchers raised two groups of mice, the first half a mile downwind of a Lake Ontario steel mill and the second 20 miles away. The mice closest to the polluted air had twice as many mutations in their DNA as the mice breathing fresh air. The researchers concluded, "Our findings suggest that there is an urgent need to investigate the genetic consequences associated with exposure to chemical pollution through the inhalation of urban and industrial air."[4]

PROTECTING YOUR LUNGS

While government, businesses, and environmental interests argue over the advantages of various economic, legislative, and technological solutions for cleaning up polluted air, the vital issue facing individuals is how best to protect their own health. Currently, over 75 million people in the United States live in counties where the air concentrations of particulate matter smaller than 2.5 microns (PM2.5) exceed safe levels.

While living away from polluted cities may seem the obvious choice, that option is not always available, nor is it always effective. Air currents and weather patterns can shift polluted air from urban manufacturing centers into rural areas where pollution may accumulate in dangerous concentrations. In addition, modern farming practices rely on mechanization, and mechanization means combustion. Engines produce pollution in the form of particulates. So, too, do wood fires (a very high source of airborne particulates), deteriorating automobile tires, agricultural chemicals, paint fumes (all those farm houses have to be kept pristine!), and thousands of other rural particulate generators.

Staying indoors is no guarantee of experiencing better air quality, either. As several studies have recently shown, much of our exposure to fine particulates occurs inside the home! With no western breezes to move polluted air out of the house and a sealed "box" that can hold only a fixed amount of clean air, accumulating particulates from deteriorating carpeting, padding, and wall surfaces may pose a significant threat.

To make matters worse, many people at increased risk of health complications following exposure to high particulate concentrations, particularly the elderly and people suffering from cardiovascular and pulmonary diseases, spend as much as nine-tenths of their time indoors, raising still *more* concerns about the effects on health in a particulate-rich environment.

AIR PURIFIERS

As indoor air pollution has grown in scope, so too has the number of people seeking air purifiers for relief from the problem. Home air filtration products come in a number of different types, all professing to do the same thing. They include electrostatic, UV radiation, water, and HEPA filtration technologies. Taking filtration one step further, a number of consumer products relying on ion-generating technology to eliminate indoor airborne pollutants, allergens, and viruses have become available.

These devices work by generating a flow of negative ions that charge and bind airborne particulate matter, which then clumps together to precipitate from the air. Ion-generating devices have been shown to be effective against dust, cigarette smoke, pet dander, pollen, mold spores, viruses, and bacteria. In addition to eliminating harmful particulates from the air, negative ions also have a number of other unique health benefits.

NEGATIVE IONS—POSITIVELY!

Just as positive ions build up in the atmosphere prior to a storm front, negative ions accumulate after the storm passes. The surplus of negative ions has long been associated with improvements in mood and physical health. Research conducted in the last decade supports the view that negative ions have an overall positive effect on health.

In one illuminating German study, mice and rats were isolated in airtight sealed acrylic cases. The researchers filtered the ambient air to remove all negative ions from the cases. After the animals were deprived of negative ions for some time, the death rate ballooned. Autopsies "strongly suggest that animal death is related to disturbances in neuro-hormonal regulation and pituitary insufficiency," the study concluded.[5]

Other researchers at the Russian Academy of Sciences in Moscow discovered that negative ions are able to help protect the body from induced physical stress. When the researchers immobilized rats and exposed them to negative charges, they found that the ions prevented the development of pathological changes characteristic of acute stress that were observed in the untreated rats. The only difference between the two groups was the protective action of negative ions.[6]

Taking the studies to a higher plane, British researchers exposed male subjects to negative ions and recorded their physiological responses, which included body temperature, heart rate, and respiration, both at rest and during exercise. The results showed that negative ions significantly improved all physiological states, especially during times of rest. The researchers concluded that negative ions are "biologically active and that they do affect the body's circadian rhythmicity."[7]

Yet another study, this one at the Institute of Theoretical and Experimental Biophysics of the Russian Academy of Sciences in Pushchino, Russia, found that subjects exposed to negative ions experienced increased levels of the protective antioxidant enzyme superoxide dismutase (SOD). The researchers also discovered minute amounts of H_2O_2 (hydrogen peroxide) and concluded, "The primary physiochemical mechanism of beneficial biological action of negative air ions is suggested to be related to the stimulation of superoxide dismutase activity by micromolar concentrations of H_2O_2 (hydrogen peroxide)."[8]

WHAT IT ALL MEANS

Although some advances have been made in the battle against air pollution, especially in reduced emissions of lead, sulfur dioxide (SO_2), nitrogen dioxide (NO_2), and ozone (O_3), air pollution in the form of particulates remains a serious health problem. As noted above, medical research has shown that in addition to damaging the lungs, particulate pollution is particularly harmful to children, the aged, and some especially sensitive populations, such as those afflicted with diabetes, cardiopulmonary disease, and other diseases.

OPPOSITE: A low, meandering spillway empties into a crystalline pond planted with flowering shrubs and dramatic palm trees and creates a healthy environment in a warm climate. *Photo © Klikk for Fotolia.*

Ponds, waterfalls, and streams—with their moving water and fracturing water molecules—help to generate negative ions, both indoors and out. Besides all of the other beneficial effects that water features provide (including psychological), they can actually help control the incidence of air pollution and counterbalance the damaging effects of positive ionization.

The negative ions that water features create, while minimal in the overall scope of air pollution and airborne particulates, help to establish a microclimate around the home, neighborhood, town, city, and wherever else water features may flow. A healthy outdoor microclimate, especially when combined with a healthy *indoor* environment, is the best means there is of combating the health hazards of air pollution on a person-to-person basis.

It's time that people begin to recognize the tremendous number of healthful benefits to be derived from both indoor and outdoor water features and to start incorporating them into individual dwellings as well as entire communities. We need to demand more indoor ponds and spillways—water cascading like lighted art against a wall, water sheeting into fractured molecules separating the kitchen from the dining room, water bubbling softly from fountains in our offices, studies, and bedrooms.

Would a water feature in every room of the house be too much? Hardly. From indoor streams, fountains, ponds, and reflecting pools to waterfalls, spillways, cascades, and aquariums, water presents an endless challenge to human development over the next generation and beyond. We need to inform our builders, city planners, and politicians of the healthful and curative benefits of fracturing water molecules and negative ionization in order to help awaken people to the illuminating benefits that only water can provide.

Water—it's a wondrous ever-changing environment of life for fish and other aquatic creatures, a horrifying and mystifying environment of death for humankind. Fish cannot survive long above its surface, and humans cannot survive for more than a few shallow seconds below it. Yet it seems that the human body cannot ever fully prosper without it.

Whether you live in the high deserts of Utah and Arizona or in the mountains of the Canadian north, whether you call home a small rental apartment or a sprawling rambling estate, you can benefit from the healthful and healing effects of moving water.

If you ask me, it's about time everyone did.

References for Chapter 18

1. Hoek G, Brunekreef B, Goldbohm S, Fischer P, van den Brandt PA. Association between mortality and indicators of traffic-related air pollution in the Netherlands: a cohort study. *Lancet,*. 2002 Oct 19; 360 (9341): 1184-5.1.

2. *JAMA,* March 6, 2002; 287: 1132-1141.

3. Zanobetti A, Schwartz J. Cardiovascular damage by airborne particles: Are diabetics more susceptible? *Epidemiology,* 2002, Sep; 13 (5): 588-92.

4. Somers, Christopher M, Yaukdagger, Carole L, Whitedagger, Paul A et. al. Air pollution induces heritable DNA mutations. Proc. Natl. Acad. Sci. USA, Vol. 99, Issue 25, 15904-15907, December 10, 2002.

5. Goldstein N, Arshavskaya TV. Is atmospheric superoxide vitally necessary? Accelerated death of animals in a quasi-neutral electric atmosphere. Z Naturforsch [C] 1997 May–Jun; 52 (5-6): 396-404.

6. Livanova LM, Levshina IP, Nozdracheva LV, Elbakidze MG, Airapetiants MG. The protective action of negative air ions in acute stress in rats with different typological behavioral characteristics. Zh Vyssh Nerv Deiat Im I P Pavlova 1998 May–Jun; 48 (3): 554-7.

7. Reilly T, Stevenson IC. An investigation of the effects of negative air ions on responses to submaximal exercise at different times of day. J Hum Ergol (Tokyo) 1993 Jun; 22 (1): 1-9.

8. Kosenko EA, Kaminsky Yu G, Stavrovskaya IG, Sirota TV, Kondrashova MN. The stimulatory effect of negative air ions and hydrogen peroxide on the activity of superoxide dismutase. FEBS Lett 1997 Jun 30; 410 (2-3): 309-12.

THE PHOTOGRAPHER AND THE CHILD

Lantau Island, Hong Kong. Summer, 1987.

Both Doug and I find our first visit to Hong Kong remarkable. From the moment I lay eyes on the harbor, I know I am in love. It is old China, *the* China, the real thing, exactly as you see on television and in old movies only more so. The smells and the sounds wash over me, carrying me back to the most exotic corners of my mind. I have always known such sensory overload existed somewhere on the planet. I had never expected to find it here.

It is early in the day, and we are heading out to catch the ferry to Kowloon. At rush hour, everyone is in a hurry to get somewhere, to work, mostly, or somewhere else. Who knows? I wait patiently in line with Doug in front of me while someone pushes me from behind. It is something I have not yet learned to adjust to, the Oriental approach to life in the fast lane—push, shove, get where you want to go as quickly as possible. Beautiful women surround me. Not beautiful women, exactly, so much as the most beautiful women I have ever seen, ever fantasized about, ever imagined existed. Each one wears a tight sheath of shimmering silk with a long slit up one side. Each has on heels, and each is made up to perfection. No one anywhere wears jeans and a T-shirt. I could die in Hong Kong (hopefully, sometime far in the future) and never regret it for a moment.

On the ferry, we hang over the rail and take in the sights. I am on assignment for *The Milwaukee Journal,* and Doug is along as a photographic assistant; so we busy ourselves snapping photos and mugging for one another.

When we reach Kowloon some 20 minutes later, we disembark and begin to walk. It is what I like to do best when I'm on assignment, walk. In time, our walking deposits us at the front doors of a restaurant. After grabbing something to eat, something authentically Chinese, something off the beaten path, something that the locals eat and not the tourists, something that is going to give me Giardia that I will be forced to battle intermittently for the rest of my life, we take a tour of the beach. I snap a photo of a woman wading in shallow water, carrying a long pole for balance in one hand and a deadly lance for spearing conch or whatever else she can find in the other.

We come across a water taxi and somehow manage to relay to the driver that we wish to go to Lantau Island. He looks confused, as if he has never received such a request before. Once we arrive, my senses are electric. I am Alice through the looking glass. Everywhere I turn, reality is suspended: fantasy reigns.

On a long bench, we pass fish drying in the sun, four or five hundred or more— fish as far as the eye can see. Each one different and each one the same, all destined for the local marketplace or for the main island—Hong Kong proper consists of several hundred islands, only a few of which are inhabited.

We pass a small group of girls coming home from school, 12 or 13 years of age I imagine, all dressed in smartly pressed uniforms, with crisp neckties and jaunty pleated skirts. The girls watch as we go by and giggle the way schoolgirls everywhere do.

We snap more photos at a building site, where a local informs us that someone is building the first high rise on the island. I am stunned that the crew is digging the foundation by hand, using picks and shovels. They throw the dirt into large wicker baskets, and a man comes along, hooks a basket to each end of a pole, and balances the pole across the back of his neck. He carries the load several hundred feet from the site, where he dumps it onto a pile before returning to do it all over again.

We gravitate instinctively toward the water's edge—the sampans fascinate me, and Doug is already shooting his thirtieth roll of the day. We wander out onto the dock and watch as a boat that has just come in from the sea opens up its baskets of fish and shrimp and squid and seaweed. A local woman shouts at a woman onboard, who in turn shouts back; when enough shouting has taken place, the woman on shore hands the woman in the boat some money, and a fish changes hands.

When we tire of this, we turn away and head out along the wharf lining the waterfront. I notice a short, thin, poorly dressed man. Doug points his telephoto lens toward the hills for a panoramic shot. I watch Short Man out of the corner of my eye, and when I see him get up from his haunches, take a drag on a cigarette, and flip the butt out to sea, I begin to get nervous.

I look behind us and realize that we have traveled several hundred feet from the activity at the pier. Short Man eyes us suspiciously and sidles up to the rail that sepa- rates us from the water, from the islands, from the rest of the world. I see a scar on his face longer than the Yangtze River itself, a deep wound made years ago that never healed properly, and I can only imagine how he got it. I see him reach into his pocket. I tell Doug to hold up for a minute. Doug stops, turning his lens inland toward some mud and brick huts not far away. I place my free hand inside my pocket and make a point of looking Short Man directly in the eyes. I stare at him, into him, glaring, demanding, intimidating, and I think for a brief fraction of a second that I notice the man flinch. I look down, spit onto the wooden planks, and look back up.

By now, my partner has turned away from the wharf and is walking along a path leading to the huts. I squint hard toward Short Man, my eyes mere slits in the early afternoon sun; and I turn slowly to follow Doug, keeping my right hand in my pocket and trying to make myself look larger than I am. I grow uneasy as Short Man moves from his place along the railing, moves into our footsteps, and steps off a few paces.

Doug is after new quarry. In an open window 50 feet before us, he has spied an old man, a grandfather with a gray and withered beard and wrinkled yellow skin. In his lap sits a beautiful young girl.

Suddenly the girl jumps down from the old man and races around to the open doorway. In a flash she is through it and running up to Doug. I pull out my camera and snap away as she comes to a stop at his boot tips. She has her hands clasped behind her and grins at him through pearly white teeth. Doug takes a pack of gum and presents it to the girl, who looks back at her grandfather and waves. The grand-father is by now standing in the doorway, and, after watching intently for several moments, he raises his hand and waves—perhaps to the little girl, perhaps to us, or maybe to no one at all, I can't quite tell.

When I look around to see if Short Man is still following us, my eyes open wide. He is gone.

Glossary of Terms

Air stone: A manufactured stone designed to produce bubbles via air pumped into the stone, used to provide additional oxygen in water.

Algaecide: A chemical used to kill algae.

Ammonia (NH3): The main waste product produced by fish, excreted from the gills as a very dilute form of urine. High concentrations of ammonia are fatal to fish.

Anal fin: The single fin on the underside of a fish immediately in front of the tail. The fin helps the fish remain upright as it swims.

Anchor worm: A parasitic crustacean that attaches to fish and feeds on the blood and tissues.

Barbels: The "tusks" located on either side of a koi's mouth. Koi have four of them, one large and one small on each side of the mouth. They use them as feelers.

Barley straw: Used as a natural method to control the growth of algae via the release of hydrogen peroxide as the straw decomposes; requires direct sun and well-oxygenated water to work. Of marginal effectiveness.

Bio-balls: Biomedia polyethylene balls with "spurs" used for growing beneficial bacterial inside filter boxes.

Brown blood disease: The binding of nitrite to the hemoglobin in red blood cells, preventing a fish's ability to absorb oxygen.

Caudal fin: A fish's tail.

Chloramines: An increasingly popular chemical used to disinfect municipal water supplies. It is extremely toxic to fish and, in high concentrations, can be fatal. Does not evaporate in time, as does chlorine, and is most often removed chemically.

Chlorine: A chemical used to kill bacteria in municipal water supplies. It is toxic to fish. It may be removed chemically. It dissipates from water naturally within 1 to 2 days.

Culling: The removal of young fish from the school because of poor color, body conformation, or deformities, making them unsuitable for sale.

Dissolved oxygen: The amount of oxygen that water contains.

Dorsal fin: The fish's top front fin.

Filter: A device for collecting debris and fish waste products so that they can be removed from the system easily.

Filter matting: Biomedia made of a polyester-based material placed inside a filter box to attract beneficial nitrifying bacteria.

Flowmeter: A device attached to a hose to calculate the amount of water that has passed through.

Fry: Newly hatched fish.

Gill fluke: A microscopic organism with "hooks" used to attach itself to a fish's gills. Gill flukes can damage gill filaments, reducing a fish's ability to absorb oxygen.

Gills: The organ used by fish to absorb oxygen into the system.

Ick: See white spot disease.

Karasu: "Crow" in Japanese, referring to an all-black koi.

Krill: *Euphasia superba,* a saltwater crustacean used as fish food. It is high in omega fatty acids and protein and is prized as an excellent "growth food."

Lateral lines: The scales on both sides of a fish's body with pores that can detect the slightest vibrations in the water.

Liner: A waterproof fabric used for the underlayment of ponds to make them waterproof.

Malachite green: A medication used for treating white spot disease (ick) and other infections in fish. Malachite green is banned in some areas because it has been shown to cause mutations by directly affecting DNA. It is also a respiratory poison and must be used with great care.

Mulm: A non-organic fish waste product, brown in color, that can be found coating filter, pipes, and other surfaces in a fishpond.

Nitrate (NO3): A form of nitrogen that is the final result of the nitrification process. High nitrate levels may result in the long-term inability of fish and other pond animals to resist disease.

Nitrification: The process by which ammonia is changed to into nitrite, which is then converted into less-toxic nitrate.

Nitrite (NO₂): A form of nitrogen that is produced from ammonia during the nitrification process. Nitrite is extremely toxic to fish.

Potassium permanganate: A medication used for treating protozoan parasites and bacterial infections of the skin and gills in fish. Toxic in water with a high pH. Use sparingly or not at all.

Praziquantel: A medication originally used to treat parasites in dogs and cats, now used as an effective treatment for fluke and intestinal parasites in fish.

Pump: A mechanical device used to draw water in one end and force it out the other. Pumps come in submersible and non-submersible models. Different sized pumps are available. The more gallons per hour the pump is capable of moving, the more force with which the water is expelled.

Silk pupae: Silkworm cocoons used as fish food.

Skin flukes: Similar to gill flukes except attached to a fish's skin. They can transmit bacterial diseases as they feed on the host fish.

Spawning: The reproductive process of a female fish laying eggs to be fertilized by male fish.

Swim bladder: A gas-filled buoyancy organ that allows a fish to remain upright at any depth.

Tubercles: Naturally occurring white raised spots that appear on a male fish when it is ready to spawn.

Ultraviolet (UV) light: A device used to sterilize algae and harmful bacteria and fungus. Water is cleaned as it passes through a tube where it is radiated with strong ultraviolet light waves.

Venturi: Named after its inventor, G.B. Venturi, it is a device that swirls water around, injecting oxygen into the water.

White spot disease (ick): A deadly killer of fish, white spot disease consists of a colony of parasites visible as white spots that grow rapidly along the fish's body and on its fins and tail. As the colonies expand, the wounds left by the parasites leave the fish vulnerable to secondary bacterial infections. This disease is extremely infectious and travels quickly from one fish to the next. It is relatively easy to diagnose and cure when treated early.

Zeolite: A type of ion exchange medium used for removing ammonia from water; generally impractical for all but small ponds and aquariums.

Supplies

Pond keeping implies a need to keep certain supplies on hand and readily available. Because of the vulnerability of fish to various diseases and chemical pollutants, you need to keep more things on hand for fishponds than for non-fishponds. Still, there are some supplies that all pond owners will want to stock, if only for the sake of convenience.

WATER ADDITIVES

AmQuel water conditioner (from Novalek): Removes ammonia, chlorine, and chloramines from water and is therefore extremely useful, especially when making large water changes or starting a pond from scratch. Widely available.

pH 7.0 Neutral Regulator (from Seachem Laboratories): Softens water by precipitating calcium and magnesium while removing chlorine, chloramines, and ammonia. Brings water pH into the neutral zone of around 7.0 and maintains it there until the water is significantly altered. Widely available.

Tetracycline: An antibiotic used to treat numerous bacterial diseases. Have enough on hand to treat the capacity of your pond two to three times. (If your pond is 500 gallons, have enough available to treat 1,000 to 1,500 gallons.)

Fungus Clear (from Jungle Laboratories): Cures common fungal diseases. Widely available. Also available in larger quantities from pond-supply stores and over the Internet.

Parasite Clear (from Jungle Laboratories): Very effective against a wide range of parasitic intruders. Widely available. Also available in larger quantities from pond-supply stores and over the Internet.

Sea salt: Used for a variety of things, from a tonic for your fish (1 teaspoon per 1 gallon of water) to an algaecide. Not toxic to freshwater fish when used in moderation.

FILTRATION

Charcoal: Used to bind chemically with ammonia and other water pollutants, neutralizing NH_3 from the pond environment. May be cost prohibitive for larger ponds.

Zeolites: Minerals with micro-porous structure, used in filters. More effective than charcoal but with the same major drawback for larger ponds.

Filter media: The stuff that encourages the growth of beneficial bacteria in biological filters. Keep extra filter media on hand for emergencies.

WATER TESTING

While numerous manufacturers make a wide variety of water-testing kits, here are some that we've found easy to use and that we keep around always.

Ammonia Profi Test (from Salifert): A complete ammonia test, testing for both NH3 and NH4, quickly, easily, and accurately.

pH Test Kit (from Aquarium Pharmaceuticals, Inc.): A fast, accurate pH test that comes with pH Up and pH Down additives for raising or lowering the pH of your water, although the amounts of chemicals are not sufficient to meet the needs of most pond owners. To adjust pH level, we suggest using Neutral Regulator (see above).

Five-in-One Test Kit (from Mardel): Uses a fast, easy water dip strip to provide five different readings for nitrates, nitrites, hardness, alkalinity, and pH. Tells at a glance if a level is safe, stressful, or potentially dangerous.

PUMPS/FILTERS

Air pump, tubing, and stones: Besides your main pump-and-filter setup, you should keep at least one small air pump, some quarter-inch plastic tubing, and a few inexpensive air stones on hand for when you might be required to infuse your water with a sudden dose of oxygen. An entire air-generating system can cost as little as $10 when purchased as a package.

Water pump: It's also a good idea to have an auxiliary submersible water pump on hand for use in the event that one of your main pumps gives out. You can purchase a good moderate-flow pump for around $30.

MISCELLANEOUS

Fish net: Make sure yours is designed for use with delicate pond fish as opposed to the landing net commonly used by fishermen. Also, as your fish grow in size, make certain that you have a large enough net to accommodate them, should you need to move your fish for whatever reason.

Skimmer net: Similar to those used by pool owners to remove fallen leaves and other debris from the pond's surface. Easier to use than a fish net for surface debris. Make sure the handle is long enough to reach as far across the pond as necessary.

Hospital tank: Sooner or later, you're going to need one. It should be large enough to accommodate your largest fish. In the case of young goldfish, that could be an inexpensive 5-gallon acrylic aquarium. You can aerate it with your air pump and stone (see above). For larger fish, plan on having a small barrel, plastic trash can, or other suitable receptacle into which you can place your ailing fish to observe and treat them. As with a smaller aquarium, have an air pump and stone ready for oxygenation.

Distilled water: Great for use in a hospital tank, when setting one up at the spur of the moment. Pure water means you won't have to worry about treating for ammonia, chlorine, or chloramines before adding your fish.

Metric Equivalents

(to the nearest mm or cm)

inches	mm	cm	inches	mm	cm
⅛	3	0.3	5	127	12.7
¼	6	0.6	6	152	15.2
⅜	10	1.0	7	178	17.8
½	13	1.3	8	203	20.3
⅝	16	1.6	9	229	22.9
¾	19	1.9	10	254	25.4
⅞	22	2.2	11	279	27.9
1	25	2.5	12	305	30.5
1¼	32	3.2	13	330	33.0
1½	38	3.8	14	356	35.6
1¾	44	4.4	15	381	38.1
2	51	5.1	16	406	40.6
2½	64	6.4	17	432	43.2
3	76	7.6	18	457	45.7
3½	89	8.9	19	483	48.3
4	102	10.2	20	508	50.8
4½	114	11.4			

INDEX